MODERN
EUROPE 1789/1914

SCOTT, FORESMAN
WORLD CIVILIZATION
SERIES

WILLIAM H. McNEILL
Editor

MODERN
EUROPE 1789/1914

By PETER N. STEARNS
Rutgers, The State University

WILLIAM H. McNEILL, *Editor*
World Civilization Series

SCOTT, FORESMAN AND COMPANY

Library of Congress Catalog Card No. 69-13661
Copyright © 1969 by Scott, Foresman and Company, Glenview, Illinois 60025.
All rights reserved. Printed in the United States of America.
Regional offices of Scott, Foresman and Company are located in
Atlanta, Dallas, Glenview, Palo Alto, and Oakland, N.J.

Foreword

Two assumptions underlie the Scott, Foresman World Civilization series: first, that there is such a thing as world history and not merely the history of separate civilizations and barbarisms coexisting in different parts of the world without important relations one with another; and second, that people learn more easily and with greater satisfaction if information is organized into a more complex intellectual framework than the bald matrix of a catalogue arranged according to proximity in time and space. Interpretation, then, with all the risks of omission and individual idiosyncrasy on the part of the authors; and synthesis, with whatever risks of error on the part of the editor, are the goals for which we have striven.

In any collaborative work, a key problem is how to reconcile expertise in detail with cohesion overall. In this series each author was invited to say whatever he thought ought to be said, but only within rather narrowly defined limits of space. The overall apportionment of space was regulated by a preliminary plan for which the undersigned was responsible. The basic architecture of that plan will be apparent from the titles of successive volumes; but choice of themes and apportionment of space within each volume were left to the discretion of the various authors.

The series itself has been organized to permit its use in a number of different ways. Books two through five, along with the first and last titles, make up a course in Western civilization; and books six through nine can also be used in the same way with the first and last titles to form a course in non-Western civilization. Taken together, all ten titles constitute the basic reading for a course in world civilization, while each individual book can be used either on its own or as a supplement to a conventional world history text.

How well this procedure permitted us to achieve our goals will be for each reader to decide.

William H. McNeill

Preface

Any textbook writer must derive satisfaction from laying down the law about so many important subjects. It is a genuinely great responsibility, from choosing and verifying the facts, to adopting and presenting appropriate interpretive slants. But the end product is also satisfying. Here is a major historical period neatly packaged, with facts, interpretations, and a number of unresolved historical controversies presented to encourage discussion. The ideas must be subjected to a critical view. To further such a view, we can begin with some doubts.

The title "Modern Europe" is prosaic enough. Yet both words are somewhat tenuous as units of historical analysis since the idea of "modern" history is open to the most obvious challenge. Some historians, usually those concerned with earlier time periods, claim that there can be no modern history at all, only journalism; for no proper historical perspective can be given to events and trends so close in time. This is special pleading. No period is exempt from biased judgments; the vast array of sources available to a conscientious modern historian helps mute his personal prejudices; and surely we do not want to be called journalists.

More relevantly, any student should ask when "modern" history begins. 1789 is not a magic date. If one looks to the history of formal ideas, a good case can be made for the 1680's as the crucial turning point toward "modernity" (though note that much of intellectual history from the nineteenth century to the present involves a challenge to the rationalism and optimism that developed at that time). In politics, 1789 is surely as good a date as any in Europe. Actual forms of government, however, can be seen in a steady evolution which the French Revolution only accelerated; while the modern revolutionary ideas such as democracy spread slowly both in application and in popular acceptance. Modern social and economic forms, such as industrial capitalism, were foreshadowed well before 1789 but had not reached full fruition by 1914. It is indeed a jumble. Yet something of a new civilization was forged between 1789 and 1914. Ideas such as the concept of progress, developed earlier, gained popular acceptance for the first time. In combination with new political and economic forms, they created perhaps the first new popular world view since the rise of Christianity (which correspondingly declined in importance). Putting it another way, the debated issues of the eighteenth century appear terribly appealing, because we recognize the validity of the leading intellectuals' ideals, and can see how desirable it would have been if the existing society had moved to correspond to them. By 1914, society had moved toward them in many ways. But all was not well — solutions and even fundamental issues were far less clear. This is another way of saying that during the nineteenth century, the modern period had begun. The First World War deflected, but did not fundamentally overturn, this period. It may be best, then, to play down the great events that mark the beginning and end of the extended nineteenth century; what is really important is that, sometime between them, a variety of factors combined to produce a new era. When this happened depends, of course, on what is meant by "modern." Hopefully, this approach to the nineteenth century will contribute to an understanding of the word.

Likewise, some doubts about the utility of the term "Europe" can be voiced. The various parts of Europe did not become "modern" at the same time or in the same degree. Geographical Europe was part of a common diplomatic system, but this is not of great help to the analysis of developments outside of diplomacy. There were some common developments, during the period, in ideologies and in governmental functions; but the gaps in economic, social, and political forms often widened during the period. All nations were different — so, indeed, were most regions within most nations. But big distinctions can be made between western and eastern Europe, with southern Europe and Germany somewhat in the middle conceptually, if not always geographically. Like most texts, this book stresses western Europe. Partly this is due to the author's own major interests, partly to the fact that in some political and economic forms western Europe was setting a trail that other areas would follow. But the drawing together was a function of the later twentieth century, not the nineteenth, and it is far from complete even now. For the period 1789-1914, the validity of Europe as a historical unit is debatable indeed. Its diplomatic unity is not a satisfactory general argument; its common Christendom, never a fully unifying factor, was becoming decreasingly relevant. It might be happier, from an analytical standpoint, to deal with western Europe and North America in common (disdaining accusations of Anglo-Saxonism, or American imperialism, or, from the American viewpoint, un-Americanism) with a book of equal importance devoted to eastern and southern Europe (with Germany treated in each book). This book does not do this; it respects the traditional unities of diplomacy and of college courses. Yet I hope it provides some materials for skepticism about Europe as an entity in any case.

I must make three acknowledgments for assistance in preparing this book, beyond those due to students who, exposed to my views, helped develop them. I am grateful to Professor William H. McNeill for his suggestions and encouragement; to the editorial staff of Scott, Foresman and Company for their advice and technical skills; and to my wife, Nancy, for support that ranged from typing through tolerance to reading the book.

Contents

MAPS AND GRAPHS

Information has been taken from government sources, *U.S. Dept. of Commerce and Labor*, Bureau of Manufacturers, Special Agents Series. *U.S. Dept. of the Interior*, Geological Survey Series, "Mineral Resources of the U.S.," Vol. I.

Introduction

An Overview
1789–1914

Between the French Revolution and World War I all aspects of European life changed fundamentally. By 1914, Germany had replaced France as the leading continental power, and the methods and means of European diplomacy had departed from eighteenth-century patterns. Further, Europe had thrust forward into unprecedented world empire. In the realm of art and ideas, the confident rationalism that was almost unchallenged in 1789 found itself under determined attack by 1914 from intellectuals in various fields who held that reason was inadequate to perceive truth, or that it was positively harmful. The challenge to the heritage of the Enlightenment had risen steadily during the nineteenth century, and not within the realm of ideas alone. Although creative intellectuals and the "general public" grew apart in many ways during the nineteenth century, the attacks on rationalism were finding a popular audience by 1914.

Indeed, the outlook of many Europeans, not themselves intellectuals, underwent a double evolution during the century. In 1789, most Europeans were still Christians of a rather traditional sort. Many still were, of course, in 1914. But the experience of the intervening decades convinced Europeans that the old outlook at least had to be modified. Their own new contacts with cities and markets, and the formal education they increasingly received, taught some the validity of much of the rationalist doctrines about the possibility for human improvement, through reason, on this earth. A new, rationalist "world view" had been developed in the seventeenth and eighteenth centuries, and it was only slightly elaborated in the nineteenth; what was decisive was that it now spread widely in society, at least in western Europe. The result was, perhaps, the most sweeping change in popular outlook since the rise of Christianity, and a major symptom of this change was the decline of Christian belief itself.

The spread of Enlightenment doctrines was not unchallenged. Many ordinary people could not accept so total a defiance of tradition, and they were open to social theories, widely preached by the end of the nineteenth century, that were not traditional but that claimed contact with the past. Others had accepted key rationalist notions but later found them inadequate. The attitudes of Europeans by 1900 were, then, divided, partly by region and social class but partly even within the same individuals. Elements of tradition persisted; there was a faith in certain Enlightenment notions of reason and orderly progress; and there was a new attraction to ideas of violence and action.

The most decisive change in general outlook concerned the idea of social, economic, and political change itself. Most people in Europe in 1789 did not believe in secular progress. They had no personal experience of progress and their Christianity gave them no basis for a more abstract belief. The French Revolution itself began, as European revolutions had in earlier centuries, by appeals to past rights, not to future gains. But the Revolution quickly turned into a modern protest, in which rights were defined by abstract and absolute standards and the revolutionaries looked to future perfection rather than to a better past. The Revolution convinced many people that change was inevitable, whether desirable or not. Time and time again, during the first half of the nineteenth century, leaders in business and intellectual life, as well as in politics, repeated the idea that change could at most be understood and guided — that it could never be thwarted. There were, of course, efforts at resistance, particularly between 1815 and 1848, but even these were undergirded by premonitions of failure, with the result that resistance often crumbled quickly in the face of renewed revolutionary onslaught. During the nineteenth century, then, most Europeans learned that change was a fact of life, and many came to believe that it was good. If, at the end of the century, there was a revival of appeals to the past, the past sought was largely imaginary and the methods suggested to attain it were radically new. Here, again, was evidence of a decisive alteration of the general outlook of European people.

The basic force for change was economic, for during the nineteenth century most Europeans developed not only new ways to produce and sell goods but also new motives for economic effort. The industrial revolution, the most decisive change in human society since the rise of organized agriculture, capped the economic development of the century, but it was preceded and accompanied by other innovations. In 1789, most people produced goods in rather traditional ways and for rather traditional reasons. Artisans by and large maintained their customs of limited, high-quality production, which protected their economic security but did not maximize their gains. Most peasants produced primarily for themselves or for themselves and their masters, without selling much on the market and without expecting significant improvements in their standard of living. Even most businessmen worked for security more than for rapid gain. Already, however, this was changing, and it was to change more still. During the late eighteenth and nineteenth centuries, population growth and alterations in land laws and taxes forced most peasants to turn to production for the market, which subjected them to new risks and required new methods. Some artisans were eliminated altogether by factory competition, and even more had to adjust to a capitalist system of manufacture in which they were employees rather than craftsmen, paid by a wage and expected to produce as much as they could. Beside these traditional producers grew the vast factory labor force, subjected to conditions that were entirely new. By 1914 most Europeans, for the first time in history, were actively part of a commercial system and were expected to behave according to commercial motives. This meant that they were expected to work harder than before; among other things, the number of holidays declined rapidly. It also meant they were supposed to take new risks. The peasant who stopped producing everything his family required and began to specialize in a crop for market sale certainly took new chances; so did the worker who, consciously or not, submitted himself to a manufacturer who relied on distant markets.

Along with economic and industrial change came a massive alteration in the size and location of Europe's population. In the late eighteenth century, population began to grow in almost all parts of the continent and Britain; between 1750 and 1900 it at least tripled. With this growth came a migration to the cities — first in trickles and then, as population growth overwhelmed the available land and urban industry offered new opportunities, in a veritable flood. Even in western Europe, only a quarter of the population was urban in 1789; by 1900, over 50 per cent of all people lived in cities (again, a first in human history). In personal terms, this meant that between 1789 and 1914 most people moved, often abandoning a village in which their families had resided for centuries.

Clearly, these vast changes were a great shock to many of the people who underwent them. New workers and many businessmen, compelled by the pressure of rising population and the force of market competition, were using new mechanical techniques and business forms against their will. Not all manufacturers embraced the new opportunities — and the new risks — of factory industry eagerly. Many refused to innovate and failed in their businesses; many tried to innovate and failed; many who succeeded did so only because they were forced to try new techniques in order to survive. The number of conscious, ardent innovators was small; yet in this new society almost everyone had to accept some novelty. The strain was great. For many people, the forces of change brought direct material suffering, at least for a time. Population growth forced peasant earnings down, because there was less land to go around. Conditions in new factories and cities were horrible in many ways. City housing and other facilities for ordinary people had never been good, and the wave of immigration to the cities made them even worse. Even in the upper levels of society there was at least relative suffering. Many aristocrats could not master the techniques of commercial agriculture and had to sell their estates. Many traditional businessmen and professional people failed as well, and many more saw their status decline as newcomers with new ideas seized the first fruits of industrialization. And economic change never let up. Small businessmen who did well in the first phase of industrialization saw their position threatened or eroded with the rise of big business. Artisans who benefited from the first expansion of the cities were later challenged by new factories.

With all this vast change, western Europe in many ways became, or seemed to become, steadily more orderly during the nineteenth century. Gradually, and at various levels, violence declined. With penal reform, punishments became less cruel and less public. After about 1830 in western Europe, city people rarely experienced the horror or satisfaction of watching bloody executions. Personal violence declined. The murder rate dropped during the century as a whole, while property crime increased. Quite probably, personal fights and beatings of wives and children became less common. On a larger scale, rioting declined in western Europe, at least after 1848. The age of revolutions was over by mid-century. Small-scale riots—the outburst of a few scores of people in a village or a few hundred in a city—decreased as well, although they had been common before. Finally, wars grew less common after the revolutionary-Napoleonic outburst.

In eastern and southern Europe, in contrast, collective violence, and quite possibly personal violence, increased after the mid-nineteenth century. Rioting in both town and countryside became more frequent and more massive, just as it was dying down in the West. Here, as in western Europe earlier, society was beginning to change enough to disturb many people but not enough to satisfy them. Population growth and the spread of new taxes oppressed a peasantry that was unable to produce substantially for a market, because of ignorance, lack of capital, or lack of sufficient land. Cities were growing rapidly and reproduced many of the foul conditions that prevailed earlier in the West.

The growth of public and personal order, then, was not uniform throughout Europe; one of the reasons that Europe was set ablaze in 1914 was because western European nations were in the diplomatic thrall of the unstable countries of the east. But for western and central Europe, there is a vital question underlying much of nineteenth-century history: why, in the face of unprecedented disruption and frequent suffering, did orderliness increase in many ways?

Some aspects of the answer are fairly obvious. At least after the first decades of industrialization, large numbers of people benefited from the new economy to some degree. Particularly during the halcyon years of 1850 to 1870, when cities were absorbing most of the population growth in western and central Europe and business was booming, the earnings of most peasants, artisans, and workers rose; this contented many of them and gave them a new stake in preserving order. But there were pitfalls. New earnings might gradually produce new expectations, and workers were clearly learning to want more than they were getting; here was an "idea of progress" in its most concrete form. Renewed economic instability after 1872 brought periodic hardship to many in the cities, and more persistent suffering to many agricultural producers. Yet, though agitation increased, violence and rioting remained relatively rare; and again, the question is why?

4

The answer must be sought in politics – in the spread of new political attitudes and in the growth of state power. In 1789 most Europeans did not have political interests in the modern sense, and few had much contact with the state save through an occasional tax collector (and many taxes were collected by private agents), military recruiter, and, more rarely, repressor of riots. For peasants, the effective political unit was the village or the manor, not the national state. Even many businessmen looked no further than city government; and urban crowds, though frequently unruly, demonstrated little political concern.

On the whole, the middle class was the first to develop some sense of political consciousness. This diverse group, composed of business and professional people, constituted about 20 per cent of the urban population; for the most part, it had enough property, in bonds or stores or real estate, to wish to avoid direct violence. The personal ethic of the class stressed respectability and self-control. The educated elements of the class were, however, open to political ideas, such as those of the Enlightenment, and even businessmen could feel that they needed a voice in the state to protect their economic interests and reflect their economic importance. On this basis, the middle class could countenance – if rarely directly participate in – violent agitation, and it did so from the French Revolution through the revolutions of 1848. Yet violence was personally distasteful to most members of the class: it could endanger property and it was bad for business. Even during the revolutionary period, most people in the middle class would have preferred evolutionary change through reforms of the existing order. It required, then, only the provision of political outlets, such as parliaments and a freer press, to convert the class to order. By 1832 in Britain and by the 1850's in western and central Europe, conservative defenders of the existing system were willing to grant this much.

Even before 1848, the middle class had done much to convert elements of the lower classes to greater order. Middle-class associations spread through schools, and pamphlets urged self-control for workers and artisans; manufacturers tried to enforce new habits in the factories. To an extent, these promptings relied on religion, the traditional sanction for order, and they had great appeal on this basis alone. There was widespread respect for authority among the lower classes, even in the cities; and new peasants coming into the cities could transfer to their employers the deference they had long felt toward the aristocracy. But the middle class also urged new forms of orderliness: temperance, control of passions, a taste for personal advancement. Many artisans and skilled workers were in fact converted, and this could powerfully contribute to public order. For example, in Britain after 1850, following three decades of periodic labor violence, a new union movement spread among the working-class elite, stressing reforms within the system and, particularly, self-improvement as the key to progress.

From the middle class, also, many workers learned a political interest. Typically, middle-class leaders sought political power for propertied elements alone, sometimes excluding the lower levels of the class itself.

But to win even these gains, lower-class support was often necessary. From 1789 to 1848, middle-class political efforts, revolutionary or not, relied substantially on lower-class agitation. Through these, gradually, the lower classes developed political leanings of their own. Here, of course, was a dilemma: how could the new political consciousness win expression? Generally — and this was crucial to the development of order after 1848 — it won expression without significant violence. Only in eastern and southern Europe, after mid-century, did political interests arise without any significant concessions to them; here was one of the bases for violence in these areas. In western Europe, political emancipation sometimes actually preceded mass political consciousness.

Many people used their new political rights to express a fundamental conservatism. Many peasants who owned land felt a stake in the existing order and were still traditionally respectful toward authority; conservatives consciously appealed to new voters in the city as well as in the countryside. The spread of democracy, then, did not simply mean a translation of grievances into political forms. Obviously, however, the most striking result of mass suffrage was the rise of socialism. Here was a clear expression of protest within the political arena from workers and others who felt real hostility to the existing order. Yet this very development helped reinforce orderliness. People who could protest through politics could realize that more violent protest was unnecessary. As their parties and political influence grew, socialist and union leaders worked to reduce disorder that might bring reprisals against their own organizations. As with the middle class before, politicization brought a certain degree of commitment to the existing system, which at least had granted the right of political expression.

In the second half of the nineteenth century, then, political change seemed to keep pace with social and economic change. More people learned to look to the state to solve their problems, and the states of western and central Europe largely responded. Well before 1848 even some conservative states began to favor middle-class business and professional interests, by developing new schools, transportation networks, and the like. Contact between the state and the broader population grew along with political rights, increasing the loyalty of many people to the state. Mass education, military conscription, and welfare programs both encouraged and resulted from the integration of the lower classes into the political system. Here again were powerful forces for order.

New reasons for contentment (particularly material contentment), new personal habits, and new attitudes toward society and the state combined, then, to work a major change in the popular outlook, stabilizing behavior in many ways despite the dizzying development of novel social and economic forms. Yet, in World War I, the nineteenth century and many of its values perished in a blaze of violence. This was not an accident, nor did it result from diplomatic maneuverings alone; its causes reached well back into the nineteenth century, into some of the very developments that seemed to encourage stability.

Not all Europeans found political outlets adequate to express their feelings of grievance and frustration. Workers were increasingly converted to socialism, and socialism did become increasingly moderate, but both of these developments depended on the continued willingness of the existing order to grant some concessions to socialist demands through a variety of welfare measures. And socialism itself taught many workers to want more than they were getting. Conservatives, who by 1900 included many members of the middle class and peasantry, had conceded almost all that they could. Welfare benefits were not allowed to reverse growing inequalities of income. Nonsocialist parties grouped together to make sure that the political concessions granted to workers did not turn into working class rule. Finally, after 1900, growing economic stagnation limited material gains for many groups and turned moderate dissatisfaction into anger. Working-class violence was on the rise again.

Perhaps more important, the very political and economic changes that partially contented many groups left others by the wayside. Throughout the nineteenth century, but particularly toward its end, it proved almost impossible to draw groups that resented modern economic trends into regular political activity, of the sort that might vent grievances and establish some sort of stake in the existing system. Broadly speaking, political changes benefited primarily those groups who were also benefiting from economic development: businessmen, industrial workers, artisans, and peasants who could make their way in a market economy. For this reason, and because political change seemed to be so much a part of an unsatisfactory "modern world," many groups nursed their grievances largely outside the political system. Many artisans and small shopkeepers who longed for a simpler economy and the return of craft traditions, many peasants who still resented market pressure, many Christians, particularly Catholics and Lutherans, who put their religion ahead of accommodation to modern society, refused to make their peace with the new order. Increasing numbers of intellectuals and professional people felt bypassed by the trends of modern society and in this case did not simply ignore politics, but turned against them. Their leadership helped rouse violent attitudes and sometimes outright violence in others who detested modernity. Anti-Semitic riots after 1870 and the popularity of many preachers of violence revealed the importance of these sentiments.

More broadly still, there were signs, at the end of the nineteenth century, that the traditional, if sporadic, human impulse toward violence had been altered rather than suppressed. There were many signs that people were bored with the sort of sedate, controlled existence they led. Even the middle class, the prime advocate of restraint, began to loosen up. Sports and hiking became more popular; the tone of sexual morality began to unbend. It was in nationalism, however, that the new mood became most apparent and most important.

The spread of nationalism almost invariably accompanied the growth of political interest, from the French Revolution onward. In existing states such as France this was perhaps a logical development, for the state was coextensive with the nation and loyalty to one might lead to loyalty to the other. From France, nationalism spread even to areas in which there was no state, in part by imitation. Nationalism took hold because it provided a respectable and intense loyalty when traditional attachments no longer sufficed, and because it helped people identify themselves. Nationalism could tell an English businessman that his efforts were not simply self-seeking, that they advanced the good of his nation; and this was surely satisfying. Nationalism could give the middle-class politician a reason for attachment to his state, or to work to create a national state, that was not tainted by religious or dynastic or aristocratic injunctions to be loyal.

From the first, nationalism provided a fairly respectable outlet for hatred and violence. This is not a condemnation; it is simply a recognition that nationalism, like socialism to a lesser extent, served to draw and politicize emotions that used to be expressed in other ways, from religious wars through riots and village feuds to—perhaps—beating one's wife. On the surface, middle-class nationalism was tame enough. French revolutionaries professed a love for all men as well as for France; Italian nationalists felt that the nation should be a peaceful unit. But French nationalists expressed their love for other men by fighting the crowned heads of Europe and their more humble supporters; Italian nationalists loved humanity but they hated the Austrians. Even businessmen explaining their role in the nation's progress used warlike imagery, for, long before Social Darwinism formalized the idea, they saw their nation's economy in conflict with the economies of others. It was the liberal, humane, middle-class press of England that helped impel that country into the Crimean War, for even English nationalism required encouragement.

After 1848, aristocratic as well as middle-class politicians and governments worked to spread nationalism to society as a whole. Increasingly, many people were drawn, because they too had been torn from traditional attachments and were open to new loyalties, particularly when preached so vigorously and from such respectable sources. Compulsory school systems, military service, and the press all served as missionary agents. In the process, nationalism became a more powerful force and a more directly violent one. Many existing nationalists, particularly the intellectual ones, were becoming more bellicose anyway, as the doctrinal and political basis of nationalism changed. Beyond this, the spread of nationalism helped consolidate a variety of grievances and emotions. Shopkeepers in economic trouble, who were carefully restrained in their personal habits and who shunned direct violence, found a respectable outlet for their feelings by supporting their country's military glory and imperial gain. Christians began to see that Nation and Church could be united as King and Church once were, for the protection of religion at home and the conquest of heathens abroad. Various degrees of nationalism reached almost everyone. Not everyone saw it as a vehicle for direct or vicarious violence, of course, but most people could at least accept violence in its name. When World War I arrived, enlightened, orderly Europe welcomed it; it was going to be great fun.

No single theme, of course, covers the complexity of a century and a quarter. Many intellectual developments had a life of their own. Political theorists—liberals and socialists particularly—played a major role in political turmoil of the century and in the spread of political interests. Many types of intellectuals and artists contributed to the evolution of nationalism. But many aspects of art and philosophy must be outlined that had little immediate relationship. Some important diplomatic developments between 1815 and 1848 had little to do with social or even political change. The following survey, then, is not simply an illustration of the thesis set forth to illuminate the main trends of the period.

Nor is there any desire to oversimplify through the thesis itself. Terms such as "popular mentality" or the "middle class" are extremely general, and they must be tested by historical fact. The notion of a gradual transfer of aggressive impulses in Europe is impossible to prove directly and must, therefore, be assessed with care. Still, much of Europe did become more orderly amid great social disruption; both diplomacy and the loyalties attached to the state did become more belligerent, as the power of the state grew. This complex evolution does convey much of nineteenth-century history, much of the changing life of the people of Europe.

From this vantage point, European history between 1789 and 1914 can be seen in several major periods. The first, running until 1848, was the classic age of revolution in western and central Europe. New political interests, particularly in the middle class, clashed with the persistent conservative effort to cling to an old regime without major change. Population growth and the spread of commerce disturbed the lower classes. Only in eastern Europe were these developments still tentative enough and the old regimes powerful enough to avoid major disorder. Elsewhere, disorder was not necessarily more frequent than before 1789, but it was more clearly focused and better organized.

The year 1848 saw the last outburst of this first period. As the result of the series of revolutions, both conservatism and liberalism had to change, and these changes were aided by a real burst of industrial development, the first significant advance outside of England. In this transitional period, a new diplomatic framework was created, partly because of the spread of political interests and the possibilities of industry. During the 1870's some fruitful accommodations were made which reduced many of the old political tensions; questions of the form of political regimes were largely solved and a new diplomatic stability seemed possible within Europe. Between 1850 and 1875, the triumph of orderly behavior seemed almost complete. The new series of wars was troubling, but they were brief and rather restrained; violence began to increase in eastern Europe, but it had yet to reach full flowering; the growth of labor agitation in western Europe, though expressed violently in the Paris Commune, still seemed manageable. The middle class was at the peak of its power and self-confidence. Its own personal valuation of order and self-control seemed generally applicable, and many other people—workers, aristocrats, and landed peasants—were coming to share it. Political reform was possible through legal action, and economic progress appeared assured. On a more personal level, the beginnings of a declining birth rate, the rise of family savings, a decrease in the abuse of children, even in some cases a decline of drinking showed that many people were able to bring their habits under greater control.

Well before 1900, however, attacks on political and social harmony mounted. The rise of socialism and trade unions troubled many, though as we have seen they did not necessarily threaten an orderly society. Attacks on modern politics and industrialism by intellectuals were more disturbing, and they coincided with an increasing, if vague, malaise among other groups. Without any clear event marking the change, a new period emerged around 1900. Social disputes grew more intense, with strikes and revolutionary efforts marking their embitterment. Massive if interrupted increases in the prosperity of industrial nations, basic to developments in western and central Europe after 1850, now seemed threatened. Russia and the Hapsburg monarchy, for different reasons, were on the verge of collapse. In diplomacy, with the outlet of empire largely closed, statesmen turned their attention to purely European interests once again. The talk was of war and preparation for war, and intensified nationalism and the popularization of some of the antirational ideals of violence and activism made the prospect of war acceptable to many people. Even before war broke out, some of the characteristics of later nineteenth-century Europe were eroding.

SUGGESTED READING

The bibliographies following each chapter in this book are intended to provide guidance to more detailed studies of nineteenth-century Europe. They are divided into topical and national histories and studies of limited periods. The stress in such brief and introductory listings is on works that provide a reasonably general coverage of a major problem and on provocative and recent studies that can indicate some of the directions and controversies of research in modern European history. The citation only of works in English excludes, of course, much valuable material, but many major topics have yet to be adequately treated in any language. The bibliographies, then, offer the basis for further study, but they also suggest some of the opportunities that remain in the field.

The *Rise of Modern Europe* series covers most of the extended nineteenth century, usually with the same periodization as that employed in this book. The series is showing its age a bit now, but it remains valuable for its comprehensive coverage; the bibliographies, which have been updated recently, are useful as well. Crane Brinton, *A Decade of Revolution: 1789-1799** (1963), is an excellent introduction to the French Revolution. G. Brunn, *Europe and the French Imperium, 1799-1814** (1963), and F. B. Artz, *Reaction and Revolution, 1815-1832** (1963), provide competent surveys. R. C. Binkley, *Realism and Nationalism, 1852-1871** (1963), is less successful in its basic approach, but C. J. H. Hayes, *A Generation of Materialism, 1871-1900** (1963), remains stimulating. In addition to this series, a fine effort at interpretation of the century is B. Croce, *History of Europe in the Nineteenth Century** (1963).

*Available in a paperback edition.

Political history is, with few exceptions, best followed through the histories of specific states; and many of the national histories contain excellent material on diplomatic, social, and cultural developments as well. For France, Alfred Cobban, *A History of Modern France** (1966), Vols. II and III, is preëminent in its coverage and analysis, but see also Gordon Wright, *France in Modern Times* (1960), for a coherent narrative history. For Germany, K. S. Pinson, *Modern Germany: Its History and Civilization* (1954), is the best survey; A. J. P. Taylor, *The Course of German History** (1946), is a long and often compelling editorial on the same subject. For Britain, a good, brief account is David Thomson, *England in the Nineteenth Century** (1950); see also K. B. Smellie, *Great Britain Since 1688* (1962). E. Halévy, *History of the English People in the 19th Century** (6 vols, 1949ff.), remains a classic.

A. J. P. Taylor's *The Hapsburg Monarchy, 1809-1918* (1965), is excellent, though it only sketches the early nineteenth century. On domestic developments, though for a more limited period, A. J. May, *The Hapsburg Monarchy, 1867-1914* (1951), offers fuller treatment. For Italy, see R. Albrecht-Carrié, *Italy from Napoleon to Mussolini** (1950), and the more stimulating D. Mack-Smith, *Italy: A Modern History* (1959). On Russia, see A. A. Kornilov, *Modern Russian History . . . from the Age of Catherine the Great to the Present* (1924), M. T. Florinsky, *Russia: A History and Interpretation* (2 vols, 1953). L. Stavrianos, *The Balkans Since 1453* (1958), is an extraordinarily coherent summary; O. Halecki, *History of Poland** (1956), is good.

There is little useful survey work on intellectual history for the period as a whole. The best essay is G. Mosse, *The Culture of Western Europe* (1962). Also useful are the relevant sections of Crane Brinton, *The Shaping of the Modern Mind** (1953), and J. H. Randall, *Making of the Modern Mind* (1940). For political theory, see G. H. Sabine, *A History of Political Theory* (1937); for economic theory, see the excellent C. Gide and C. Rist, *History of Economic Doctrines from the Physiocrats to the Present Day* (1948). General surveys of the history of science include J. Jeans, *The Growth of Physical Science** (1948); T. M. Lowry, *Historical Introduction to Chemistry* (1936); and C. J. Singer, *The Story of Living Things: A Short Account of the Evolution of the Biological Sciences* (1931). A. Hauser, *The Social History of Art** (Vol. II, 1950), is a useful summary.

For an overview of diplomatic history, see R. Albrecht-Carrié, *Diplomatic History of Europe Since the Congress of Vienna* (1958). Also see Theodore Ropp, *War in the Modern World** (1962), and G. A. Craig, *Politics of the Prussian Army, 1640-1945** (1955). For church history, E. Hales, *Catholic Church in the Modern World** (1960), is a very pro-Catholic account, J. B. Bury, *History of the Papacy in the Nineteenth Century* (1964), a very hostile treatment, and J. M. Moody, *Church and Society* (1953), though less comprehensive, somewhere in between. See also J. J. Altholz, *The Churches in the Nineteenth Century** (1967).

Economic history can be surveyed through W. Bowden, M. Karpovich, and A. P. Usher, *An Economic History of Europe Since 1750* (1937), H. Heaton, *Economic History of Europe* (1948), and Vol. II of the *Cambridge Economic History* (1965). More specialized studies for the whole period include J. Clapham, *The Economic Development of France and Germany** (1961); J. Clapham, *An Economic History of Modern Britain* (3 vols, 1926-1938), and W. Henderson, *The Industrial Revolution on the Continent* (1961). For demography see A. M. Carr-Saunders, *World Population: Past Growth and Present Trends* (1936); A. Weber, *The Rise of the City* (1963); and R. E. Dickinson, *The West European City: A Study in Urban Geography* (1951). For social history, see P. N. Stearns, *European Society in Upheaval* (1967), and G. D. H. Cole and R. Postgate, *The British Common People, 1746-1940* (1947).

*Available in a paperback edition.

Chapter 1

The French Revolution

The French Revolution dominated the decade following its outbreak in 1789. The Revolution aimed directly at altering the social as well as political structure of France, but its effects were not confined to these goals. Revolutionary governments imposed their laws on neighboring territory, particularly in the Low Countries; groups in various states agitated for comparable reforms on their own. There was also a quick and general reaction against the Revolution, leading to various repressive measures even in parliamentary England. In short, the fact of revolution in France soon became the leading internal political issue in other countries. The Revolution quickly dominated diplomatic considerations. From the 1790's until the 1840's, diplomacy was first and foremost a tool to foster or prevent revolutionary gains. The Revolution also affected Europe's intellectual concerns; an intellectual reaction to the Revolution took shape in the 1790's and made coherent various indirect protests against Enlightenment philosophy that had risen earlier. A fairly formal conservative philosophy developed as a result. The Revolution was an almost unimaginably intense experience in France. Although its impact diminished with distance, its excitement reached out to people at all social levels, to Russia in the east and to the United States in the west, either to inspire or to repel.

Yet, for all its importance in the revolutionary decade and later, it is difficult to define the Revolution precisely. It was not avidly sought in advance. Most people in France wanted a variety of political and economic changes, but they were not revolutionaries. The Enlightenment philosophers, who so clearly helped prepare the way for revolution, were predominantly antirevolutionary, and those who still lived, such as Condorcet, generally opposed many aspects of the Revolution. More basically, there were several large groups in revolt, for quite different things. The aristocracy led the revolt, only to be consumed by it; middle-class people, particularly from the professions or from government bureaucracy itself, shaped the Revolution more than any other group; but peasants rose for their own goals, with substantial success, and urban shopkeepers and artisans, the *sans-culottes,* had yet another list of grievances for which they agitated for several years. The Revolution would have been impossible without all these groups, yet they acted largely without mutual contacts or understanding; and often they attacked each other. Finally, the Revolution underwent three definite stages, partly because the groups in power varied. The initial, liberal phase lasted until 1792; a radical phase, the Terror, followed until 1794; then a period of retrenchment ensued, which tried on the whole to recapture the spirit of the liberal period but under conditions of much greater internal and external stress.

CAUSES OF THE REVOLUTION

Revolution was to become a familiar event for the sixty years after 1789. It should not be forgotten that it was always difficult to begin: revolution involved physical risk, danger to property, violation of normal, peaceful habits and chains of command. Particularly in this, the first and longest of the European revolutions of the period, the combination of causes had to be massively compelling; and an element of accident and miscalculation was essential too.

Two related developments set the stage for the outbreak of revolution: a discontented aristocracy and a weak, financially desperate centralized government. Like all eighteenth-century governments, the French monarchy devoted most of its expenditures to the maintenance of the military and to payment of past war debts. The debt burden had been greatly increased by France's participation in the American war for independence. Approximately half of the annual expenditures of the state were swallowed by interest payments; and, though France was the richest country in Europe, the tax structure could not bear this burden. The government's problems called the whole social regime into question, for two groups were exempt from direct taxation: the nobility and the church. Though the church made small payments in lieu of taxes, almost the entire tax burden fell on the peasantry, whose meager incomes allowed little margin above subsistence in most cases. The result: an impoverished, overcommitted government and a system of privilege which could be criticized not only because it was unjust but because it did not work.

The Estates-General. The monarchy, aware of the difficulties of the system, tried reform repeatedly in the latter half of the eighteenth century. Reform was always blocked by aristocratic interests, however, since it would have eliminated the immunities of privilege and taxed those groups who controlled most of the landed wealth of the country. In 1788 a new finance minister, Calonne, called an "assembly of notables" which he hoped would agree to a general tax. But the aristocracy had long seen in the weakness of the state opportunity to regain a share in real political power, to push back the dominance of the centralized, absolutist monarchy. The King, Louis XVI, tried to force through the program despite aristocratic resistance, but the nobles threatened virtual revolt and began to form agitation groups throughout the country. In so doing, they roused other people to an awareness of grievance and impelled the calling of the Estates-General, a body which had not met for over 150 years but which now turned into the agency of revolution. On July 5, 1788, Louis XVI called the Estates-General and invited the various classes to draw up lists of grievances.

The causal pattern in revolutions for the next sixty years can be easily seen in France in 1789. A weak or at least hesitant government was one precondition. An economic crisis was needed to prod elements of the lower classes into violence; but there were deeper lower-class grievances as well, which called the social system into question. Finally, politically conscious leadership was essential, drawn from confident, established groups, possessed of elements of ideology, loath usually to participate in actual rioting but willing and capable of using such agitation to establish a new government.

The French peasantry was massively discontent in 1789, though it was in a far better position than most of its European counterparts. France was already a country of small holdings. That is, most peasants were able to buy and sell their plots of land and could farm them as they pleased instead of working on great estates. However, peasants were still burdened with remnants of manorial obligations, a major source of the wealth of church and aristocracy; the peasants wanted to attack these continuing restrictions above all. They wanted the abolition of the taxes they owed the local nobles; they wanted abolition of other noble rights, such as exclusive hunting privileges; they wanted abolition of the obligatory tithes owed to the church; and they wanted a fairer general tax system. French peasants, like peasants in later risings in Europe, felt that the land was theirs by right and wanted only to be left alone to cultivate it. Moreover, rural population had been rising rapidly, putting pressure on existing holdings; the majority of peasant plots were too small to support a family without some extra agricultural or manufacturing labor as a supplement. Hence many peasants looked enviously at the estates of church and aristocracy, which still comprised at least a fifth of the arable land in France.

Artisans and shopkeepers in the city were aggrieved also. They suffered particularly from the intense economic crisis in France between 1787 and 1789, for high bread prices and unemployment brought stark misery to the urban poor. Crises of this sort often caused urban rioting in France and elsewhere. Furthermore, some artisans and shopkeepers had a sense of "natural justice," defined in terms of a fairer sharing of wealth, that could lead them to attack the rich and the noble. Before 1789 their grievances had not been directly political, but their traditions of protest could be turned toward more political goals.

Lower-class Participation. The common people, both rural and urban, provided the muscle for actual agitation during the Revolution, yet only a minority were actively involved. We do not know how many peasants participated in violent protest between 1789 and 1793. Their grievances were widely shared, for they appeared in most of the lists of complaints drawn up in every area in preparation for the Estates-General. Many were too poor to be able to agitate, a few were too wealthy to want to, and many were ignorant of any possibility of change. Probably many of the leaders were not ordinary peasants, but men who had some contact with cities through rural manufacturing work. Among the urban lower classes, too, only a minority was ready for a riot. Again, the very poor could not ordinarily participate, not only because they were constantly busy with problems of mere survival, but also because they lacked both the expectations and the sense of community necessary for most riots. The urban riots were staffed primarily by artisans — carpenters, bakers, and the like. These groups alone could produce thousands of demonstrators in Paris.

Middle-class Enthusiasm. The French Revolution was a middle-class revolution above all. Almost all the revolutionary leaders were middle class; the most articulate and certainly the most political demands were middle class; the enduring results benefited the middle class most clearly. Yet, in 1789, there was no easily definable middle class at all. Indeed, the Revolution itself played a major role in creating the class by providing a common political heritage (however diversely interpreted) and by attacking some of the more traditional forms of urban economic activity. To be sure, it can be noted that in 1789 about 5 per cent of the national population were business or professional people. This group may have shared personal values, like hard work and moral respectability, that suggested some social unity already. In politics and economics, however, the group was deeply divided.

Many businessmen and professional people were satisfied with their lot. Many were traditionally deferential to authority, including the aristocracy which some rich businessmen preferred to imitate rather than attack. Businessmen played an insignificant role in the Revolution, for they were concerned above all with their economic ventures. Furthermore, many business people were content with the economic structure of the old regime. Big financiers were attached to the old order by the tax exemptions they, too, received and by their profitable loans to the state. Many little merchants and manufacturers liked the protection that guilds gave against new methods and undue competition. Only a minority of businessmen were venturesome capitalists.

The leading bearers, in 1789, of what *became* middle-class values were professional people, particularly lawyers, and bureaucrats. This group was fully as numerous as the business element, which helps account for its influence. It had political awareness, through contacts with at least local governments. Many professional people were acquainted with the writings of the *philosophes,* who criticized traditional religion and aristocratic privilege and who demanded freedom of thought and equality under the law. This group resented aristocratic control of the upper positions in church and state. Because aristocratic prelates and government officials often used their offices simply as a source of gain, many professional people believed that their kind alone was capable of good government. Professional people were also concerned with freedom of thought and the press, against church as well as state controls. Their rationalist ideology, their own desire to get ahead, and, often, frustrating experiences in the state bureaucracy led many professional people to seek economic reforms as well, particularly the removal of most tax privileges, on grounds not only of justice but also of fiscal solidity. They also attacked limitations on trade, most notably the tariffs which many provinces still levied on internal commerce and the government-enforced guild restrictions on the movement of labor and the methods of manufacturing work.

How did the enthusiasm of many (not all, of course) professional people turn the French Revolution into a middle-class revolution? Even in 1789 the grievances of lawyers were shared by some businessmen, and as the Revolution wore on more and more business people saw the utility of economic and legal reform. These same reforms, such as the attack on economic restrictions, weakened the most conservative business elements. Furthermore, professional people quite early began to speak in the name of a larger middle class. In attacking aristocratic incompetence and the unfairness of aristocratic privilege and exclusiveness, professional people claimed both that most wealth was being produced outside the aristocracy and that wealth was a key sign of competence. They did not use the term middle class, but they implied one and in so doing helped create one, for businessmen might well come to agree with them. All of this took time, of course. "Middle-class" revolutionaries initially spoke in terms of the whole nation. Most of them felt that the proper leaders of the nation were the wealthy and the educated, but they did not say this directly; hence the wide initial suffrage granted, if only in a limited way, by the first revolutionary assembly. Some middle-class individuals were among the most ardent democrats, for political groupings knew no precise social boundaries. Only with the experience of the Revolution itself, and then incompletely, did some common middle-class political attitudes develop, close to the principles of the discontented professional people in 1789.

In sum, at least a minority of most the major segments of the French population felt active grievances in 1789, and these grievances referred to problems that affected far larger groups. The grievances added up to a sweeping attack on traditional, state-enforced privilege: the privileges of the aristocracy in tax and land; the privileges of nobles in state offices; the privileges of the church in censorship; and the privileges of guilds and provinces. This attack proved to be the essence of the Revolution.

Lack of Political Sense. The French Revolution, like any revolution in the strict sense of the term, was political, directed against the existing state. Yet, before 1789, few of the potentially revolutionary groups had a clear political sense. Many of the demands for reform, particularly in rural areas, were accompanied by protestations of loyalty to the King. The peasantry never developed directly political demands, though rural agitation was translated into political terms and rural grievances solved by political means. Once peasants had won their release from manorial obligations, they dropped out of the Revolution, and the revolutionary governments were just as remote for most of them as the monarchical regime had been. For artisans and others in the cities, the Revolution was a decisive political experience. Particularly in Paris, the example of upper-class protest and, perhaps, some direct leadership, prompted many poor people to turn their economic grievances against the state, as early as July 1789. They developed a dislike of aristocrats, the church, and the monarchy that was not necessarily new, but that was clearly and politically expressed for the first time. The experience of the Revolution taught them positive political goals as well, such as republicanism and democracy. The French Revolution marked a first step in the politicization of the urban lower classes, in France and elsewhere in western Europe, for it held out the possibility that political power was the answer to social and economic problems.

Before the calling of the Estates-General, most business and professional people had only vague ideas of political participation. They knew the state was important, of course, and they wanted governmental reforms, but they were accustomed to expecting initiatives from above, from the king, rather than demanding a share in the initiatives themselves. However, many of them saw that aristocrats were asking for political rights against the monarchy and wondered if they might do the same. The calling of the Estates-General, a political body, forced many middle-class people to think in new ways. Quite suddenly, many realized that they *did* want political rights as well as reforms; some of them wanted political rights for everyone. Again, the rights they demanded had potential applicability well beyond France, and they spread political consciousness to many different areas. For many decades, the chief result was a heightening of protest, for the political demands were not easily met; but they carried the seeds of a greater stability as well, for the middle class sought above all a forum for the legal expression of grievances, and this could affect even the rest of society.

Composition of the Estates-General. The political question in 1789 that turned the general movement of protest into revolution was the composition of the Estates-General. Very simply, the Estates-General was a medieval body, and many now urged that it be turned into a modern parliament. The estates had traditionally represented not individuals but legal categories of the population: the church, the nobility, and the third estate (which was meant to cover everyone else, at least indirectly). Each estate had the same number of representatives and had only one vote, which meant in 1789 that the nobility would rule, for aristocratic prelates controlled the first estate, of the church, and the second estate, which represented the nobility directly. What many people, including some churchmen and a few aristocrats, now wanted was a parliament representative of the whole population, not of separate, privileged orders; and they wanted this parliament to have sovereign power, rather than merely the right to advise the king. This meant revolution.

In January 1789, the Abbé Sieyès wrote "What Is the Third Estate?"

blasting the nobility and declaring that the nation as a whole should rule. Bowing to pressure, Louis XVI broke precedent even before the estates met, by allowing the third estate to have twice the number of representatives of each of the other two. But the King agreed with the aristocracy that the estates should meet separately and that each should have one vote. From the first meetings of the estates, in May 1789, the representatives of the third estate refused to acquiesce in this arrangement. On June 17 the third estate declared itself the "national Assembly"; and on June 20, after the King had closed their meeting hall, the representatives met on a tennis court and signed the Tennis Court Oath, affirming that they constituted a National Assembly wherever they met and vowing to remain until they had drafted a constitution. This Oath did more than overturn the traditional, privilege-based organization of the estates; it claimed sovereign power for the new Assembly, and it claimed the intent to remake the state. The Revolution had begun.

The Revolution was confirmed by subsequent outbursts in Paris and in the countryside. Louis XVI backed down and allowed the Assembly to meet, but he called in troops and intended to disband the body during July. This frightened the residents of Paris, already disturbed by the economic crisis and the resultant influx of beggars and criminals, and many Parisians began to arm themselves. Crowds gathered in front of arsenals and public buildings; on July 14 they assaulted the Bastille fort and overthrew the city government—and neither the King nor the army acted against them. The King dropped the idea of disbanding the Assembly.

Late in July wide sections of the countryside flamed into riot, spurred by rumors of brigand bands. Peasants burned manor houses and records of fees and dues, seeking to overturn the remnants of manorialism by force. Their actions impelled the Assembly to take the first giant step toward the abolition of the old regime on August 4. Finally, on October 4 a Paris food riot was diverted to Versailles, where the mob beseiged the palace and forced Louis XVI to come to Paris, thus subjecting the King to more constant supervision by the revolutionary forces.

THE LIBERAL PHASE

With the existence of a national, constituent assembly assured and with representatives both protected and prodded by popular agitation, attention could turn—had to turn—to the construction of a new regime. The Assembly sat until September 1791 and enacted four major pieces of legislation. These laws summed up the character of this first, liberal phase of the Revolution. They created problems which altered the later course of revolution. With one later emendation, they formed the most enduring portion of the revolutionary heritage.

On the night of August 4, a handful of liberal nobles led scores of their fellows, and upper churchmen, to renounce their old rights: manorial dues and work services, church tithes, manorial courts, tax exemptions, and provincial privileges. In other words, the Assembly gave the peasants approximately all they demanded, for though compensation was required for some of the dues, out of respect for property rights, little was ever paid. A strong, independent peasantry was the result, distinguishing France from many other nations in which full peasant emancipation came later and was less liberal. The most important step toward replacing privilege with equality under the law had been taken.

The Declaration of Rights. On August 26, 1789, the Assembly issued the Declaration of Rights of Man and the Citizen, proclaiming man's natural right to freedom and to legal equality. All people were to be free from oppression in thought and religion; the nation was sovereign, and only the people or their representatives could make laws; laws must bear equally on all citizens; and security of property was assured. The document affirmed liberty and suggested the basic principles of democracy. It remained to translate both into fact.

By 1790 the revolutionary assembly sought to make an appropriate arrangement with the church. Legislation following the night of August 4, by abolishing tithes, deprived the church of about half its income; the Declaration of Rights proclaimed full religious liberty. During the next months, the government seized church lands. This was done primarily to maintain the solvency of the state, for with the lands as guarantee, ultimately to be sold, the government hoped to issue new currency and meet all debts. But there was also a reforming interest in reducing the wealth and independence of the church. The Revolution could not bear to let the church go its own way, for the tradition of church-state association was strong and there were real fears that an independent church might attack the Revolution. Also, many sincerely religious deputies wanted to use the opportunity to reform church practices. Hence, the Civil Constitution of the Clergy (1790) put churchmen on a state salary, provided for the election of bishops by the citizens of their diocese, with non-Catholic citizens allowed to vote, and curtailed the rights of the French church to communicate with the papacy. In separate legislation all monastic orders were disbanded. Here was a radical effort to reduce and dominate the church. When the Pope condemned the Civil Constitution and the entire Revolution, the government required an oath of loyalty from the clergy which half of them refused to give. The war between church and Revolution, which was to last through the nineteenth century, had begun.

In September 1791, the constitution for the state was finally completed. All the old provinces and municipalities were disbanded, for they embodied the system of privilege and inequality; the new regional units, the departments, were given substantial powers of local government. At the center was a single legislature, chosen by a two-stage electoral process, in which the majority of adult males could choose electors but a minority of the richest citizens in practice selected the legislators. The executive branch, headed by the King, was weak, partly because Louis XVI could not be trusted; the King could delay but not prevent legislation desired by the Assembly.

First Stage Summarized. The first stage of the Revolution can be seen as a vast effort to replace group privilege with individual equality. Regional loyalties were attacked along with church and aristocracy. There were to be no barriers save individual rights between citizen and state. For example, not only were guilds destroyed—they had been functioning so badly that almost no one regretted their passing—but also all combinations of workingmen were prohibited by the Le Chapelier Law of 1791. This law based its prohibition not on the need for order alone, as the old regime had done, but on the economic necessity of untrammeled individualism. Each individual was to follow his economic self-interest, free from the restrictions both of the state and of private associations. But individuals were not entirely equal, even under the new revolutionary law. Most notably, the effective suffrage was restricted by property qualifications, despite bold talk of the sovereignty of the nation. Here was a crucial problem, for though the Revolution had destroyed some of the abuses of the common people, it had also destroyed some defenses, such as the possibility, for some, of associating in guilds for economic protection; and yet there was no adequate political outlet for protest. While many people, artisans as well as professional people, were gaining experience in local elections, national elections were largely dominated by the rich. Late in 1791, in fact, the Assembly formalized the association of wealth and national voting rights by introducing far higher property requirements for suffrage. This was a middle-class system, though certainly other groups, notably the peasantry, gained from it. Merchants and professional people even bought up many of the church lands offered for sale over the next several years, making the middle class an agricultural as well as commercial class. And laws eliminating guilds, banning unions, and removing local restrictions of trade were potentially a great boon to business.

Yet the first phase of the Revolution had been liberal and liberating. The destruction of manorialism and the curtailment of the church were massive accomplishments. Unfortunately, each revolutionary act drove many into opposition. By the end of 1791 thousands of aristocrats had fled the country, in hostility to the attack on manorial rights. Loyal Catholics were opposed to the Revolution, and churchmen at home and abroad were already attempting to foment attacks on the new government. Many others felt the Revolution had gone too far in one or another respect and were eager to strike back.

The new government itself was weak. Decentralization, a liberal reaction to absolute monarchy, limited the powers of the state. The King, responsible for heading the executive, was in virtual rebellion; he had even attempted to flee in June 1791. The problem of combining a real parliament with an effective executive was to haunt France from this time onward, for the perfectly reasonable solution that the new constitution proposed, a constitutional monarchy, depended on a willing king.

By 1791, the Revolution was beginning to stir resistance abroad. From the first, great attention had been focused on events in France, both because of the traditional preëminence of France in politics and culture and because of the magnitude of events themselves. There was widespread initial sympathy for the Revolution. Many businessmen in Britain and the Low Countries, anxious for political reform, were inspired by the revolutionary principles to feel that a new order was at hand; some workingmen in western Europe and in the German states were roused also. Even in eastern Europe there was limited enthusiasm. There were reports that some peasants, for example, were thrilled at the news of the end of manorialism. On the whole, however, aristocrats rather than common people found utility in the revolutionary principles in the east for only they were politically aware. Polish nobles sought to defend their government (run by an aristocratic Diet) and the territory remaining in Poland against encroachment by neighboring monarchs. Bohemian and Hungarian nobles had been alienated by the centralizing policies of Joseph II, in the Hapsburg empire; they sought restoration of local rights and aristocratic diets. It was early discovered that revolutionary ideals of liberty and national determination could be invoked to support traditional privilege. Only in western Europe, then, did the Revolution inspire large bodies of adherents; in the east it served mainly to give a modern vocabulary to aristocratic interests.

European Opposition. Hostility to the Revolution arose from the first also. Catherine the Great of Russia, whose enlightenment had always been a façade behind which the country was plunged into an increasingly rigorous feudal system, now dropped all pretense of reform; she even banned further translations of her erstwhile correspondent, Voltaire. The Prussian government was relaxing after the rigors of Frederick the Great's rule. Its expenses mounted; its bureaucracy became less efficient; and its king, Frederick William II, was hostile to the French influences which his predecessor had favored. The Hapsburg monarch, Leopold II, was busy trying to reduce the widespread opposition that had arisen against the reforms of his predecessor, Joseph II. He granted substantial autonomy to Hungary, including restoration of the aristocratic diet; he established a chair in Czech at the University of Prague, to pacify Bohemian interests; and he was even able to regain control of the rebellious Austrian Netherlands.

In all three of the powers of eastern and central Europe, then, the age of enlightened despotism was over, for kings had lost the taste for further reform, and opposition from the aristocracy could not be overcome. In the Hapsburg monarchy particularly, there was a pronounced return to more traditional regional rights. No more would eastern monarchs proclaim a reforming zeal, though they might work to improve the economy or the educational system gradually. Everywhere in eastern Europe the hold of the aristocracy on government and society was confirmed or increasing: two years before the French Revolution, the Russian government gave noble landlords the right to inflict any punishment on their serfs short of death. The reaction against the principles of enlightened despotism was not primarily due to the Revolution in France, but it inevitably colored official attitudes toward the Revolution. And the Revolution helped turn the reaction into a formal conservatism, which dominated the diplomacy as well as the internal policies of the eastern states for fifty years.

Political Stirrings in Britain. The situation was different in Britain, where the industrial revolution had been underway since about 1780. Factories and steam-driven machinery spread rapidly, particularly in the textile industry. Agricultural methods were being modernized at the same time, under the aegis of aristocratic landlords. The enclosure movement was in full swing; backed by Parliament, the owners of large estates were able to incorporate vast new lands into their holdings and to isolate these holdings from plots tilled by traditional methods. As a result, drainage could be improved, new crops and methods introduced, and the age-old fallow system displaced by the use of nitrogen-fixing plants. Commerce and banking naturally expanded under the influence of agricultural and industrial growth. This general economic surge was the principal preoccupation of the middle and upper classes, and the prosperity it brought was immensely satisfying.

Britain, then, was undergoing social and economic changes far greater than those in France. The changes brought hardship to many. Large numbers of rural laborers lost their land to the enclosure movement and population was rising more rapidly than available jobs. The standard of living for common people in the countryside fell significantly; their increased numbers were supported largely by the spread of the potato, a cheap crop that had the dubious merit of keeping people alive even if in considerable misery. Workers in the new factories suffered long hours, harsh discipline, and abuses of child and female labor. Yet, though there was scattered agitation among both rural and urban laborers, protest was surprisingly infrequent. Many were too poor to risk a protest, and others were so confused by their new condition that they could not formulate clear goals. New factory workers, particularly, were handicapped by their strangeness to each other and to factory and urban life. These groups had never been politically conscious, so that when they did riot it was for immediate economic demands alone.

There were, however, political stirrings in Britain, more intense in some ways than those in France before 1789. As in France, but independently, many artisans began to develop some sense of politics as early as 1760. They were roused by expanding population, which meant more jobs for the urban crafts; by a concomitant fear of new forms of employment (for they were increasingly being treated as paid laborers rather than as independent craftsmen); and by the threat of factory competition. They were spurred, also, by outside leaders, for occasionally politicians in Parliament and elsewhere saw the utility of lower-class support. They too began to glimpse the advantages of political rights, for though their conditions were changing rapidly they had enough education and sense of group solidarity to meet their problems in new ways. The most persistent support for the principles of the French Revolution came from the Corresponding Societies founded by the London cobbler, Thomas Hardy, and spread over England by hundreds of artisans.

Clearer grievances existed in the English middle class. Even before the French Revolution a variety of groups had been formed to protest the limited composition of Parliament, which represented only the aristocracy and a few traditional and wealthy merchant groups. Parliamentary districts did not reflect the rising centers of industry, and in some "rotten" boroughs two or three voters elected a representative. Small wonder that new manufacturers, such as James Watt, the inventor of the steam engine, sympathized with the French Revolution.

Yet there was no revolution in Britain, and sympathy with developments in France faded rather quickly in the middle class. In part this was because the leaders of opposition, including most businessmen and even many artisans, were profiting from the new commercial economy and wanted no disturbance that might interrupt their gains. In addition, the confusion of the masses of the poor limited the support for direct agitation. Even more clearly, the British government was strong and it could be flexible; it could prevent revolution and, in the long run, it was able to make it unnecessary. Until the 1790's, the government was moderately reformist. William Pitt the Younger improved the administration and tightened up the collection of taxes and tariffs, so that many imposts could be lightened. The government favored business; there were no internal barriers to trade, no guild restrictions, no real limitations to free enterprise. And there was a parliament, however unfairly constituted; Pitt even hoped to revise the borough system to extend representation, though he failed in that task. The British government seemed to be working well. In many ways, the first phase of the French Revolution could be viewed as an imitation of Britain's parliamentary monarchy. But already there were those who pointed to the subversive, un-British character of the French uprising. Edmund Burke wrote his *Reflections on the French Revolution* in 1790, castigating the French for violating their traditions, for seeking to construct a government on unrealistically abstract principles, and for attacking their church and aristocracy, the bastions of social order. He could see only anarchy or despotism as the result of France's folly, and he feared that these evils might spread to the rest of Europe.

Even in Britain, then, there were many for whom the principles of the Revolution were irrelevant, and many to whom they were repugnant. Pitt and his government sought moderate reforms, but they could not countenance radical change. No state in Europe was prepared to sympathize with the new government in France.

Initially, however, there was no disposition to interfere with the Revolution. Catherine might fulminate against it, but Russia was too far away to act and had every reason to enjoy the distraction of the great powers to the west. Prussia was weak, incapable of maintaining the brave front it had manifested in previous decades. Pitt sought to develop his reforms in peace. Leopold had his own problems of consolidation to consider, including the termination of a costly war with the Ottoman Empire. But it was on Leopold that the pressure to intervene against France bore most strongly, and it was from Leopold's efforts to meet this pressure without going to war that, ironically, war came.

Leopold was brother to the French queen. The Hapsburg monarchy had for over a century stood as the principal counterpoise to France in Europe; it was the other Catholic great power. For these reasons, aristocratic refugees from France flocked to the Austrian court, where they urgently pressed the government to march against the Revolution in their homeland. Leopold was also head of the Holy Roman Empire, of which Alsace was a part; and the French revolutionary government had cast aside feudal rights in Alsace, without consultation with the Empire, as part of its general movement against the aristocracy. Finally, when Louis XVI attempted unsuccessfully to escape in June 1791, all pretense that the Revolution was acting in accord with the monarchy had to be abandoned. Leopold had to do something to demonstrate his antirevolutionary stance.

In August 1791, Leopold met at Pillnitz with the Prussian king, and issued a declaration pledging action against France if all other powers joined. He was confident that his statement of intent would pacify the French *émigrés* in Vienna without causing war, for he relied on Pitt to keep Britain aloof. The declaration had an incendiary effect in Paris, however, where the revolutionaries were already haunted by fears of aristocratic and monarchical conspiracy at home and abroad. A war party arose within the Jacobin organization, a nation-wide group of the most devoted revolutionaries. The party, the Girondists, had two motives for their belligerent policy. They honestly felt that the Revolution could never be safe in France until it had spread to the rest of Europe and the world; for them, the Declaration of Pillnitz showed that Europe's crowned heads would league against the Revolution. And they felt a mission to spread liberty and equality to their fellow man, by a crusade in which gifts of the Revolution would be brought to neighboring states by the French army, aided of course by local risings. This feeling of mission, an early and distinctive form of French nationalism, became now an important part of the revolutionary tradition. Only a handful of revolutionaries opposed the movement, and on April 20, 1792, the French Assembly declared war on "the king of Hungary and Bohemia."

From this point, clearly, the French Revolution became intertwined with the whole of Europe. The revolutionaries did not realize their dream of liberating the world, but they did spread their government well beyond French borders. Sympathy for various revolutionary principles continued outside France, which would help motivate agitation well after the upheaval in France was over. In the short run, however, the conservative reaction to the Revolution seemed to be its most important consequence outside France. Edmund Burke was the first of many political philosophers who sought a system immune from revolution and radical change. States everywhere adopted a more repressive tone; even Britain and, more briefly, the United States, entered a period of watchful defense against any possible subversion. Diplomacy changed. The war against France maintained many aspects of the traditional jockeying among states, but superimposed on this was a clear ideological purpose as the monarchies of Europe sought to remove the revolutionary cancer.

THE RADICAL PHASE

Soon after the declaration of war, and in considerable measure because of it, the Revolution entered its second, most radical phase. On August 10, 1792, the artisanal quarters of Paris rose in revolt, supported by many provincial troops brought in for the war. The mobs stormed the royal palace and killed many of its guards, seized and imprisoned the King and the royal family. The city government of Paris was again overturned and replaced by a revolutionary "commune"; the legislative assembly was disbanded, the constitution abrogated, and a new constitutional convention elected by universal male suffrage. By the standards of the age, the liberal phase of the Revolution had been radical enough. In this new phase, the government sought still further reforms and some groups, in the cities, developed or expressed demands that were more radical yet, looking toward state protection for the poor and perhaps an attack on private property.

There were many reasons for the radicalization of the Revolution. Many lower-class groups had not obtained what they had wanted from the liberal assemblies of the previous two years. Peasant demands had not changed — there was no radicalization in this sense in the countryside — but many peasants were angry that seized lands were not distributed more widely. Sales of church estates and holdings of emigrated aristocrats proceeded rather slowly, and the estates were sold usually in large allotments, which only middle-class buyers could afford. Peasants also resented government efforts to collect taxes and redemption payments. In addition, there was widespread antipathy to the financial measures of the revolutionary regime. The government had begun printing paper money in 1789, and almost immediately the value of the money declined. Lack of confidence in the government caused much of the decline; the uncertainties and distractions of the Revolution limited production anyway and heightened distrust of paper money. In response, the government printed more and more paper money, to try to meet its own expenses, and the value of the paper *assignats* fell ever more rapidly. As a result, many peasants stopped all production for the market, preferring to maintain their own subsistence rather than work harder for an uncertain reward. The rural economy was severely disrupted and many peasant producers were discontent.

All of this had repercussions in the cities. Lack of food and near-worthless money drove the prices of all staples up. The price rise meant direct hardship for the lower classes, a hardship compounded by widespread unemployment, as the market for manufactured goods dwindled due to increased expenditures on food. The Revolution had not met the expectations of artisans and shopkeepers for higher and more secure standards of life. It had taken away the guilds but had not replaced them with organizations any more sensibly designed to protect collective bargaining power and security of employment. And the Revolution, despite its talk of national sovereignty, had withheld full political rights from the masses. Yet in Paris particularly, the excitement of the Revolution brought political consciousness to many in the lower classes. The mob, then, was not goaded by economic hardship alone. It was composed of respectable artisans and shopkeepers, not of the most impoverished or criminal elements of the city. It was devoted to the Revolution, but convinced that revolutionary change had only begun.

Lower-class agitation also found much sympathy and leadership from above. Some revolutionaries sought personal power by sponsoring demands for further change; far more saw opportunities to carry through the democratic ideals of the later philosophers of the Enlightenment, most notably Rousseau. The radical phase of the Revolution was under constant pressure from the urban masses in Paris; it attacked the wealthy segments of the middle class as well as aristocrats and priests. But the leaders of the Revolution were still mostly lawyers and professional people, and revolutionary Jacobin clubs throughout the nation were filled by men of the same type. As a result, even the radical Revolution did not violate certain basic middle-class interests; in particular, it ignored demands for a redistribution of wealth. It stemmed not only from the lower orders, but also from the intense enthusiasm of middle-class elements themselves.

Subversion and War. Two factors, internal subversion and foreign war, conditioned and channeled the revolutionary excitement at all social levels. There was a growing fear of counterrevolution at home. Almost all aristocrats had renounced the Revolution, half the priesthood had done so, and the King himself was demonstrably disloyal. Hence the King had to be removed, on August 10, 1792; in September over a thousand priests and other counterrevolutionaries were dragged from prison and executed after drumhead trials. And the fear of counterrevolution fed itself throughout the radical phase and beyond. Each new, radical step created new enemies for the Revolution. By late 1792 revolutionaries in the liberal, constitutional monarchist tradition of 1789 were enemies; by 1793 the Girondists, who supported the war but wanted no major internal changes beyond the proclamation of a republic, were enemies. There was severe popular unrest as well. In 1793 a rising against recruiters for the revolutionary army began in the Vendée, where peasants remained attached to church and nobles. There were antirevolutionary riots in several cities. Small wonder that the defenders of the Revolution felt that radical defensive measures were necessary; small wonder that their excitement, their passionate loyalty to a new France, grew ever more intense.

The war itself brought all this various pressure for radicalization to the surface. Disloyalty to the Revolution, dangerous in itself, was unendurable when the foreign enemy was at hand. Throughout much of 1792 the enemy was advancing inexorably, as Prussian troops moved toward Paris. The tide was turned when the French won a confused artillery battle at Valmy, in September, but the sense that the Revolution and the nation itself were battling for survival remained very real. Subsequent victories against Prussia and Austria simply increased revolutionary enthusiasm. Common soldiers prayed in 1792: "God of all justice, take into Thy protection a generous nation which fights only for equality." A religious type of exaltation was a major motivation for participants, however humble, in the new revolutionary experiment.

France Becomes a Republic. The first step in the radicalization of the Revolution was the change in political form. The monarchy, symbol of all that was left to the old regime, was abolished; the King was suspended, tried for treason, and by a narrow margin condemned to death. Here was a decisive blow against the form of government that had prevailed virtually unchallenged on the continent for centuries. France was now a republic, ruled in theory by a democratically elected Convention, a single legislative body that met first in October 1792. In actuality, however, the democracy proved hollow. The democratic basis of the Convention failed to operate effectively, for only a small number of eligible voters participated in the elections—voting was an unfamiliar experience for most people—and the elections were not repeated. More important, the Convention was too large and unwieldy to deal with the problems of a besieged France. The radical phase of the Revolution, founded in principle on legislative supremacy, made its greatest mark by establishing the machinery for a strong centralized executive.

The Convention was profoundly divided. Girondist leaders who in the previous assembly had been the republican warhawks now had achieved their goals; they sought to stabilize the gains of the Revolution but also to avoid any further change. For the most part they represented provincial business and professional elements, anxious to see an end to disorder. Their timidity was now challenged by the left wing of the Convention, backed by the mobs of Paris. This new group, called the Mountain because its members preferred to sit in the highest seats in the assembly halls, resented Girondist hesitancy in executing the King and in creating a strong war government. They seemed receptive to the demands of Paris crowds for economic reforms and were certainly permeated with the revolutionary fervor of the city. In May 1793, they won control of the Convention and seized and executed most of the Girondist leaders.

The leader of the Mountain was Maximilian Robespierre, a lawyer from northern France. From the beginning of the Revolution he had been an ardent democrat, and in the 1792 elections he ran in a Paris constituency. Robespierre became a symbol of bloodthirsty demagoguery, and he has since been viewed as a forerunner of totalitarianism. Yet he valued liberty and democracy and sought an ideal France in which all men would be inspired by a spirit of virtue. Personally incorruptible, Robespierre's fanatical devotion to the defense of the Revolution and to the rational restructuring of all aspects of society determined much of the character of the radical phase and its Terror.

The machinery of the republican government was established before Robespierre came to power. The Committee of Public Safety was created in April 1793 to deal with the day-to-day administration of government; its twelve members, soon to be headed by Robespierre, were elected monthly by the Convention. This Committee rapidly took control of the whole government, and the republican constitution approved by the Convention in June, which provided for universal suffrage, was suspended indefinitely in favor of the emergency regime. Under the Committee, the government began to send representatives "on mission" to all parts of France. Initially these representatives supervised military affairs alone, but their powers were later extended to cover most aspects of local administration. The concentration of government functions at the center was under way, though it would be completed by Napoleon. In certain respects it continued the centralizing traditions of the monarchy. Manorialism was abolished, however, and with it the many local governmental powers that aristocrats had maintained over their peasants. Gone were other local units with political functions, such as guilds and corporate towns. Gone, finally, were the traditional provinces themselves, and their many special rights and duties. All this, accomplished by the first phase of the Revolution, had been intended as a liberation, and so it was. But it also allowed the government to reach the citizen directly, particularly now that the concern for municipal and local governments had been overridden by a zealous effort at central control. The corollary to increased political consciousness was the expansion of the political apparatus.

The radical government not only created the machinery of a centralized state, but also established a theory to justify it, based on the presumed political interests of citizens. Robespierre was certainly committed to defense of liberty, though he held that liberties might have to be sacrificed to the national emergency. He was more interested, however, in creating an active bond between citizen and state, by which the citizen would have a voice in government, would receive benefits from it, and would owe in turn an active loyalty. This concept of an active and, if necessary, total devotion to the national state, not to a monarch or a feudal lord, was a new one. The radical phase of the Revolution produced in many Frenchmen a primary devotion to revolutionary France that was really nationalistic.

Campaign Against the Church. To carry through these ideas the government waged an active campaign against all aspects of Christianity, which was after all a competing loyalty, and through the church, an institution in potential competition with the state. Many priests were attacked and killed. The Convention replaced the Christian calendar with a republican, rational one which removed the old Christian holidays, set up new months of thirty days each, and substituted a new week based on the rational unit of ten for the old seven-day one, with its Sunday. Moreover the government, backed by many revolutionary groups, tried to establish a new worship of reason. Robespierre, fearful that de-Christianization would alienate the masses and anxious to tie religious sentiment clearly to the republic, introduced a "Worship of the Supreme Being," in which the existence of God and immortality of the soul were recognized. All of these efforts were short-lived, and served mainly to alienate Christian sentiment still further. They indicate, however, the extent of the interest in refocusing the loyalties of Frenchmen.

The most characteristic and enduring effort of the republican government to reach for new contacts with the entire citizenry was through military conscription. The principle of universal military service, the *levée en masse,* was proclaimed, calling on all able-bodied men to serve their government and their country. By the spring of 1794 the republic possessed an army of 800,000 men, the largest ever raised, to that time, by a European state. The government requisitioned food and supplies for the army. It recruited leading scientists to develop armaments and munitions. In military structure, most clearly, a modern state was being created, a state with the machinery to rouse masses of its citizenry.

Because of the war effort, the government directed many aspects of the economy. It controlled the supply of gold and so manipulated finances that inflation ceased. Maximum prices and wages were decreed, though here the government lacked sufficient enforcing administration. On the whole, the government believed in and supported free enterprise, but it showed a clear intent to introduce controls where necessary to the state.

The effort to create a central, national government and to mount a war effort of unprecedented scope was the greatest accomplishment of the radical phase. Techniques of government operation were created that endured in France and could be copied elsewhere. But the reputation of the radical phase, understandably if unfairly, was summed up in the Terror. The expansion of the powers of government included a massive effort to eliminate opposition, both of individuals and of whole regions such as the Vendée. And, as Robespierre proclaimed, the emergency of war made treason unthinkable and justified any measures taken to combat it. At the center, in Paris, this meant an active campaign against all opposition elements. Following the destruction of the Girondists, leaders on the left were attacked. A number of groups arose in 1793 and 1794 which sought a further, social revolution to the benefit of the urban lower classes. Leaders like Hébert, an officer of the municipal government of Paris, waged attacks on the rich and demanded a redistribution of wealth. In Robespierre's eyes, these efforts were fully as counterrevolutionary as any clerical conspiracy, and their authors were seized and punished. Outside Paris, revolutionary armies moved forcefully against the Vendée and other rebellions, though they were not fully successful. And capping the whole effort, a series of revolutionary tribunals were established, in which normal legal procedures were waived and summary judgments issued against presumed traitors.

This, then, was the Reign of Terror. It killed possibly 40,000 people, mostly in the military efforts against rebellion; the special courts executed perhaps 4000. Most of the victims were common people—peasants and workingmen in the areas of counterrevolutionary insurgency. Many priests and aristocrats were killed as well, but, interestingly, an even larger number of wealthy business and professional people went under the guillotine. Revolutionary groups, led by the national Jacobin Club, vigorously sought out possible traitors; and private hates were vented in successful accusations. The horror and the frequent injustice of the Terror cannot be denied. By modern standards, however, the methods used and the number killed can seem relatively moderate. Certainly, the most important result of the Terror was the creation of a myth. Its depredations were quickly exaggerated by the opponents of the Revolution, and its excesses drove many liberal men everywhere into hostility to the Revolution. The Revolution could easily seem, now, a monster, and revolutionary leaders such as Robespierre classic examples of power-hungry fanatics or creatures of a depraved mob.

In the long run, conservatism was immeasurably strengthened by the knowledge of revolutionary excess. Liberals, then and later, might hesitate in their quest for political change because they knew that change, if pushed too far, might bring revolution, and revolution might unleash the mobs and create a new terror. The timidity of many nineteenth-century revolutions owed something to the example of the Terror.

Accomplishments of the Radical Phase. Yet the Terror should not obscure the other characteristics of the radical phase of the Revolution. The extension and standardization of government activities represented a far more enduring accomplishment. There were plans, many of them unrealized at this point, for further uses of state power to the benefit of the citizenry. The radical phase was shaped by the pressure of the mobs, but it was not mob rule; the government tried to suppress agitators. The government also defended property rights against the inclination of the crowds to attack the rich; measures such as the ceiling on wages, justified by the need to stop inflation, were directly contrary to the demands of workingmen.

There was a zeal for reform within the republican government, however—a real desire to improve all aspects of French life. Peasants were freed from the obligation to pay compensation for manorial dues, and purchases of small plots of land were facilitated. Pamphlets were issued on the most modern agricultural methods. If little was done for urban workers, the end of inflation was certainly a boon and the government tried to encourage manufacturing. It opened a number of trade schools and planned a system of universal elementary education. Slavery was abolished in the French colonies. Robespierre even considered a system of graduated taxes by which incomes could be redistributed to the benefit of the poor. A concept of a state active in social reform, short of social upheaval, was clearly developing, though for the most part it lapsed when the government was overthrown.

Aside from the improvements in administrative machinery and the evil reputation of the Terror, little endured, in France, from the radical phase of the revolution. The regime, for all its excitement, was short-lived. It could not match the achievements of the first stage of the Revolution, in which the foundations of the old regime were overturned. Despite the fervor of the Jacobins, there was too little support in France for principles such as democracy and social reform. The majority of the Convention itself, though apathetic and easily cowed, grew hostile to Robespierre's radicalism. To an extent, the republicans defeated themselves, by removing many of the factors that had earlier impelled an intensification of the Revolution.

By the summer of 1794 the war was going well; economic difficulties had subsided; the peasantry, at last satisfied with its gains, largely withdrew from active interest in the Revolution; and the threat of counterrevolution seemed more remote. Further, widespread fatigue followed the excitement of the radical effort, and even many Parisian revolutionaries sought a return to more normal pursuits. The excesses of the Terror alienated many. And the lower classes in Paris increasingly realized that Robespierre was not their creature and that the government was not going to introduce massive economic reforms in their interest. When, on July 27, 1794 the Convention impeached Robespierre, no one rose in his support. The radical phase of the Revolution was over.

EUROPEAN IMPACT

Outside of France, the influence of the radical phase of the Revolution was profound. It extended the war against France, dragging almost the whole of Europe into the conflict. The initial attack on France was led by Prussia, with some support from Austria. Only after the execution of Louis XVI did Britain enter, early in 1793, soon to be joined by Spain, Holland, Sardinia, and Tuscany. France was indeed surrounded by its enemies.

Yet, apart from the initial setbacks against the Prussians, when the French armies were still disorganized, and a few later reverses, France easily won the war against the First Coalition powers. Fed by the masses of conscripts, often highly motivated by devotion to the Revolution and love of country, France's military also benefited by the leadership of bright young officers, who had been trained under the old regime. The French army developed improved supply facilities, superior artillery, and a speed and mobility that defied the careful march-in-line tactics of the eighteenth century.

Disunity among the allies and the financial weakness of Prussia and Austria were essential to the success of the French army. There was, certainly, an element of antirevolutionary crusade in the First Coalition, a war against the evils and excesses of the Jacobins. There was a growing fear of the annexationist intentions of the revolutionary government, which seemed bent on gobbling up as much territory as possible. But at first, the European states saw the Revolution as an opportunity to shift the balance of power in their favor. Until 1793, at least, it was widely felt that the Revolution had dislodged France from great-power status for the time being. Catherine of Russia held that a mere 10,000 men could march from one end of the country to the other. Obviously, there were spoils to be gained from this situation. Plans were circulated apportioning French border territories among various powers, after the eighteenth-century fashion of balanced gains by several great states. It was easy, in this situation, for the Coalition to founder on the conflicting ambitions of its members.

Furthermore, a territorial grab was undertaken in another and more genuine power vacuum, which directly conflicted with a united effort against France. Poland had already been partially dismembered, but from 1788 onward its government attempted a major internal reform to preserve what was left. The excessive powers of the aristocratic diet were curbed, feudalism modified, and a hereditary monarchy established. This vigorous activity frightened Catherine of Russia, who saw the chance to intervene while her rivals, Prussia and Austria, were distracted by France. Russia accordingly invaded Poland in 1792 and forced a second partition, to the benefit of itself and Prussia. A Polish national war resulted, until 1795, that compelled intervention by Austria and Prussia as well as by Russia. Poland was crushed, eliminated by a third partition.

France benefited greatly from the several years' diversion of its enemies. France was able not only to beat back attack, but also to invade neighboring territories. French armies seized Belgium; took Savoy from Piedmont; and invaded the German Rhineland. The French government began to talk of France's natural frontiers — the Pyrenees, the Mediterranean, the Alps, the Rhine, and the Atlantic — and succeeded in incorporating much of this new territory by 1795. In this effort, again, the missionary zeal to spread the Revolution was joined to a newly vigorous nationalism.

The zone of territory immediately surrounding France was, therefore, most intimately touched by the radical phase of the Revolution. French commissioners followed the French army, to administer the conquered areas. They encouraged the formation of indigenous Jacobin clubs, to spread enthusiasm for revolutionary reform and to stir sentiment for French annexation. In all the territories involved, many merchants and professional people needed little prodding to support the invaders' cause. Nationalism was as yet unknown, save perhaps in Belgium, where it was largely anti-Austrian and thus favorable to France. The French cause meant the elimination of aristocratic privilege and the modernization of commercial laws. Furthermore, the neighboring territories had social structures similar to those of the French. They possessed relatively strong middle classes; in addition, peasants in Rhineland Germany, the Low Countries, and northern Italy were small-holders, burdened only with remnants of manorial obligations, as the French peasants had been before 1789. There was no strongly entrenched aristocracy to resist the spread of revolutionary legislation, and the peasantry proved highly receptive to it. Only loyal Catholics could mount significant opposition to the incorporation of these areas into France.

Incorporation meant, of course, the full application of French laws. The occupation administrators abolished manorialism, seized church lands, destroyed guilds, proclaimed religious and other personal liberties, and removed traditional trade restrictions. To be sure, in 1795, the French hold over western Germany was far from complete, and Italy aside from Savoy had scarcely been touched. But already the revolutionary zone had been extended, by a combination of outside force and local cooperation. The Revolution was accepted in these areas, particularly when France eased its attack on the church after 1795; and the major gains of the Revolution were never rescinded in this borderland belt.

European Conservatism. Outside the territory contiguous to France, the impact of the continuing Revolution and the war was far different. In varying degrees, sympathy for the Revolution continued among certain groups; but the preëminent fact was the spread of a conscious reaction against all agitation and all change. Monarchs or their ministers established or increased censorship, augmented the activity of political police, and increased the prohibitions against private associations. In most of Europe beyond the revolutionary zone, a policy of deliberate, repressive conservatism was being established that would last, with minor interruptions, until at least 1830.

These developments were most marked in Britain. Active sympathy for the Revolution continued there despite the widely publicized excesses of the Terror. But the sympathy was increasingly confined to the lower orders of society, that minority of artisans and shopkeepers who were eager for political gains. Agricultural laborers, weakened by population pressure and the enclosures, might riot, as in 1795, but without political overtones. And even larger groups, including the growing factory labor force, were calm. An interest in revolutionary reform, if not in revolution itself, did spread to many craftsmen and to some other workers; the result was a recurrent and intense pressure against the government's policies of reaction.

At the upper levels of society, where political power lay, sympathy for the Revolution almost disappeared. Merchants and manufacturers joined the landed gentry in seeking preservation of order and successful prosecution of the war against France. The largely middle-class reform movement was cut off, damned by the stigma of earlier sympathy for the Revolution. A few politicians in the Whig party tried to hold out in the interests of reform, but most of the members of parliament, and most of the voting public, coalesced around a new Tory grouping, first formed under Pitt, that was to rule for forty years.

The British government not only avoided reform, but also reacted vigorously against the possibility of agitation from below. Pitt and his colleagues were genuinely frightened by the continuation of political clubs favorable to France and eager for a formal constitution and universal suffrage. Reformist demands became treason in the eyes of the established order, no matter how peacefully presented. The government began to create a network of police spies against subversion, and subsidized the press to channel news in approved directions. In 1795 and 1796 the Two Acts were passed, stipulating that treason could be accomplished in speech as well as in writing, and so could be prosecuted. A large number of presumed agitators were arrested and tried. In 1799 the Combination Acts were passed outlawing all secret political associations and even trade unions; and press censorship was established. Britain by 1800 possessed a government as strong as any on the continent, and fully as dedicated to the preservation of the existing order.

Nowhere on the continent, outside of the revolutionary zone, was there as much sympathy for the Revolution as there was in Britain; and nowhere else, save in Holland, did a revolutionary political consciousness penetrate the lower orders of society. Workers and peasants in southern Italy and in Silesia agitated against their misery, but their cause had nothing to do with political revolution. At most, there were vague references to "doing as the French had done." Some peasants were in fact roused against the French Revolution; Sardinian peasants, for example, demonstrated against the immorality and anti-Christianity of France. What sympathy for the Revolution there was came in the upper levels of society. In Italy and the German states, particularly, but to a degree in Austria and Spain, some state bureaucrats, professional people, and even occasional nobles formed Jacobin clubs or other groups. In a few cases they really approved of the radical phase of the Revolution, but more commonly they were interested in the liberal gains of the earlier stage: a constitutional monarchy, guarantees of liberty, and abolition of manorialism. Nowhere were these groups large enough to pose a real threat to order; only occasionally did they even plot revolt.

The absence of any real internal menace did not deter continental governments from taking increasingly rigorous repressive measures. Catherine and her successor in Russia found scarcely any opposition to repress, but they did ban Masonic orders and even officially removed the Russian words for "citizen" and "fatherland" from the language. The Prussian government tightened its censorship and in 1794 issued a new legal code that confirmed feudalism and the existing social hierarchy, with such measures as that forbidding nobles to marry outside their class. This was, again, a continuation of the reaction against the reforming tone of enlightened despotism, but it now became more rigid, more specifically repressive. This trend was even clearer in Austria, under the new and highly conservative emperor Francis II. The chief minister, Thugut, felt that all measures were justified against the possibility of revolution, for "only the axe can put out the fire." The government increased censorship and held a number of show trials against revolutionary sympathizers in the bureaucracy and army. Similar measures were taken by the Italian states. The war against revolution in France lagged, but by the late 1790's the war against radicalism in other parts of Europe was in full swing — even where there was virtually no radicalism to war against.

In France, the Revolution was over by 1795. A period of consolidation and defense of the central revolutionary gains began and lasted on and off until 1815. The Directory, the government established after the disbanding of the Convention, was ineffective in many ways, but it set the main lines of stabilization that Napoleon was to follow with greater success.

The Directory quickly undid the most radical measures of the Convention period. Not only did the Terror end, but many conservative politicians returned to public activity. The price maximum was dropped and inflation briefly resumed, to the benefit of many speculators who sought to gain from war expenditures and military conquests. Suffrage was again restricted by a system of electors, so that only 20,000 wealthy citizens had an effective vote for regional officials and members of the national legislature. This was a far smaller electorate than that of the 1791 constitution and showed the firm intent of the new government to rely on purely upper-class rule. The de-Christianization movement was called off and some gestures of accommodation were made toward the church.

A number of fruitful measures were taken in the fields of economic policy and education. With great difficulty, the inflation was gradually brought under control again, and France returned to a currency based on precious metals. The government improved tax collection and raised taxes on consumer items which burdened the poor but aided the budget. It increased protective tariffs, particularly against British goods; this was partly a war measure, of course, but it reflected a conscious desire to use the state to defend the nation's economy. A number of technical schools were established, setting the basis for one of the best systems of engineering training in Europe during the nineteenth century. Finally, the government began the codification of civil and criminal laws, for the sake of standardization itself and as a means of incorporating the principles of legal equality and commercial liberty into the whole legal framework. The Directory's efforts at consolidation were not, then, simply a matter of backtracking from the Terror and trying to conciliate some of the opponents of the Revolution. Fundamental principles of the Revolution were maintained or extended, providing a basis for Napoleon's more famous efforts along the same lines.

Failure of the Directory. Nevertheless, the Directory failed. It did not develop great leaders, and indeed it was marred throughout by bickering and personal rivalries. It was desperately pressed by internal dissent, partly because it seemed the creature of the wealthy elements of the middle class alone. Leftist opposition developed rather quickly. In 1796, "Gracchus" Babeuf organized the Conspiracy of Equals, to abolish private property in the name of a communist equality. The movement was small and easily crushed, but it was one element of the instability that haunted the regime. More important, royalists were also active, and they too organized riots. On several occasions the military had to be called in to repress disorder. Finally, the legislature itself became increasingly royalist with successive elections; and this the former Jacobins could not endure, if only because they feared reprisals for their part in executing Louis XVI. France was profoundly divided. Some elements wanted the Revolution to go further; far more wanted to return to the old regime, encouraged by the exiled heir to the French throne, later Louis XVIII, who promised to destroy all the acts of the Revolution and punish all their perpetrators. Faced with these schisms, the weak Directory government could not survive.

Furthermore, the government was confronted constantly with the problems of a continuing war effort. It refused to seek peace because it feared that a restoration of the monarchy would be part of the peace settlement, and also because it depended on the war for spoils and prestige. Furthermore, rather early, the government lost control of the military. General Napoleon Bonaparte was given command of an army in 1796 and quickly drove the Austrians from northern Italy. He set up a new republic in the conquered territory, signed a peace treaty with Austria on his own responsibility, and began to plan further conquests. Napoleon was only one of several independent generals, each carving out his own territory. The hold of the generals on the Directory increased after 1797, when the army forced annulment of the elections that had favored the royalists, in return for continued government backing for a policy of expansion.

Briefly, in 1797 and 1798 France was at peace with the entire world except England. Austria recognized Napoleon's Italian republic, and also French annexation of Belgium and the left bank of the Rhine; in return, Austria received Venice and its hinterland, one of the oldest independent European states, and also was to obtain territories in central Germany. The remaking of the European map had begun. However, peace did not last. Napoleon sailed off to conquer Egypt, ultimately to lose his army, and thereby frightened the Ottoman government, of whose empire Egypt was a part, and Russia, who resented any interference in the Near East. And French armies continued to nibble in Italy, alienating the remaining Italian states and also Austria. The result, under the prompting of British diplomacy, was the formation of the Second Coalition in 1798, which grouped Britain, Russia, Austria, Naples, Portugal, and the Ottoman Empire against France. By 1799, France had been driven from Italy and Switzerland. There was no threat to France itself, but the sense of defeat weighed heavily on the Directory.

On October 9, 1799, Napoleon returned to France, alone, from Egypt; one month later he was master of France. The difficulties of the war — Russian armies were in Switzerland — and the troubles in France, where counterrevolutionary guerrilla activity had flared up again, convinced many political leaders that a new regime was vital. Aided by military force, which chased parliament from its chambers, Napoleon accomplished a coup d'état and established a Consulate with himself as First Consul. The need for strong authority to quell disorder and prosecute the war was now to be fulfilled.

The French Revolution and reaction to it do not sum up the entire decade of the 1790's. The principles of the Revolution were to alter social structure profoundly, but many features of the change remained unclear even within France. The Revolution had an undoubted impact on intellectual life, but it fit into a broader tension within the intellectual community, aspects of which had nothing to do with politics.

Structure of French Society. If one excludes law and politics, it can be argued that French society was not too different in 1799 from what it had been in 1789. The peasantry was now free from manorial obligations and possessed most of the cultivable land outright, in small plots. But the manorial obligations had been relatively limited before, and for all practical purposes France had been a country of predominant small holdings. There were no startling changes in agricultural methods in the decade, for most peasants were content with their land and anxious to follow traditional procedures; government efforts to promote agricultural improvements met with apathy and outright resistance. The middle class had moved into almost complete control of government positions, had benefited from the newly established upper schools, and had certainly translated their principles of legal equality and economic freedom into law. Many individuals gained by rising in the bureaucracy or by purchasing church lands. In both cases, the gains on the whole continued and confirmed prerevolutionary developments and led to the creation of a conservative bureaucratic-landowning group that was to dominate middle-class politics for most of the next century. The business community, by modern standards the leading element of the middle class, did not gain nearly so much. New laws might free trade and manufacturing, but the disruptions of the Revolution distracted from economic advance; several prerevolutionary factories, for example, had to be abandoned. And for the urban lower classes, finally, the Revolution brought disruption and the very important legislation against guilds and unions, but beyond this prompted no vital changes in conditions. At most, elements of the artisan class gained a political consciousness that was new and important, even if their hopes were not realized in this period.

The destruction of the political and much of the economic base of the aristocracy, however, was a major development. The way was open to middle-class leadership in society, in ethics and culture as well as politics. There were, also, important indications of a democratization of social manners, such as the growing popularity, even among the upper classes, of the long trousers of the workmen. Traditional social hierarchy was breaking down in France, and this would gradually affect the style of life even of the common people.

Outside France, social changes were under way that in some ways were more basic than those prompted by the Revolution. The tightening of the feudal system in Prussia, Russia, and Austria was significant, bringing an increase of aristocratic political and economic power and a corresponding subjection of the peasantry. At the same time, in eastern Europe, there were signs of economic change; some aristocrats began to improve agricultural methods, in the English pattern, and there was a general spread of rural manufacturing, particularly in textiles. Underlying these developments, a major population increase was under way, particularly in Germany. In Prussia, for example, the population increased by an average of .66 per cent per year in the last decades of the century, leading to a 50 per cent rise in total population between 1750 and 1800 and a 40 per cent increase in the density of population. In Britain, of course, the pace of broad social change was even more rapid, with extensive population growth, modernization of agriculture, and the rise of factory industry. Everywhere social change brought protest, particularly in the countryside, prompted by population pressure and by the growing dominance of large estates—a dominance now as characteristic of England, through enclosures, as of Prussia. Much of the social impact of the Revolution came later, then, particularly when revolutionary principles were applied to societies whose structures differed from the French.

Intellectual Trends. In intellectual life, as in society, the French Revolution affected developments but did not determine them, and the leading trends cannot be dated by the decade of the Revolution itself. Even before 1789, a major conflict was arising, on many fronts, between the advocates of reason and their diverse opponents, who were, generally, developing the equally diverse tenets of romanticism.

The rationalists believed that man possessed, in reason, the faculty for understanding the physical universe, moral principles, and social and political truth. Their activities during the 1790's were varied. Major scientific advance continued, particularly in France, with the discovery of the functions of oxygen by Lavoisier, and by Laplace's synthesis in astronomy. The French adoption of the metric system, in 1800, was both a product of and basis for scientific inquiry. Rationalist political philosophy continued. The defenders of the French Revolution argued generally in terms of the ability of human reason to construct a better society; and they were not confined to France. Thomas Paine wrote a ringing denunciation of Burke in his *Rights of Man*. Jeremy Bentham continued to assert that in all aspects of society man could rationally determine what would serve the greatest good of the greatest number; his proposals ranged from education to penal reform.

Clearly, proponents of the rationalist tradition in various fields were by no means on the defensive; their continued vitality was fully as important a part of the intellectual scene as the growing attack on reason. On the whole, however, the more dynamic developments of the decade were antirational or arational to some degree. France did not yet participate in this movement, but Germany, Britain, and Italy did.

Part of the early Romantic Movement ignored, rather than directly attacked, the principles of reason. In art and literature the enemy was classical style and its canons, and the weapons were unconventionality and appeals to sentiment. In the fine arts, the most popular styles were rigidly classical, from the epic paintings of David in France to the imitations of Palladian architecture popular in London. Only in the rural scenes of Constable and others was there much hint of the supple style and sentimental interest of the Romantics. In literature, the great figure of the decade was Goethe, who tried to balance a new interest in classicism with a continued concern with sentiment and irrational yearnings. In this decade Goethe began his work on Faust, whose limitless striving was to express much of the mystic quality that Romantics found in the human personality. Late in the 1790's also, a new generation of Romantic writers began their work in Germany; and 1798 saw the first major publications of Wordsworth and Coleridge in Britain, which attacked the stylistic conventions of the eighteenth century and sought instead to capture sentiment and a mystic quality.

The major development in the movement against rationalism came, however, in philosophy, with the work of Immanuel Kant. Kant was sympathetic to the rationalists in many ways, and he admitted that reason could know a certain order of truth. But it could never grasp absolute truth, he felt, for it was confined to the sphere of transitory phenomena. For reason to claim to know God or to construct a set of political principles was impossible, and rationalists who purported to be able to do so were acting on faith. Logic plus empiricism, for example, could not show that man was naturally free. Fortunately, there was another category of knowledge, which Kant rather confusingly called pure reason; this was, in essence, personal intuition, which conveyed absolute truth in ethical matters. Here was a fruitful principle for those, in all fields, who sought to elevate the emotional aspect of man's nature and who found truth in their feelings.

Little of this had anything to do with the French Revolution, though Kant came to oppose its excesses and Wordsworth first favored and then turned against it. In the realm of political philosophy, however, the Revolution inspired a clear reaction to the rationalists. Edmund Burke held that man was irrational and needed the restraint of a traditional, hierarchical society and of religion. Efforts to reason out political principles were futile and dangerous, he felt, because they ignored man's nature. By the end of the 1790's other political philosophers began to think in this vein.

Furthermore, the Revolution began to produce an anti-French intellectual nationalism that, on the whole, fed the antirational movement, for France had been and remained the center of rational philosophy and of classical artistic standards. Italian writers, appalled by the Revolution, began to shake off French tutelage in literature; if not yet pro-Italian, they were certainly anti-French. German writers such as Herder had already asserted the distinctiveness of German culture, and the reaction to the Revolution began to heighten this movement. In political philosophy directly, Burke asserted the confidence in English traditions and institutions that many of his contemporaries shared. All of this was still rather tentative, but the Enlightenment principles that all men were basically the same no matter where they lived and that intellectual endeavor should be international and uniform, were coming under attack.

The effects of the French Revolution were, in later decades, increasingly intertwined with the impact of the two other "revolutions" that were taking shape in the 1790's: the economic upheaval centered in Britain and the intellectual reorientation centered in Germany. Revolutionary legislation against manorialism and the guilds and for more standardized commercial law were vital for the spread of industrialization on the continent. The antirational movement, with some exceptions, sought to oppose revolutionary principles and assumptions; and the heirs of the early Romantics in the late nineteenth century condemned reason, the political heritage of the Revolution, and industrial society in the same breath. In sum, developments in the 1790's set much of the tone for the nineteenth century.

Opposition to or advocacy of the central purposes of the Revolution became the focal point of politics for most of the following century. The Revolution meant parliamentary government instead of powerful monarchy, with the parliament based on extensive though not universal suffrage. It meant equality of the law and elimination of officially privileged groups and bodies. It meant an attack on church powers and, to a degree, on religion itself. It meant a strong state, demanding active loyalty from the nation as a whole, with a bureaucracy open to talents more than to privileges and a legal and financial system that was uniform and relatively efficient. The Revolution was liberal and helped make liberalism a formal movement, and it gave birth to nationalism and, in a limited way, to socialism. It accustomed a whole generation to expect change, and it made further change inevitable.

SUGGESTED READING

An ample and controversial literature is available for the French Revolution. Several generations of skilled French historians have offered general interpretations. H. Taine, *The French Revolution* (3 vols., 1878-1885), and P. Gaxotte, *The French Revolution* (1932), offer conservative attacks on the purpose of the Revolution. The classic liberal scholarship on the Revolution is represented by F. V. A. Aulard, *The French Revolution, A Political History, 1789-1804* (4 vols., 1901). For a more radical view, see A. Mathiez, *The French Revolution** (1928), and *After Robespierre, the Thermidorean Reaction** (1931). By far the most balanced and useful treatment is G. Lefebvre, *The French Revolution* (2 vols., 1962-1964); see also Lefebvre, *The Coming of the French Revolution** (1947), for a succinct analysis of the social forces involved. Recently aspects of Lefebvre's approach have been challenged by the stimulating A. Cobban, *The Social Interpretation of the French Revolution* (1964), which asks whether the Revolution actually changed much in France. A great deal of the recent work on the French Revolution attempts a social analysis, particularly of the lower classes. A convenient introduction to this work is J. Kaplow, *New Perspectives on the French Revolution** (1965); see also A. Soboul, *The Parisian Sans-Culottes and the French Revolution* (1964); and, for treatment of a broader topic of which the Revolution was part, G. Rudé, *The Crowd in History, 1730-1848** (1964).

*Available in a paperback edition.

There is much interesting work on revolutionary parties and leaders, with emphasis on the radical phase. See R. R. Palmer, *Twelve Who Ruled: The Committee of Public Safety During the Terror** (1941); Crane Brinton, *The Jacobins* (1930); J. B. Sirich, *Revolutionary Committees in the Departments of France, 1793-1794* (1943); J. M. Thompson, *Robespierre* (2 vols., 1935). An important interpretation of the radical revolution, extending beyond the period, is J. R. Talmon, *The Rise of Totalitarian Democracy* (1952). On the church in this period and beyond, see A. Dansette, *Religious History of Modern France* (1961).

The problem not only of the meaning of the Revolution but also of its relation to the rest of Europe is dealt with excellently by R. R. Palmer, *The Age of Democratic Revolution* (2 vols., 1959-1964); see also E. J. Hobsbawm, *The Age of Revolution, 1789-1848** (1963). For greater specificity, see G. P. Gooch, *Germany and the French Revolution* (1920); W. T. Laprade, *England and the French Revolution, 1789-1797* (1909); and A. Cobban, *The Debate on the French Revolution* (1950). The early industrial revolution in Britain is treated by T. S. Ashton, *The Industrial Revolution, 1760-1830** (1948) and P. Deane, *The First Industrial Revolution** (1965).

*Available in a paperback edition.

40

Pitt: The Granger Collection   Sieyès: The Granger Collection

PITT AND SIEYÈS

William Pitt the Younger (1759-1806) was the master of the House of Commons, and thus of the British government, from 1783 until his death, except for the years from 1801-1804. The Abbé Joseph Emmanuel Sieyès (1748-1836) played a far more fleeting role in politics; he was unknown before 1789, and he lost all political influence after 1799. Yet Sieyès typifies the early leadership of the Revolution in France insofar as such a diverse grouping can be typified; he won his fame as the enunciator of the central demands of the Revolution.

William Pitt was no revolutionary. He was born to political prominence, as the son of the Earl of Chatham, who had organized Britain's victory in the Seven Years War. He was an inferior orator to his father but had greater political influence. Pitt entered Parliament at the age of twenty-two. A year later he was offered a subordinate post in the government, which he arrogantly refused. After still another year, in 1783, he became Prime Minister. Pitt's guiding passion was to lead the House of Commons. Through this, he hoped to improve Britain's governmental structure, but he was no crusader for principle; he valued political power for its own sake. He was a man of real personal integrity, and he sought to curtail parliamentary corruption, but he lavishly distributed peerages in order to control the House of Lords. He continued his father's effort to reform the parliamentary boroughs but was blocked by the King and never pushed his proposals with great vigor. Pitt was interested in abolishing the slave trade and granting full freedom to Catholics, but again, the opposition was too much for him and again he yielded without complaint. Pitt's main success in reform was in the area of finance. He reduced the number of functionless offices in government, funded the debt, and lowered and consolidated the tariffs, all of which improved British credit substantially.

The French Revolution changed the tone of Pitt's administration. A mild reforming impulse was replaced by repression. Pitt turned all his energies to the war against the French and to capturing every possible colony for Britain in the process.

Sieyès had as great an interest in politics as did Pitt, but it was an interest born of theory. Forced to be a priest by his family and against his will, his priesthood was only nominal, and by avocation he was drawn into the circle of the *philosophes,* though he was known only in local intellectual circles. As an adherent of the Enlightenment, Sieyès believed in reason and natural law and in the possibility of human progress and perfectability; and on this basis he constructed a general system of government, a full scheme for reforming the present order. When the Estates-General were called, he saw the opportunity for offering his plan for society. He elaborated his system in four pamphlets, including "What is the Third Estate?" which won national fame. He asked for what most of the politically aware in France wanted: a declaration of the rights of citizens, a written constitution with a representative assembly and separation of executive and legislative branches, and an end to the special privileges of the nobility. He spoke for the growing sense of importance and competence of the middle classes.

Sieyès did not preach revolution, but he accepted it when it came, for reform was necessary at any cost. Elected to the Estates-General from Paris, he helped create the national assembly and had great influence in framing the constitution of 1791, which expressed many of his principles. He sat in the Convention also, and after 1795 was one of the five Directors, but he had little power in the governments he served. His last political act was to help arrange Napoleon's coup in 1799, for like many of the original revolutionaries he had wearied of disorder and he wanted to increase France's military and diplomatic strength.

The political goals of Sieyès and Pitt were not very different. Sieyès was an intellectual and believed that a theory of government could be rationally derived, whereas Pitt was a pragmatist who worked for reforms that were necessary in practice; in this, of course, there is great contrast. But both men believed in representative government; both believed in human rights, though both also found these could be modified where national interests required; and both believed in order. Although Pitt was born to politics, Sieyès was outside the government of the old regime and subjected to a profession he did not want. And Pitt's goals were largely realized in the existing British system, while Sieyès had to advocate sweeping changes. So Sieyès became a revolutionary, though he abhorred violence and disorder; and Pitt became the leading opponent of the Revolution, though he was part of a political system that was already radical by continental standards. ■

Chapter 2

The Napoleonic Era

Napoleon's central goals were the establishment of a Bonaparte dynasty and virtually unlimited territorial expansion. His regime brought an unprecedented challenge to Europe's diplomatic order, and the boundaries of the continental states changed with bewildering rapidity. The powers that gradually drew together to oppose the French dictator could not efface many of these changes, and the resultant realignment of powers set the stage for the diplomacy of the next fifty years.

Diplomatic and military developments between 1799 and 1815 drew attention away from activity in other fields. In particular, the tide of political unrest seemed to recede. Napoleon had to consolidate the Revolution in France to provide a base for his territorial ambitions, and his achievements contented many Frenchmen. In administering his vast conquests he introduced a variety of political and social reforms to new regions, and again, many people were satisfied. A reduced pace of economic change encouraged greater internal stability. Britain stepped up its industrialization to meet the French threat, but largely along preëstablished lines. Some landlords in eastern Europe tightened their control over the peasantry in order to produce more for the western market, where regular supplies were disrupted by the wars. In general, however, the wars reduced the possibilities for economic change, by diverting capital and labor to military efforts. Wages rose in the cities and the countryside because so many men were away in armies. Military sales prompted most entrepreneurs and farmers on the continent not to innovate, but rather to extend existing methods wherever possible.

However, beneath the surface important changes were taking place, though they bore fruit only in later decades. In France and elsewhere, a number of "new men," from various classes of society, found new opportunities in the military and civilian bureaucracies of Napoleonic Europe, and when the wars ended some of them applied their talents to business. The wars, by disrupting European society, brought great energies to the surface, and this prepared further change. Napoleonic legislation opened the way to economic innovation in western and central Europe, even if the response was delayed. Napoleon's accomplishments also forced his enemies to seek new sources of strength by reforms of bureaucracies, armies, and agriculture, which again heralded new economic developments when peace was restored.

Napoleon also helped spread political consciousness. His reforms, and those undertaken in reaction in states like Prussia, roused the aristocracy to a new defensiveness in many areas. The same reforms convinced many middle-class people that they had a stake in politics, to preserve and possibly to extend rational principles of government. Even more obviously, French occupation roused resistance in many countries. Not all resistance was politically inspired, but many people fought Napoleon in the name of national liberty. At the same time, many Frenchmen in Napoleon's armies gained a new taste of national power. The spread of new political loyalties had only begun in 1815, but this was to be the most important fruit of the reshuffling of the map of Europe.

NAPOLEON

Napoleon Bonaparte was born in 1769, of a lesser noble family in Corsica. He studied in French military schools and became an army officer before the Revolution, but his rapid promotion was due to the Revolution alone. His military specialty was the use of artillery, which he turned to good service in 1793 in helping to drive the British from Toulon—this won him a brigadier generalship—and in dispersing a riot in 1795 with a "whiff of grapeshot," which helped him gain command of an army the following year.

Napoleon was a child of the Enlightenment, and his regime indeed resembled an enlightened despotism of the eighteenth-century type, though leavened by the freedom from aristocratic restraints and the other reforms that the Revolution had produced. He was a rationalist, with an orderly mind and a desire to create order about him; he had no use for religion or moral restraints, save as they might be made to serve him. Yet there was a mystic quality about Napoleon that was later to entrance romantic intellectuals. He claimed to follow a personal "star" that would lead him from victory to victory. Highly intelligent, a born leader, he was capable of quick decisions and a rapid grasp of complexities. By temperament and ability, he was eminently suited to provide the authority that France now seemed to want; but he served himself, not France, and he inevitably used his authority to plunge the country into new adventures.

Napoleon was indifferent to the principles of the Revolution, except as they promoted a strong state. He sought in many ways to create not only a new dynasty but also a new aristocracy to adorn it, by allying himself with the Hapsburg house, in 1810, and by ennobling many of his army officers. Yet he confirmed the Revolution beyond recall in many aspects of French life and spread its principles as far as Poland and the Balkans. Napoleon had no interest in traditional boundaries or in national units; he seized territory for his own sake and to provide thrones for his brothers and sisters, to whom he felt loyalty that was only occasionally overcome by his disgust at their incompetence. Yet he resurrected several national units and approximated certain others. He had no interest in economics, yet he took several measures important to the economic expansion of western Europe. Constantly there was a disparity between the intentions and effects of Napoleon's acts. Certainly, his intentions proved far less important than what can be seen, in retrospect, as his enduring accomplishments. However, the paradox should not be carried too far. If Napoleon's goals were those of an aspiring dynast on a European scale, he understood the forces of his times. He recognized and used the power and efficiency of the middle class, the loyalties of nascent nationalism, and the new principles of legal equality and opportunity open to talent. Napoleon is a classic example of the problem of the great man in history. He did not, in the long run, accomplish what he really intended, though he certainly raised a ferment in trying. He did not fight against the basic forces of his age, and he achieved much along some of the lines suggested by the Revolution and Enlightenment. Would these developments have occurred without him? Would Europe, not in 1815 perhaps, but by 1830 have been much different if Napoleon had never lived?

CONSOLIDATION IN FRANCE

Napoleon came to power in a badly divided country and set about quickly to repair the worst rifts. He altered the structure of government so that there would be no power to compete with his own. Napoleon liked to affirm the sovereignty of the people; he was the first despot specifically to claim authority from the popular will. Several times during his rule he held plebiscites in which constitutional proposals were submitted to the people with no alternative—in which a hostile vote would be a vote for nothing. In the constitution of the Consulate, universal male suffrage was granted, but not for government offices directly. The voters simply chose a list of 10,000 "notables," from which the government in turn selected legislative representatives. Finally, the legislative bodies themselves had no power; one of them could vote for or against laws without discussing them, and another could discuss but had no enacting power. It was significant that a façade of democracy and parliamentary structure was maintained, for it helped legitimize the regime in the eyes of the supporters of the Revolution; but quite clearly, a façade was all that Napoleon allowed. The proclamation of Napoleon as Emperor of France in 1804 was no more than a recognition of the power he had long maintained.

The executive branch was the real government of France. Building on the system created by the Jacobins, Napoleon greatly increased the powers of the central bureaucracy. Each regional unit was put under the charge of a prefect, named by the ministry of interior, with powers over police, education, transportation, and economic development. Local autonomy was virtually nonexistent. This centralized structure was one of Napoleon's greatest achievements, for it resisted all efforts at modification in France and was copied by many other countries anxious to create a strong government quickly. Napoleon also established a powerful secret police to supplement the other forms of political control.

Combined with the new authority of government was a deliberate policy of reconciliation. Napoleon used in his government former royalists and former Jacobins. He invited most of the émigrés back to France, so long as they remained orderly, and many did return. He ended the rebellion in the Vendée. Most important, he made an uneasy peace with the church. There was no question in all this of undoing the central revolutionary achievements against privilege; Napoleon was careful to make the old Jacobins feel secure. But with relatively few concessions he proved able to win partial acceptance of the revolutionary changes in France from those who had suffered most from them.

The Concordat of 1801 with the church was a necessity. France could not survive outright warfare between Catholics and revolutionaries, for neither side could win. And the church itself needed peace; it could not contemplate permanent opposition to the established order. Therefore, the Vatican accepted the loss of tithes and church lands and full toleration for all religions in France, though the Concordat stated that Catholicism was the religion of the majority of Frenchmen. In signing the document, the Pope virtually recognized the Napoleonic regime. In return, the church gained state salaries for its clergy, a papal right to depose French bishops (whom the state still named), and a firmer hierarchical structure within France. These seemed meager gains to many churchmen, but at least Catholics could now worship publicly. Napoleon later revived Catholic ire by his conquest of Rome and virtual imprisonment of the Pope and by increasing police supervision of the church in France, but never did French Catholics risk outright resistance.

Achievements of the Regime. With his regime fully established, Napoleon went on to build a clear legal and administrative framework for the new France, and in so doing confirmed some of the key gains of the Revolution. Since 1789 taxes had been theoretically levied on all citizens, but only under Napoleon did the government actually begin to collect the taxes it assigned, with professional collectors rather than local concessionaires. Within the government, orderly accounting procedures were introduced. All of this helped the war effort, which was the principal goal, but it also stabilized the currency and strengthened the whole financial system. In law, the regime's great achievements were Napoleonic codes, in which civil, criminal, and commercial laws were collected, condensed, and made consistent, replacing the welter of laws of the old regime onto which revolutionary legislation had been grafted. The principle of equality before the law was carried through the codes almost completely; the major exception was that a worker's word could not be accepted in court against that of his master. Private property, particularly land, was rigorously protected, which gratified peasant owners as well as the middle class. Laws of contracts and indebtedness facilitated private enterprise. The ban against labor unions was repeated. Here was a rational, uniform code that facilitated the operations of government and pleased the propertied elements of French society.

The final enduring achievement of the regime within France was the establishment of a state-controlled system of education at the secondary and university levels. Napoleon cared nothing for the education of the common people, so long as they were taught to be loyal. But he needed trained professional cadres for the government bureaucracy. Except for dabbling with the creation of new aristocrats, Napoleon preserved the principle of the "career open to talents" in government and military, untainted by the power of privilege or the purchase of offices. To obtain the talents he needed, he sought a training system, uniform for the whole of France, rationally graded so that secondary schools led directly into the higher schools, and state-run to insure uniformity and loyalty. The University system, as the whole enterprise was called, monopolized education at the higher levels. So well did the system serve the interests of the state that it has scarcely been modified to the present day. During most of the nineteenth century the University represented yet another gain for the middle class, whose sons dominated the student body, and it produced exactly the sort of competent if standardized bureaucracy that Napoleon had intended.

Napoleon faced almost no opposition in France during any part of his regime. Though his police and censorship certainly contributed to this fact, he was genuinely popular among most segments of society. To France as a whole he brought much-needed order, and early in his regime he seemed to be bringing the external peace he had promised. When his wars resumed they seemed so glorious, so inexpensive to France, and were so well publicized by Napoleon himself that again there was no reason to complain. The middle class, willing to accept a lack of real political freedom, was gratified by the law codes, financial stability, and educational system. The wars provided much opportunity for profit. Napoleon himself ignored the economy except as an aspect of war, but manufacturing prospered in his regime and in a few areas factories began to take hold. To the peasantry Napoleon brought order and confirmation of property; and peasants filled the ranks of his armies and reveled in the excitement of conquest. Again, Napoleon had no interest in agriculture, except to introduce sugar beets when France was cut off from the West Indies, but the wars offered fine opportunities for agricultural sales. For the workingmen, Napoleon offered almost nothing directly; indeed, he feared labor disorder and frequently took repressive measures against workers. Only a few tentative gestures of conciliation were made, such as the establishment of arbitration committees for labor grievances. These were outweighed by efforts to increase government control over labor, such as the system of state licensing for workers that Napoleon introduced. And certainly the law codes discriminated against the working classes. But workers, too, were tired of strife and incapable of combating government repression; further, the manufacturing boom and the drain of able-bodied men to the armies caused a rapid rise in wages. No group in the Empire had the combination of strength and motive to cause trouble, and many elements of the population long retained fond memories of the emperor.

FOREIGN POLICY: THE ASCENDANT

Through his popularity and the efficiency of his government, Napoleon had a solid home base from which to undertake military adventures. He long possessed a number of military advantages over other European states, including his own genius. He recruited talented officers and inspired enthusiasm in his men. Universal military conscription gave him large armies, for France was, with Russia, the most populous nation in Europe and Napoleon could call on conquered areas for troops as well. Technically, Napoleon's chief innovation was the use of light, mobile field artillery, which gave a decisive edge to French troops until their enemies began to imitate French guns.

While building his power in France, Napoleon sought to bring the war with the Second Coalition to a successful conclusion. Russia dropped out of its own accord; it had entered the war only because it feared French gains in Egypt, which might threaten its own ambitions in the Near East. When Britain defeated Napoleon in his Egyptian campaign and later took over the island of Malta, to keep it from Russian hands, Britain replaced France as Russia's main enemy. In this case and often later, coalitions foundered on the conflicting ambitions of their members. Napoleon was even able to find allies among the other powers, because of their rivalries. Only very slowly did a consensus emerge that Napoleon was the chief enemy of all.

With Russia out of the picture, Napoleon easily invaded Italy once more and defeated the Austrian armies. Austria signed a new peace in 1801, and even Britain came to terms in the Treaty of Amiens in 1802. By these treaties France retained Belgium and the left bank of the Rhine and gained recognition for satellite republics in Holland, Switzerland, Genoa, and the Po valley. Britain withdrew from most of the colonies it had seized during the previous decade of conflict; its withdrawal benefited Holland and Spain as well as France, for Britain had shown little concern about whom it despoiled. Napoleon had won a great victory, and Britain had been decisively thwarted. Not only were its colonial ambitions restrained, but it had surrendered its key diplomatic stake in Europe, the freedom of the Low Countries from any great power control which might bring a direct threat of invasion. Quite possibly Britain could not have endured a lasting peace on these terms, but it was Napoleon's continuing ambition that provided ample pretext for renewed fighting.

Aggrandizement Provokes War. Napoleon's limitless ambitions showed clearly in 1802 and 1803, for peace to him was simply an opportunity for further gains. He sent an army to Haiti, with the thought of reviving a French empire in America. He seized more direct control of the puppet states in northern Italy and Switzerland. He supervised the continued rearrangement of Germany, a process that the 1797 treaty with Austria had begun. Ever since France had taken the left bank of the Rhine, the German princes who lost territory as a result sought compensation among the tiny states of the right bank; and they fawned upon the French to aid them in their scramble. Most of the free cities and church states disappeared, as Prussia, Bavaria, Württemberg, and Baden particularly expanded. And the enlarged states depended on Napoleon's good will for their maintenance.

The scope of Napoleon's aggrandizement was too much for Britain, and in May 1803 war was declared. Within a year, Austria and Russia had joined the coalition. Both were aided by British subsidies, but they had their own grievances against Napoleon. The reorganization of Germany had been accomplished without any real consultation with Francis II of Austria, despite his position as head of the Holy Roman Empire; Austrian influence in Germany was radically reduced, and there were grave doubts that an Austrian monarch could ever again be elected emperor. In this situation, Francis virtually abandoned the Holy Roman Empire and proclaimed a new Austrian Empire, to maintain the status of his regime. He had every reason to join in the effort against the upstart Emperor of France, for French gains in Italy and the Low Countries, as well as in Germany, had weakened Austria more than any other power. Russian motives were more complex. The new emperor, Alexander I, believed he had a mission to reorganize Europe along constitutional and humanitarian lines. It was easy for him to confuse extensions of Russian influence with gains for humanity, and in essence he continued the expansionist program of his predecessors. Naturally, he saw Napoleon as his chief rival; he was sincerely shocked by Napoleon's brutal violations of the sovereignty of states.

Napoleon's first efforts against the new coalition centered around a possible invasion of England. The schemes for American empire were abandoned, and he sold the Louisiana Territory to the United States. He assembled a large fleet of barges on the channel. Britain was seriously frightened and appointed many watches along the coast; with a traditionalism that Burke might have admired, many of these posts persisted for decades thereafter, and a few men were paid to watch for Bonaparte into the twentieth century. The invasion was never attempted. Russian and Austrian armies moved west in 1805, forcing Napoleon to shift his troops, and in October Lord Nelson annihilated the French fleet at Trafalgar. Here, of course, the real limitation to Napoleon's ambitions was revealed.

Like many of his French predecessors, he could not consider building a navy that would really rival Britain's; therefore, he could not attack Britain or throttle its foreign trade. By this time, the British were vowed to his complete defeat and the reduction of French influence in the Low Countries and Germany. By themselves they could not succeed, but neither could Napoleon eliminate their pressure.

Napoleon's Power Grows. Despite the setback against Britain, Napoleon was near the apogee of his power. Austria and Russia were defeated in the great battle of Austerlitz, in December 1805, and Austria made peace, surrendering the territory of Venetia to Napoleon's Italian kingdom. Napoleon raised Bavaria and Württemberg to the status of kingdoms, thus defying Austria further and solidifying his German influence. The Holy Roman Empire was now officially dissolved; if its structure had been increasingly empty, its demise, after a millennium of existence, symbolized Napoleon's intent to restructure Europe. In place of the Empire, Napoleon began to organize a West German confederation under his protectorate. This action drove Prussia into the Third Coalition in a masterpiece of mistiming. By promising it various territories, Napoleon had held Prussia back for two years, but the Prussians could not tolerate French control in Germany. Napoleon easily defeated the famous Prussian army and marched through northern Germany into Poland where, in June 1807, he beat the Russians again for good measure. Alexander now backed down; he felt that the British were using him as a pawn to protect their own interests, and he could not risk a French invasion of Russia that might bring a revolt against his rule.

At Tilsit, on a raft in the middle of the Niemen River, the two emperors met, while the Prussian king paced fearfully on the bank. Napoleon captivated Alexander with pictures of a Russian empire extending to the east, to India; and France and Russia became ostensible allies against England, with Alexander accepting Napoleon as an emperor of the West. Napoleon let Prussia continue to exist, but maintained the occupation of Berlin and gave all Prussian territories west of the Elbe to the new kingdom of Westphalia, which became part of his Confederation of the Rhine. Napoleon was now the virtual master of continental Europe, with a territory directly in his power larger than that of any previous European conqueror.

Napoleon might have been able to hold his great gains, had he worked solely to consolidate them rather than trying to push still further. Britain was of course still at war, but it could not act by itself against France's land power. Prussia and Austria were theoretically hostile, perhaps, but too weak to be a threat. Russia was only marginally and tentatively in Napoleon's sphere of influence, but while Russia might be regrettably independent, events had proved that it was no match for France in the rest of Europe. But it was not Napoleon's nature to be content; there were still areas to be probed, such as southern Italy, where the absence of any real barrier to expansion could only attract Napoleon's appetite for territory. Further, Napoleon was increasingly trapped by his desire to defeat

Britain. Unable to gain victory directly, he mounted an economic war; to win this in turn, further conquests were necessary and allies such as Russia had to be forced, against their interests, to participate. The specter of an insatiable conqueror became ever more real, and Napoleon extended himself further and further to preserve his authority. In terms of real power, then, Tilsit represented the peak of his achievement, for difficulties increased steadily thereafter. But there were still five more years before the collapse began, years in which revolutionary changes were pushed through within the French Empire and, in imitation, outside it as well.

THE NAPOLEONIC EMPIRE

Napoleon's conquests reached their greatest extent in 1810 and 1811. His armies moved into Portugal and Spain during 1807 and 1808, though his control in fact remained incomplete. In 1809 Austria proclaimed a war of liberation against the French emperor. The Austrian government feared the same treatment that had been meted out to Spain, whose king had been summarily deposed, and it hoped that the continued fighting in Spain would distract the French. Austria also thought that Russia could be drawn in to put an end to French advances. But in fact Austria stood alone and was defeated without great difficulty; the only immediate result of the war was a cession of still more territory to Napoleon. Part of Austrian Poland was given up to Napoleon's Grand Duchy of Warsaw; some territory was ceded to Bavaria; and in the south, parts of Dalmatia, Croatia, and Slovenia were combined in the French-controlled Illyrian provinces.

Napoleon now dominated the entire European mainland except the Balkan peninsula. His sphere consisted of three layers. Russia, Prussia, Denmark, and Sweden were allies; and now Austria became one, with the marriage of Napoleon to the daughter of the Austrian emperor in 1810. There were a variety of smaller, dependent states, under some direct control from France. These included Switzerland, which remained a republic in form, and the Illyrian provinces, which were really administered as a part of France. There was also the new Duchy of Warsaw, created from Polish portions of Prussia and Austria, which was given to an ally, the king of Saxony. The most important dependent states were organized in the Confederation of the Rhine, which included all of Germany between France and Prussia and Austria. There were now twenty princes in this region, led by four newly made kings, one of whom, in Westphalia, was Napoleon's brother Jerome, who ruled an entirely new state composed of parts of Prussia and other areas. There was also the kingdom of Spain, given to Joseph Bonaparte, another brother; the kingdom of Naples, given to Napoleon's brother-in-law Murat; and the kingdom of Italy, including Lombardy, Venetia, and most of the former Papal States, with Napoleon as king but under the administration of his stepson. Finally, there was the French Empire itself, which had long embraced Belgium and the left bank of the Rhine. By 1810 it also included Holland and the northwestern coast of Germany, for Napoleon wanted direct control over the Dutch and German ports to prevent trade with Britain. Similarly, the French Empire now extended down the west coast of Italy, giving Napoleon the port of Genoa and the imperial prestige of controlling Rome. The entire Empire was administered by French prefects reporting to Paris, under the system established for France itself.

With the exception of the Iberian peninsula, then, Napoleon controlled the whole of western Europe directly. Much of central Europe was given to rulers completely dependent on him for their eminence and the extent of their territory. In the many thrones given to relatives, Napoleon sought more than reliable allies. He was trying to create a dynasty. His marriage to the Austrian princess was designed to legitimize his regime through alliance to one of the leading royal families, and to provide an heir. When a son was born, in 1811, Napoleon made him "King of Rome," harking back to the imperial traditions of the city. When the Pope objected to this, he was taken prisoner and interned in France. In addition to Napoleon's own glory, two of his brothers were kings themselves and a sister was queen in Naples. The Bonapartes' mother was installed in the Emperor's court and was called Madame Mère; she was said to mumble to herself constantly, "If only it lasts." Around the imperial courts were a flock of newly titled aristocrats, drawn from Napoleon's chief aides and endowed with extensive estates as well as ducal or princely titles. Napoleon himself became ever more pompous.

Administrative Policies. Napoleon's dynastic policies were an important indication of his political goals and increasingly commanded his time and energy; but they were not the most important aspect of his imperial rule. In all the states under French domination, including most of the dependent states, French armies were followed by the establishment of new governments, under French control but aided by the cooperation of local people eager for a new regime and for the favor of the powerful conqueror. New constitutions were drawn up everywhere, sometimes sent out by Napoleon directly. Real reforms proved impossible in Spain, because of continued fighting against Spanish guerrillas, and in the Duchy of Warsaw, which was really merely an armed outpost against Russia. But in Italy and Germany political and legal reforms were extensive. Napoleon forced changes to increase the efficiency of the regimes under his control. He also saw himself as a reformer, and he was indeed an heir of the Enlightenment in many ways, for he sought rationally constructed, uniform systems of law and government across Europe. He wanted these systems to be consciously planned, not simply inherited from the past in a jumble of traditional practices. There was no need to allow for differences in local needs, for he considered all people basically the same. Finally, Napoleon saw in his reforms, precisely because they were universally applicable, a means of winning widespread popularity for his rule.

The Napoleonic reforms were directed, first and foremost, against all elements of feudalism. The Napoleonic law codes were introduced, establishing the full legal equality of individuals and also giving governments more complete control over individual subjects, for the restraints of local and group privileges were wiped away. Nobles lost their tax exemptions, and careers were "opened to talents" in the army and government offices. Manorial fees and controls were abolished, freeing the peasantry in law and depriving the aristocracy of important revenues as well as of jurisdictional rights. Where peasants already controlled the land in small plots, as in Belgium, the Rhineland, and parts of northern Italy, the reforms created an entrenched class of small farmers similar to the French peasantry.

Outside western Europe, however, the changes in law tended to increase the power of landlords, particularly when some aspects of the reforms were rescinded after 1815. Most of the land in places like Poland or southern Italy was held in large estates, and peasants were not given new holdings as they became legally free. Further, they were obliged to pay indemnities to the nobility for their former dues, which provided aristocrats with important revenues and forced many peasants to sell what land they had, which they were now legally able to do. They could move freely under the new laws, but at this point there were few cities to move to, so increasing numbers became mere agricultural laborers. The disruption of traditional dues did force landlords to develop new methods to make their land pay off, particularly through sales to the market, and some of them were not able to adapt; but there was no gain for the peasantry in all this, and not enough disruption of the aristocracy to free eastern or southern Europe from their control.

As part of the attack on feudalism the church lost its special position in law and on the land. Napoleonic officials abolished tithes, restricted church courts, and dissolved or strictly regulated monastic orders. Toleration was granted to all religions and to unbelievers, for Napoleon was bent on creating a secular state in which rights did not depend on beliefs or birth. Church property was seized, forcing the church into economic dependence on the state.

Traditional restrictions on commerce and manufacturing, such as guilds and internal tariffs, were removed. The Napoleonic codes provided uniform commercial laws and the administrators standardized weights and measures as well. Napoleon's government imposed new controls on the economy, but it claimed for itself alone the right to regulate. The principles of uniformity and destruction of private privilege were clearly proclaimed.

Government systems themselves were rationalized, through the institution of careful accounting procedures and the substitution of state agents for private contractors in the collection of taxes. High salaries attracted government personnel and guarded them from corruption, and hereditary office-holding was eliminated. Military conscription was extended and systematized.

In sum, Napoleon introduced all the basic principles of the Revolution to western and central Europe, except the goal of self-government through elected legislative bodies. Instead of political freedom, the newly efficient states extended police supervision and censorship. But massive repression was seldom necessary, for many people were satisfied by the Napoleonic reforms. Enlightened nobles joined professional people and businessmen in welcoming measures which accorded with the philosophy of the eighteenth century. Many peasants and artisans welcomed their new freedom. This support for Napoleon's system extended the popularity of revolutionary principles, for groups which, in the previous decade, vaguely sympathized with the Revolution now knew first-hand some of the benefits of revolutionary legislation. As a result, in many areas the reforms could not be undone; where the reforms were rescinded, powerful interests were ready to advocate their return.

Function of Reforms. The impact of the reforms varied, of course, with the region. Northern Italy, the Low Countries, and western Germany were most profoundly touched, both because the French rule was longest and firmest there and because urban and rural social structure, similar to the French, allowed the full assimilation of the new systems of law. In these areas, a revolution occurred without violence, for manorialism and group privilege were overthrown for good. In these areas, correspondingly, there was no need for a social upheaval in the nineteenth century; unrest might arise over political or nationalist issues, but basic changes in social structure were not sought. This must be remembered when comparing later revolutions in these areas to the great French model.

In southern and eastern Europe, reforms largely confirmed the existing social structure, and many of them were rescinded later. Polish nobles welcomed the revival of part of their nation, but they carefully preserved their basic power. Estate owners in southern Italy and in Spain were really untouched; if they lost some feudal rights permanently they regained local political powers after 1815 and never surrendered their economic hold over the peasantry. In Spain particularly, French attacks on the church led the peasantry to rebel in many areas. Resentment against French control affected even middle-class groups that sympathized with principles of liberal reform.

In all areas the Napoleonic reforms served also as weapons of war. Freer and more efficient states could collect more taxes and conscript more men. In the dependent states as well as in the Empire itself, both men and taxes went to feed Napoleon's war effort. Even the expenses of the army could be largely defrayed by taxes in the Empire outside France, which reinforced French contentment with Napoleon. Further, the efficiency of Napoleon's principles of government, their direct relation to military success, forced governments outside his immediate control to introduce some similar measures.

OUTSIDE NAPOLEON'S EMPIRE

There was some spread of sympathy for revolutionary and Napoleonic principles on the edges of Europe. In some Balkan areas, contacts with

France increased during the period. Even in the eighteenth century trade with western Europe had increased as growing cities provided greater markets for agricultural goods. Trading possibilities expanded during the Napoleonic wars; Greek merchants, for example, were able to extend their Mediterranean fleet because Britain was distracted by the conflict with France and the French fleet was virtually wiped out. The new, small merchant class found French principles attractive in many ways, not only because they promised political and economic liberties but also because they suggested national loyalties. The merchants were eager to rid themselves of inefficient Ottoman rule and to replace it with national states that would be their own. A nucleus of revolutionary sentiment developed in the western Balkans that was to dominate the region in later decades.

In Serbia, a revolution actually broke out in 1804. It was encouraged by several merchants, and it received temporary support from Russia and Britain, who attacked the Ottoman Empire when the sultan allied himself with France in 1806. The revolution was also backed by the Serbian peasantry, which resented the harshness and inefficiency of Ottoman rule and, particularly, efforts by Ottoman landlords to dislodge traditional peasant small holders. The revolutionaries won a substantial victory, and in 1815 an autonomous Serbian government was established, with its own chieftain, its own army, and a national assembly. From the Serbian success, from the continued expansion of commerce, and from the equally continuous inspiration of French revolutionary principles, the basis for Balkan unrest developed.

The extension of interest in revolutionary ideas was not the principal motive for reform outside the Napoleonic empire; even the Serbian revolution was due primarily to local factors. In Prussia particularly, and to a degree in Russia and Austria, a reform effort was mounted by men who detested France. The leading reformers found some revolutionary principles just, but they were motivated primarily by a desire to strengthen their states. To resist French domination, some of the basic factors in French success had to be imitated; only because of this need was reform accepted by the ruling aristocratic class in eastern Europe. The result was a significant modernization of state government structures and some legal change for society as a whole; but the fundamental social hierarchy was not touched.

The Prussian government had grown progressively weaker after the death of Frederick the Great; a renewed vigor was overdue. The spectacular defeat by Napoleon in a single battle, in 1806, provided ample motive for energetic action. Many Prussian territories were seized and what remained suffered the indignity of French occupation. Talented Germans from the west flocked to Prussia as a haven from direct French control elsewhere. As the only purely German state outside Napoleon's immediate orbit, the stature of Prussia as a possible savior of German liberty and honor grew, a part of the long process of association of the cause of Germany with the cause of Prussia. More immediately, the non-Prussian Germans provided political and intellectual leadership for the Prussian revival.

Baron Karl von und zum Stein came from west of the Rhine, drawn to Prussian service by the promising reforms of Frederick the Great. Stein was never narrowly Prussian, never lost his attachment to Germany as a whole, but he worked for civil reform in Prussia as the key to a German revival. He long administered territory in western Prussia, where feudalism was lighter than in the east and where there was more manufacturing. His inspiration clearly came from the west, though from Britain and Holland rather than from France. As Minister of Trade from 1804 to 1807, Stein sought to free commerce and reform the state bank, but he came to realize that improvement in the state bureaucracy was an essential precondition to all further change. Beyond this, he sought an active sense of citizenship in the people of Prussia, rather than mere subjection to a central government. Returned to office in 1807 and 1808, he drafted the basic measure in his campaign, the liberation of the serfs; for, as serfs, peasants could never be active or responsible citizens. He was unable to obtain a full liberation, but he did grant the peasant personal freedom and he modified the legal basis for a caste system. Non-nobles could buy land, nobles could engage in trade, and the peasant was freed from some personal obligations to his lord. Stein also established some independence for municipal governments, as a first measure of self-government in Prussia.

Prussian Military Reforms. From the standpoint of the king and the nobility, military reform was the leading need in Prussia. Some of Stein's goals were relevant to this reform, for Prussian soldiers had to be made as actively loyal and inspired as their counterparts in Napoleonic France seemed to be. Most important, the French mass conscription had to be imitated. Prussia established universal military service, with every male serving either in the active forces or in a reserve unit. The government opened the officer corps to some members of the middle class, removed inefficient officers, improved training, and established promotion by merit.

The military reforms were the most enduring results of the Prussian rejuvenation. They not only encouraged a vastly improved machine for war, but also removed some features of the caste system by mixing middle-class officers with traditional aristocrats. In addition, Stein's successor, Hardenberg, seized some church endowments, made internal trade freer, and granted greater liberty to the Jews. Education at all levels was revised and a university was established in Berlin. All of these measures shook Prussia's traditional social structure and particularly encouraged the middle classes, by opening greater opportunities for business, by allowing the purchase of land, by freeing city governments, and by improving the training and opportunities of talented professional bureaucrats. Yet many aspects of the old order survived. The nobles retained some local judicial powers over the peasantry, and they kept their economic power. Laws of 1811 and 1816 allowed peasants to rid themselves of all feudal obligations, but only by surrendering much of their land to the lord, and as a result, large holdings increased in size. The reform era provided Prussia with many of the tools for modernization, particularly in the economy, and greatly increased the efficiency and military power of the government. A modern state arose in advance of major social evolution, and this reduced the need for agitation and political protest when society did change. Prussia was distinguished from western Europe at this time, and from much of eastern Europe later, by the low level of political awareness of most segments of the population.

In other countries outside the direct French orbit, reform was far more limited than in Prussia. In Russia, Michael Speranski served as a reformist chief minister from 1809 to 1812, when he was sacrificed to conservative opposition. Like Stein he hoped to create some representative institutions for the expression of opinion, but he failed; he also was unable to carry through his plan for greater regional and municipal autonomy. Speranski did rationalize the central bureaucracy to some extent, by establishing a central council to aid the Emperor in drafting legislation and by expanding university training for bureaucrats.

In Austria, there was no move toward reform, despite the defeat of 1809. The government relied still on professional armies and preferred diplomatic maneuverings to internal revival. Klemens von Metternich became foreign minister in 1809 and immediately repaired Austrian relations with France. Metternich believed that Austria could be saved by a skillful foreign policy, and he shared his monarch's hatred of significant political or social change. From this time onward, Austria retained its position as a great power primarily through its ability to form protective alliances — unlike Prussia, whose strength lay in the rising efficiency of its government and army.

The government of Britain, the other power outside the French orbit, had no need to contemplate major reform. Political agitation had already been suppressed, and Pitt's earlier improvements in government accounting and finances held good. Trouble in Ireland, which threatened to affect the war effort, in the late 1790's, was met by an Act of Union in 1800 which suppressed the Irish parliament and placed Ireland under more direct British control. This was the only constitutional change which the conflict with France prompted. Pitt continued to remodel the fiscal system, having earlier introduced an income tax to meet the huge expense of the war. On this basis Britain was able to support a more than sixfold increase in public expenditure from 1792 to 1815. But the real changes that the war brought were not in the realm of state action. War needs spurred many segments of the economy. Improvements in agricultural methods were accelerated; factory industry grew to provide the uniforms and weapons of war. Commerce, partially blocked from the continent, spread to the Middle East and Latin America. The war played a significant role in extending and confirming the economic transformation of Britain; and this transformation, in turn, allowed Britain to sustain a massive war effort of her own and to subsidize the efforts of her allies.

The impact of the Napoleonic era outside the French empire thus varied. The Prussian revival copied some French measures, but without developing a revolutionary context. In Britain, conservative politics were joined to rapid economic change. Austria and, with minor exceptions,

Russia sought to meet the Napoleonic challenge without disturbing their internal order, first by allying with Napoleon, which Prussia and Britain never did, and then by allying against him. Divided between Napoleon and Prussia, Germany was partially introduced to rationalized laws and bureaucratic procedures and to freedom for economic advance. Despite later alliances of the German states with the advocates of unaltered conservatism, Austria and Russia, this already set Germany apart and opened it to further change. Despite Britain's conservative alliances against France, the structure of British society distinguished it even more definitely from the defenders of the old regime.

NATIONALISM AGAINST NAPOLEON

The relationship between Napoleon and the spread of nationalism in Europe is an obscure one. By shaking traditional boundaries in Europe, Napoleon undoubtedly prompted a desire for further reconstruction along national lines. This was particularly true in the Duchy of Warsaw and in northern Italy, where Napoleon most clearly played on a hope for national existence. The French enthusiasm for their country and their Emperor, the national sense that the Revolution created, may have inspired emulation, as seems to have been the case with some Balkan businessmen who traded with France. Measures against the church as well as against traditional rulers doubtless weakened customary loyalties, although they did not necessarily replace them with nationalist attachments. Nationalism may also have risen in resistance to France, either on the part of conservatives who sought to free their nation from French-sponsored reforms as well as from France itself, or on the part of liberals who saw national liberty as a counterpart to personal freedom and who realized that both goals now demanded resistance to France.

There is reason to doubt, however, that extensive nationalist sentiment was roused either by or against Napoleon. Nationalism involved an active loyalty to a complex entity. The nationalist could define his nation by culture and tradition, often where no political boundaries existed at all. In Germany and Italy, this meant a loyalty to something above the established states. The loyalty could not be merely passive; the nationalist had to feel real membership and participation in the nation and the national culture. But few people yet sensed a national culture, for their attachment remained local and religious. Moreover, few states outside of France (and, to a degree, Britain) yet encouraged any substantial sense of active citizenship.

Furthermore, there were many reasons to oppose Napoleon besides nationalist ones. Conservative nobles in eastern Prussia were angry at the reforms Napoleon had indirectly induced. Liberals in southern Italy formed a secret society, the Carbonari, to resist French influence, but they acted in the name of individual freedom, not for the sake of Italy. Liberals in Spain, similarly, drew up a constitution and called for a parliament to resist Napoleon, but they did not appeal directly to a nationalist sentiment. Conservatives in Spain, from priests to peasants, formed numerous guerrilla bands to resist the French in the name of religion and their local freedoms. In many areas there was resistance to the French as foreigners, but this did not mean there was a positive sense of nationhood in contrast. Indeed, some of the areas that were later to lead in nationalist movements, such as northern Italy and western Germany, were largely satisfied at this point with the benefits of French rule. Most of the internal resistance to Napoleon came, as in Spain, in the name of tradition, not of nation. The peasants who filled the armies that battled Napoleon fought because they were accustomed to obey authority, as did many in the polyglot forces of Napoleon himself.

Nationalist Sentiment. With all this, French invasion did rouse some nationalist sentiment, among intellectuals especially and primarily in Germany. The reformers in Prussia, such as Stein, knew there was such a thing as Germany and felt that they were acting in Germany's behalf. The final Prussian war effort against Napoleon had overtones of a national German liberation, and, even if much of this was simply propaganda, the propaganda itself was significant. German intellectuals increasingly looked to a distinctive German culture, and a nationalist sense became intertwined with German Romanticism and idealism. Against Enlightenment, universality, and rationalism, the Romantics stressed the diversity of mankind and the importance of tradition. Friedrich von Savigny founded, in this period, the school of historical jurisprudence, which stressed that laws should not be created all at once, but should emerge gradually from distinctive national traditions. Johann Fichte, initially an admirer of the French Revolution, appealed in his *Addresses to the German Nation* (1807-1808) to the distinctiveness and superiority of German people and culture, and cited the need to create a common patriotic feeling so that Germans would fulfill their historic mission to lead in the development of mankind. The cultural nationalism now being expounded by German Romantics was important in itself, for a belief in a distinctive national culture provided the basis for other more political forms of nationalism in Germany and elsewhere. For its part, nationalism was colored by its association with German Romanticism and with opposition to a rationalism that was presumably foreign. The superiority of German culture was seen by most of the nationalist intellectuals precisely in its defiance of classical forms in literature and of rational standards in philosophy.

The efforts of the Romantic nationalists, then, ranged from propaganda pamphlets to literature to law. The movement was unquestionably the most important intellectual development in the Napoleonic period, especially because French intellectual life was largely stifled by Napoleon's censorship and his insistence on classical styles. Even some French intellectuals began to look to Germany for inspiration. Mme de Staël, for example, stressed the beauty of contemporary Romantic literature and of medieval German folklore. Partly inspired by the German movement, some French writers began to look to their own traditions for an alternative to rationalism; François René Chateaubriand, most notably, praised the aesthetic satisfactions of Christianity.

In the turmoil of Napoleonic Europe, then, nationalism took shape as an intellectual movement, even if it did not yet inspire widespread political loyalties. Its strength among German intellectuals and its association with the leading cultural movement of the period assured its propagation to broader groups and distant regions. This propagation, along with the massive reshuffling of boundaries and governments, was the main legacy of this period to later nationalism.

THE DEFEAT OF NAPOLEON

Napoleon's attempt to isolate Britain economically led him to efforts that drained his strength and roused the hostility that brought his downfall. Behind both his attempt and the hostility was the overweening ambition that could not let him rest.

Ever since they entered the war against France, the British had blockaded France and its allies, not to deprive them of needed materials but to destroy their commerce and, through this, their revenues for war, and in the long run to monopolize world trade. As part of this campaign, which annoyed many powers besides France, the British sought to flood Europe with British goods, particularly the cloth that they now produced by machines in ever increasing quantities.

Napoleon, in 1806, undertook a similar campaign against his enemy, hoping to destroy British commerce and drain its credit and gold. By the Berlin Decree of 1806 and the Milan Decree of 1807, Napoleon prohibited the importation of British goods to the continent and threatened any neutral ships that dealt with the British. In place of British trade, Napoleon hoped to build up the continent's economy with France as its center.

This Continental System proved a failure. There was widespread grumbling at the lack of British and colonial goods, especially such items as sugar. Port cities atrophied for lack of trade. Moreover, without command of the seas, the system depended on inland transportation that was simply inadequate. Eastern Europe suffered from the curtailment of manufactured products, which had previously been brought in from England. The British were not harmed; they replaced lost European trade with exports to other parts of the world, and they continued to penetrate the Continental System with much of their merchandise.

Napoleon's military activity after 1807 was largely determined by his commitment to a continent closed to Britain. The invasion of Portugal and takeover of Spain were designed to close off areas easily accessible to the British fleet. The continuing resistance of the Spaniards inflicted some of the first defeats on Napoleonic troops and required a major military commitment from that time onward. Discontent spread in Belgium and Holland, both injured by the closing of the ports; the Dutch actually rose against Napoleon in 1813, with the approach of allied troops, and declared their freedom under their legitimate ruler, William of Orange. Sweden broke away from the alliance with Napoleon in 1811. Most important, Russia was increasingly annoyed by Napoleon's insistence on obedience to the Continental System, as well as by his pro-Polish efforts and general expansionist policy; in 1811 Russia formally withdrew from the Continental System. This action, in turn, determined Napoleon's disastrous invasion of Russia in 1812, in which the largest army ever assembled was drawn farther and farther into the giant country and decimated by starvation and cold and the harassment of Russian troops. Five hundred thousand men, five sixths of the Grand Army, died or were imprisoned in the campaign.

Napoleon's Defeat. The end then came quickly, despite heroic defensive efforts by Napoleon. Prussia and Austria now joined Russia, though Metternich distrusted both the czar and German nationalism; and the British pushed quickly through Spain. Napoleon's newly assembled army was defeated at Leipzig in 1813, and Napoleon was chased back into France. At this point the allies threatened to split once again, but the British foreign minister, Castlereagh, established a Quadruple Alliance, based on the common fear of France and Napoleon; Russia, Prussia, Austria, and Great Britain bound themselves against France for twenty years and agreed to enforce such peace terms as they might decide. Napoleon abdicated in 1814, and when he returned to power briefly in 1815 he was defeated by allied armies at Waterloo. The Napoleonic era was over; it remained to put Europe back together again.

THE CONGRESS OF VIENNA

The settlement of the Napoleonic wars was based on several partially contradictory principles. There was a general desire to restore as much of the old order as possible and to reëstablish the sanctity of legitimate monarchy; hence the Bourbon dynasty was returned to France. But the Revolution could not be entirely undone, and the new king, Louis XVIII, granted a constitutional charter confirming the major gains of the preceding twenty-five years: legal equality, eligibility to public office regardless of class, the Napoleonic law codes and settlement with the church, and a parliamentary government based on very limited suffrage. Clearly, the restoration of the monarchy did not mean a restoration of the old regime, and most Frenchmen were satisfied with the government—and with peace—for the time being. Several deposed dynasties were restored outside of France, notably the Bourbons of Spain and of southern Italy; and here

Empire of Napoleon

States under Napoleonic Control

States allied with Napoleon

Independent States

RUSSIAN EMPIRE

BLACK SEA

OTTOMAN EMPIRE

BALTIC SEA

KINGDOM OF PRUSSIA

DUTCHY OF WARSAW

EMPIRE OF AUSTRIA

SWEDEN

DENMARK AND NORWAY

CONFEDERATION

OF THE

RHINE

ILLYRIAN PROVINCES

KINGDOM OF NAPLES

KINGDOM OF ITALY

SWITZERLAND

KINGDOM OF SICILY

NORTH SEA

UNITED KINGDOM OF GREAT BRITAIN AND IRELAND

EMPIRE OF THE FRENCH

P. of Lucca

KINGDOM OF SARDINIA

MEDITERRANEAN SEA

SEA

ATLANTIC OCEAN

KINGDOM OF SPAIN

PORTUGAL

EUROPE IN 1812

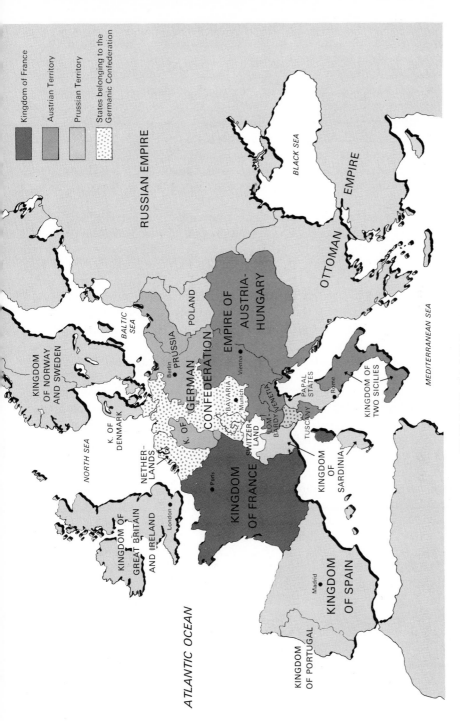

EUROPE IN 1815

Kingdom of France

Austrian Territory

Prussian Territory

States belonging to the
Germanic Confederation

RUSSIAN EMPIRE

BLACK SEA

OTTOMAN EMPIRE

POLAND

EMPIRE OF AUSTRIA-HUNGARY

PRUSSIA

Berlin

Vienna

GERMAN CONFEDERATION

BAVARIA

Munich

BALTIC SEA

K. OF DENMARK

KINGDOM OF NORWAY AND SWEDEN

NORTH SEA

NETHER-LANDS

K. OF

SWITZER-LAND

LOM-BARDY VENETIA

PAPAL STATES

Rome

TUSCANY

KINGDOM OF TWO SICILIES

MEDITERRANEAN SEA

KINGDOM OF SARDINIA

KINGDOM OF GREAT BRITAIN AND IRELAND

London

ATLANTIC OCEAN

KINGDOM OF FRANCE

Paris

KINGDOM OF SPAIN

Madrid

KINGDOM OF PORTUGAL

63

the monarchs began quickly to attempt a full return of the old order. A vigorous conservatism was one of the keynotes of the settlement of 1815 and also one of its most important legacies.

The problems of territorial settlement could not be settled simply by a return to the old order. To be sure, Prussia and Austria recovered almost all the areas they had lost and were compensated for the rest. But there was no thought of restoring all the little states of Italy and Germany. In restructuring the European map, three interests predominated: the desire to limit France on all sides; the desire of Prussia, Russia, and to an extent Britain for territorial gains; and the desire of Austria and Britain to make sure that no gains would be so great as to disrupt a basic balance of power in Europe.

The buffer was created around a France essentially confined to its pre-revolutionary boundaries. A united Kingdom of the Netherlands was created on the north, combining Belgium and Holland under the Dutch ruler, who in accordance with the new concern for strong monarchies was made a king. On the south the kingdom of Piedmont was revived and expanded. Finally, two great powers were placed near France's borders. Prussia was given virtually the whole German left bank of the Rhine; the other power, Austria, not only recovered its lost Italian territories in Lombardy and Tuscany, but took over Venetia as well. In addition, the restored rulers in the smaller Italian duchies and to a great degree the Papal States were dependent on Austria.

The acquisitiveness of three of the powers showed in many ways. Britain refused even to discuss the islands and colonies it had taken during the war, though the Netherlands Indies were returned. Britain had gained, then, increased holdings in India, the island of Ceylon, Malta, the Cape of Good Hope, several West Indian islands including Trinidad, and a few other areas. Britain stood, in 1815, as the only large and expanding imperial power in Europe, and with this empire and its industrial pre-eminence its world supremacy was long assured. The Russians kept Finland and Bessarabia, which they had acquired in fighting Sweden and Turkey when both were allied with France. Prussia, of course, gained the Rhineland; and Prussia and Russia competed for larger shares of Poland or for compensating territories. Alexander proposed a united Poland with himself as king, joined through him with Russia; Prussia agreed but only if it was given Saxony in return for its lost Polish holdings. Here Metternich called a halt and broadened the principle of balance of power in Europe. He feared both Russian and Prussian expansion, so close to Austria's borders, and Castlereagh joined him in resisting Russia; they both allied secretly with France to prevent the proposed aggrandizement. Thus was France even in defeat brought back into the European balance. News of the alliance caused Russia to back down and accept a smaller Poland. Prussia and Austria regained the rest, and Prussia had to be content with only two fifths of Saxony.

There were several principles that the Congress of Vienna quite consciously did not pursue. Liberal demands for constitutions and guarantees of rights were ignored in the new or restored regimes, except for the concessions in France and in some south German states. Nationalist ideals were scorned, particularly by Metternich, who feared their impact on Austria. Neither Germany nor Italy was united, and Austrian power in Italy made prospects for national independence seem dim. Germany was now composed of thirty-eight states, a vast reduction from pre-Napoleonic days, and the kings of Bavaria, Würtemberg, and Saxony were able to keep their crowns. A loose confederation was formed, with Prussia and Austria as members, which had few powers over individual states; this was the closest approach to a recognition that there was a Germany.

Conservatism Prevails. Instead of liberalism and nationalism, an energetic conservatism ruled the day. In response to Napoleon's return in 1815 and the renewed threat of revolution and war, the Quadruple Alliance powers reaffirmed their pact and pledged to meet periodically in congresses to preserve the established order. Alexander, now motivated by a vague religious idealism, proposed a Holy Alliance, devoted to the Christian principles of charity and peace; all rulers save the English regent and the Pope signed the document. In practice, the Holy Alliance represented more than a statement of peace. It signified the union of Prussia, Russia, and Austria—all monarchies, all conservative, all vigorously Christian—in defense of the established order not only among the nations of Europe but within them.

Within a generation, liberals and nationalists abounded who protested the conservative, antinational tone of the Vienna settlement; their strivings represent one of the principal themes of the political history of the next decades. Diplomatic attention, too, was primarily devoted to the problem of keeping order. Ultimately, neither the liberal nor the nationalist current could be repressed. Damaged already by 1830, the conservative aspect of the Vienna settlement was destroyed between 1848 and 1870.

The settlement was a clearer success in three other, related respects. A number of traditional problems were resolved, at least for a half century; these included the rivalries over Poland, rivalries over colonial empire, and Austrian-Prussian disputes over power in Germany. France was effectively hemmed in, and the period of recurrent French thrusts for greater power in Europe was over. If, then, future diplomatic problems, the problems raised by the new "isms," were not anticipated, past problems were effectively solved. Most important, the Congress of Vienna really did balance European powers, particularly because Britain was drawn to colonial expansion and wanted nothing more than a true balance in Europe. Prussia, greatly increased in territory and now possessing the most advanced parts of Germany, the Rhineland, and northern Saxony, was more than ever a power to be reckoned with, capable of restraining Russia as well as France. France was not destroyed, not dismembered, so that its government could play a full role in maintaining a balance. Most of the traditional vacuums of power in Europe were filled—by Prussian expansion in Germany, Austria's hold in Italy, and the full partition of

Poland. There was neither room nor great desire for further gains in Europe. The Vienna settlement kept the peace in Europe for fifty years; and there was no general war until 1914. It was an amazing diplomatic success after a quarter-century of turmoil.

Until 1848, at least, the Vienna settlement dominated European diplomacy. There were, véry simply, no major diplomatic problems; the few clashes of interests that did occur took place outside Europe. Within the peaceful setting — in part because of it — attention could be turned to internal politics and to economic development. Here, the legacy of the Revolution and of Napoleon could not be so easily controlled; and the spread of industrialization from Britain to the continent added to political pressures. Napoleon was to write, in his exile, a fraudulent memoir claiming that his whole purpose had been the spread of liberty, national independence, and democracy to all of Europe. He had neither done so nor intended to do so. But he had spread basic legal reforms well beyond French borders; he had encouraged a desire for further change, including real liberty and real nationhood. Within five years of his defeat, men who had opposed Napoleon were rising against the governments that had taken his place.

CONCLUSION

How much did the life and outlook of Europeans change between 1789 and 1815? Perhaps rather little, with a few obvious exceptions, for the revolutionary and Napoleonic periods prepared more basic changes than they accomplished.

How, for example, did a French peasant at the end of the Napoleonic wars differ from his counterpart when the Revolution began? Clearly, he was less aggrieved. He generally possessed a small plot of land outright and owed dues to no one but the state. Yet his methods of farming had changed little, and his economic expectations were no higher. Was he more politically aware? His attachment to the monarchy may have declined from simple loss of the habit of looking to a monarch, though there were many monarchist peasants still and many others whose attitudes changed little because the monarch had been for them rather unimportant before. Some peasants were attracted to Napoleon, for they had served under him in the armies and cherished their memories; but it is not clear that this was a decisive interest or that it was much more than a surrogate monarchism. More important changes had occurred beneath the political level. Many peasants had lost their religion, if only because church services had been interrupted in large areas for a full generation. Relatedly, many were beginning to limit their birth rate, a clear defiance of tradition, in the interest of protecting their landed holdings against too many heirs. In some ways this was merely a new way to defend traditional attachment to the land.

Peasants elsewhere in Europe had changed even less. Population pressure was continuing, but protests about conditions were still infrequent and traditional in form; they had nothing directly to do with politics. Legal changes stemming from the Revolution or other reforms contented many peasants, particularly in western Europe. A small number of peasants as far east as Prussia were now able to expand their holdings, through purchase of new land, and to produce for the market; this meant that some of the most dynamic peasants were directly opposed to agitation. In eastern and southern Europe, peasants were too poor and dependent to protest significantly, and the few reforms that had been introduced simply increased their helplessness.

The cities, too, were not greatly changed, outside of Britain. They had not grown much, nor had their economic functions been altered. The abolition of guilds and associations among artisans in western Europe opened the way for more capitalist methods of manufacture, but these were introduced only gradually. The prosperity of the Napoleonic period allowed many people to profit by traditional methods so that the implications of legal changes were not fully realized. In France, artisans and members of the middle class had undergone decisive political experiences, which would be remembered. But they had been willing to accept Napoleon's rule, partly because they were tired of strife but partly because they remained tolerant of effective government even when they had no role in it; they accepted the restored monarchy in 1815 on much the same basis. Outside of France, Britain, and the Low Countries, there were few signs that the urban lower classes had changed at all. In Naples, riots into the 1820's scarcely differed from those of the eighteenth century, and they were certainly no more political. In central Europe, the lower classes evinced even limited political awareness only in 1848. Members of the small middle class in Spain and southern Italy had been roused by the experience of Napoleonic rule to want real liberty, but they did not have general support. The French middle class seemed bent on enjoying the gains they had won since 1789, which did not include extensive political rights, and only slowly awakened to a new political interest in the later 1820's.

In most of continental Europe, then, the social bases for conservatism, in 1815, were extensive. Most people — even outside the peasantry — were still traditionalist in economic practices, religious, and politically apathetic. This is why the conservative settlement lasted so long. Small groups in Spain, Italy, and Russia were newly enthusiastic about the principles of the Revolution, but they could make no headway. Elsewhere (with the exception of Britain, where social changes impelled a rapid resurgence of political protest after 1815) most people had either won what they wanted or had no basis for agitation.

Yet the twenty-five years of Revolution and Napoleon bore fruit within the next two decades. Within France, many groups recovered quickly from the fatigue induced by disorder and war, and returned, if hesitantly at first, to the political interests they had developed earlier; and they would not abandon them so easily a second time. Elsewhere on the continent, the principles of the Revolution had real meaning still, for there were so many liberal and national goals to be achieved.

Aside from the direct inspiration provided by its various principles, the Revolution unleashed or promoted several forces that promised new political activity. The reaction of 1815 was novel, for governments, churches, and aristocracies were more closely allied than they had been for centuries. However limited their achievements, governments in the eighteenth century had been reforming agents, but they were no longer, because the Revolution seemed to show the danger of change. Even Prussia called a substantial halt again. At the same time, many governments had gained new powers during the revolutionary-Napoleonic period, to tax directly, administer the state religion, and recruit soldiers. They now had more immediate contact with their subjects, for part of the protective buffer of feudal and guild activities had been withdrawn. In sum, governments could rouse new political grievances because of their failure to reform, because they no longer seemed guided by enlightened principles, and because they had cut into older privileges and traditions.

Within a few months after the final defeat of Napoleon in 1815, new kinds of brigandage arose in the Papal States, directed in part against the government itself, and continuing off and on for fifty years. Several years of French rule had given many people a taste of political reform. Population growth and the slow spread of commerce after 1815 discontented many as well, even some who were basically conservative, because novelty was not stopped by the restored papal government. And some of the popes themselves experimented with more efficient taxation systems that created still more grievances—without being efficient enough to set papal finances on a sound footing. Agitation in the Papal States was unusually intense, both on a political level and beneath. Yet the pattern was not unusual: a conservative government that adopted some new measures to increase efficiency; a small number of people inspired by the French Revolution; and a larger number aroused occasionally from apathy by changes beyond their control.

Apart from setting political examples, the French Revolution had its most enduring effects by encouraging economic change, in combination with the compelling model of British industrial success. Countless individuals in countries such as France and Belgium had been inspired by the confusion of the previous decades to make their own mark, by setting up new economic ventures. France may have been surprisingly apathetic politically between 1815 and 1825, but it was in this very period that its commercial and manufacturing personnel were being radically renewed— the majority of wealthy Parisians were "new men" by 1830—and were adopting new techniques. Economic innovation revived the significance of revolutionary political principles for the middle class, throughout western and central Europe, and spurred elements of the lower classes to look to the revolutionary heritage of radicalism.

Outside the peripheries of Europe in the south and east, the revolutionary period seemed, in 1815, to have made its principal mark in the fierce new conservatism. The calm was deceptive. People are born every year, but occasionally in history one can talk of political generations. A new generation had arisen between about 1785 and 1805. They were too young to lead, in 1815, though some might agitate as students. But they had been born or raised during the revolutionary era, and even if they had disliked it they knew it was a fact. They were bound to dispute with the old men who returned to power in 1815, for they sought something new in the economy and the bureaucracy of their country; indeed, they sought a nation. After 1815, it was not only intellectuals who proclaimed the importance of nation, for even businessmen felt their own importance in contributing to a nation's strength. This new generation helped disrupt the habits of society generally and inadvertently helped inspire a growing dissatisfaction among the common people.

SUGGESTED READING

Controversies on the nature of Napoleon's efforts and the quality of the man are admirably presented by P. Geyl, *Napoleon, For and Against** (1949); the best biography is J. M. Thompson, *Napoleon Bonaparte* (1952). On special topics, see E. Heckscher, *The Continental System* (1922); S. Zweig, *Joseph Fouché, The Portrait of a Politician* (1930); and H. Cachard, *The French Civil Code* (1930).

British reaction to Napoleon is treated by C. Oman, *Britain Against Napoleon* (1944); see also J. H. Rose, *William Pitt and the National Revival* (1911), and *William Pitt and the Great War* (1911). For Germany: R. Aris, *History of Political Thought in Germany from 1789-1815* (1936); R. R. Ergang, *Herder and the Foundations of German Nationalism* (1931); G. S. Ford, *Stein and the Era of Reform in Prussia, 1807-1815* (1922); W. M. Simon, *The Failure of the Prussian Reform Movement, 1807-1819* (1955); W. O. Shanahan, *Prussian Military Reforms, 1786-1813* (1945); and for the modern period generally L. Krieger, *The German Idea of Freedom* (1957). Also useful for the Napoleonic era: W. C. Langsam, *The Napoleonic Wars and German Nationalism in Austria* (1930); A. A. Lobanov-Rostovsky, *Russia and Europe, 1789-1825* (1947); E. Tarlé, *Napoleon's Invasion of Russia, 1812* (1942).

For diplomacy, consult H. Butterfield, *The Peace Tactics of Napoleon, 1806-1808* (1929); C. K. Webster, *Britain and the Reconstruction of Europe* (1931); and H. Nicolson, *Congress of Vienna; A Study in Allied Unity, 1812-1822** (1946).

*Available in a paperback edition.

Hegel: Brown Brothers   Bentham: Culver Pictures

HEGEL AND BENTHAM

The diversity of philosophic activity in the early nineteenth century is clearly illustrated by two of the leading thinkers of the period, Georg Wilhelm Friedrich Hegel (1770-1831) and Jeremy Bentham (1748-1832). At the same time, the two men illustrated the difference in intellectual traditions developing in Germany and England. Hegel's idealism, his search for basic forces in history, long colored German intellectual life; and Bentham's rationalistic pragmatism was equally influential in shaping British political theory in the nineteenth century.

Hegel was the son of a civil servant in Württemberg. He was trained in Protestant theology and served as a private tutor before turning to philosophy. Initially attracted to rationalism and the French Revolution, Hegel early developed his philosophic mission: to combine the ideal and the actual, the natural and the moral. He turned against liberals and bitterly criticized the revolutions of 1820 and 1830, because they sought reform by abstract reason. He urged, instead, an historical reason that would recognize the natural growth of government and society. Here was the antirationalist side of Hegel, where a sense of the variations of history was to underlie any comment about society. But Hegel was also an absolute idealist, who felt he possessed, *a priori,* the key to the divine plan of creation. He developed a scheme of the constant evolution of society, an evolution to be capped by the rise of the Prussian state.

Within this broad framework, Hegel sought to reconcile human freedom with social order. He held that the state was the source of all good and that morality came from the state and not from individual conscience. War was a spiritual good, for it expressed the power of the state and so of the citizen. Punishment for crimes actually carried out the will of the criminal, by attuning him to the ethical demands of the state. And the state itself was to be orderly, monarchical, and strong. Hegel, whose work won him a post at the University of Berlin, was a favorite of the Prussian government. Most of his followers and students maintained his conservative stance; but some, including Marx, seized on his sense of evolution to work toward quite radical goals.

Jeremy Bentham had no idea of an underlying plan for history. He prided himself on his pragmatism, and his school of political theory is called utilitarian. Bentham believed that human reason could be constantly and fruitfully applied to the organization of society. Like the scientists who derived laws of the physical universe and went on to control this universe, so the reformer could apply experimental reasoning to society and invent quite practical methods for its improvement.

The goal of the reformer was the same as the goal of society itself: the happiness of the greatest possible number of citizens. Here was the test for all reform proposals. Bentham devised some wild schemes, such as a highly disciplined organization of poor relief, called the Panopticon. But he was at his best in proposing specific, practical improvements in Britain's legal system, in local governments, and in health measures. He had a modest private income and devoted his life to the disinterested investigation of all aspects of British government. He maintained contacts with every type of reformer, from Tory politicans to democratic radicals; and he inspired two generations of politicians and social theorists, including John Stuart Mill.

Bentham and Hegel had a common frame of reference in the Enlightenment. Hegel attacked the abstract reasoning of the Enlightenment and denied any rational basis for social reform. Bentham remained optimistic about the powers of human reason, but he abandoned the Enlightenment's interest in broad social theories and its discussion of abstract, universal rights. But where Bentham turned to a piecemeal and pragmatic approach to social problems, Hegel developed a higher idealism, an intuitive sense of the basic force of history. By associating this force with the power of the state Hegel could justify the rigorous authority of state over individual. Bentham had his abstraction too, the very simple one that the state must serve its citizens. This assumption, never really analyzed, allowed him to devote his whole attention to practical investigations and proposals.

Hegel's influence helped maintain Germany's clear leadership in formal philosophy in the nineteenth century; Bentham's approach was destructive of elaborate systems. Bentham encouraged the common-sense reformism that has so obviously dominated modern British politics. Hegel encouraged the devotion to abstractions, like the state but also like the proletariat, that commanded German political thought. Both men, of course, reflected their different national climates of politics and philosophy; it would be too simple to see them as basic causes of the differences. But the two thinkers were both involved in the breakup of Enlightenment political thought. With this standard gone, a number of different approaches were possible; and these approaches would have great influence on politics as well as on intellectual life. ■

Chapter 3

Reaction and Revolution
1815–1848

After a brief pause for breath following the Napoleonic wars, European political conflict spread more widely than before. In fact, conflict came to dominate the years between 1815 and 1848. The basic struggle was between liberals, willing to countenance revolution to achieve their goals, and conservatives, bent on holding the line against all political and social change. Revolutionary efforts of various sorts burst forth from France to Russia; although Britain avoided a revolution in the period, it did not avoid massive and diverse agitation. Diplomacy was clearly subordinated to political strife, particularly before 1830; foreign policy became an adjunct of the effort to repress protest at home. Intellectual activity grew closer to politics than it had in the previous decade, and there were intellectuals on both sides of the political fence. The most notable development was the establishment of a series of conservative philosophies, based on traditional values such as religion, but also on the rising wave of Romanticism. But Romanticism could lead to a radically liberal view; there was no unified intellectual approach to politics. Indeed, the movement toward liberalism of most intellectuals, Romantics or not, became increasingly general after about 1828 and before 1848.

The increasing pace of social and economic change was the basis for the new unrest. Industrialization, which came to dominate British society by mid-century, had its influence on political conflicts in the period; but, although the beginnings of industrialization did prove unsettling on the European continent, far more important were economic changes leading to but falling short of actual industrialization.

Both peasants and artisans in western and central Europe had to grapple with the aftermath of legal changes brought by the Revolution and Empire and by reformers like Stein. In Germany, many peasants lost their land through the partial abolition of serfdom, while others faced new taxes. They had to try to earn money, which meant producing for the market, but they often lacked the knowledge and equipment to do this successfully. Other peasants in Germany and eastern Europe were still serfs, sometimes burdened with rising labor obligations to their landlords as market agriculture spread to the estates. Everywhere, outside of France and Britain, population pressure increased in the countryside. Urban artisans were also faced with new numbers, as cities grew, but there were new opportunities as well. Artisans, too, were troubled by new economic forms; some had been deprived of their guild organizations and many were employed in larger firms than before—firms in which the owner treated them as paid labor rather than as fellow craftsmen. For peasants and artisans alike, recurrent food shortages brought general economic recessions, at least once a decade, that caused great misery. Protest against immediate hardship and against the more basic changes in the situation of the common people was inevitable. A growing wave of strikes and riots supplemented the frequent revolutions of the period. Some of the protests sought simply to restore the old social order, for many people could see no other goals. Many protests, certainly, had nothing to do with politics. With increasing intensity, however, particularly in the cities of western Europe, common people learned to fight for new goals, including political rights.

The forces of order, then, had much to contend with. There were liberal groups who remembered their gains under the Revolution and empire; there were, after a decade at least, the most vocal segments of the intellectual community; and there were the various groups disturbed by the changes in economy and society. Against these dissidents, the conservatives had only political and military weapons, but they were willing to use these weapons with vigor. Nowhere, during the period, did conservatism yield save in Britain and to a degree in France and Belgium. There were vital differences among both the supporters and the opponents of conservatism, but during most of the period the lines seemed clearly drawn, to conservatives and liberals alike. Both sides arrayed themselves for war.

THE METTERNICHIAN SYSTEM

The leader of the conservative forces throughout the period was the Austrian foreign minister, Prince Metternich. Under his forceful leadership, Austrian policy dominated much of the internal order of the German and Italian states, as well as the varied holdings of the Austrian Empire itself. In trying to enforce conservative political interests, Metternich was responding to a well-developed conservative creed shared by many people after two decades of confusion. Metternich believed that the first duty of states was to preserve order and therefore, in his own day, to resist the impulse to revolution that he saw was active still. For him, the French Revolution meant only anarchy, for he believed its doctrines that society could be reformed by a rational plan and its faith in the power of each individual to reason were fatally in error. Metternich thought that man needed controls of the sort provided by a traditional state. It was in the general interest, not simply for the benefit of a ruling class or the state itself, that every effort be made to prevent and repress disorder; any means might be justified for this. On the other hand, Metternich was not opposed to gradual change, to limited reforms in state structure and economic policy. Ironically, the author of an international conservatism was not the most conservative statesman in his own land.

Francis I, who lived until 1835, resisted even the most minor change: as he said in 1831, "I won't have any innovations. Let the laws be justly applied; they are good and adequate." Only fitful and limited efforts were made to rid the Empire of the old economic restrictions, including internal tariffs. The bureaucracy was left with a welter of redundant agencies, though some improvements were made in army administration; and there was no financial reform, so the imperial debt mounted steadily. To support the regime, increasing overtures were made to the church, which had been seriously limited during the eighteenth century; the Catholic hierarchy gained substantial powers in education and censorship. Finally, a repressive police system was extended throughout the Empire. Police spies opened even Metternich's correspondence; there were many arrests and secret trials of presumed subversives. Press censorship was rigorous. Teachers and students were constantly watched, and students were forbidden to attend foreign universities. Here was a system that had to be rigorous to survive, for there were many reasons for grievance and no peaceful channels for their expression.

Although Metternich had little to do with policies within the Empire, he had much to do with encouraging and directing their adoption elsewhere. He had agents and spies all over Europe, ready to report any hint of subversion so that their master could press the appropriate government to take action. In addition to protecting order in itself, Metternich used his system to make sure that Austria's place in Europe would not be diminished.

Metternich and Germany. The first challenge to Metternich came in Germany. Disappointed by the Vienna settlement, nationalistic university students began forming political clubs, the *Burschenschaften,* and held a nation-wide congress in 1817. Although the clubs did not pose much of a threat to the existing order, they did provide Metternich with an opportunity to introduce repressive legislation. He had no direct authority in Germany, save through Austria's membership in the weak German Confederation. He had great influence, however, and he was careful to conciliate the leading states, particularly Prussia, whose rulers were almost as anxious as he to repress dissent. In 1819 the principal German rulers agreed on the Carlsbad Decrees, which provided for the dissolution of the *Burschenschaften* and the imposition of strict censorship over the press and the universities throughout Germany. In 1832 the Diet of the German federation, alarmed by liberal agitation in 1830, further enacted that no representative assembly could limit the power of its prince. Other conservative measures were taken by individual states. Prussia abandoned its reformist impulse and, by imposing the large compensation in land on any peasant who sought freedom from his manorial obligations, bolstered the aristocratic landlords. The usual measures of press censorship and police surveillance of all liberals, particularly in the universities, were rigorously applied. The Prussian king also tried to use the force of religion to support his regime, by bringing the churches under greater state control and by uniting, by fiat, the two leading Protestant denominations.

However, the German states on the whole cannot be described as purely conservative in the Metternichian sense. Metternich was unable to persuade the southern German states to abandon the constitutions they had granted right after 1815, or the weak representative assemblies for which the constitutions provided. Prussia improved its central administrative system still further, expanded its universities, and worked for rapid economic growth. The government established model factories with British machinery and rapidly extended roads and canals; in the 1840's it even abolished the restrictive practices of the guilds. Prussia and other German states were among the continental leaders in railroad development in the 1840's—far ahead of France and certainly of Austria. Some German states built and owned the railroads themselves, and all the governments provided funds and central direction for the effort. Finally, Prussian leadership prompted a major tariff reform, which spurred the entire German economy and ultimately proved vital in uniting Germany. The Prussian tariff of 1818 was carefully devised to encourage all elements of the economy, framed in the belief that moderate tariffs brought the greatest revenues precisely because they facilitated trade. Gradually, beginning in 1828, other German states took similar measures and some united with the Prussian system. In 1833 most of the major states joined Prussia in a customs union, the *Zollverein*.

In sum, German conservatism was different from Austrian, despite common participation in a Metternichian framework. The repressive apparatus was all there, though modified by a greater freedom of expression in the parliaments of south Germany. In the 1840's the new Prussian king, Frederick William IV, made a few concessions, by moderating the censorship and calling a joint meeting of provincial diets to discuss financial matters. But he believed firmly in divine right monarchy and had no intention of allowing any challenge or limitation to his power. Still, the German governments did not simply try to stand pat. Economic progress and improvements in administration helped compensate for the absence of political freedoms, and if a gap between Germany and the West remained, in politics, the gap between Germany and Austria grew also. Austria's resistance to the *Zollverein* was more than symbolic; it showed the difference between a concerted, if limited, effort at reform under conservative auspices and a conservatism that was simply immobile.

Conservatism in Italy. Austrian conservatism was more completely followed in Italy than in Germany, though both were parts of Metternich's system in politics and diplomacy. It was true that the states under

Austrian control and direct influence followed relatively enlightened policies, compared to the rest of Italy or to Austria itself. Police control and censorship were prominent, of course, but the Napoleonic reforms were not undone. This meant that the administration was efficient and honest, that serfdom was not restored, and that the powers of the church were limited. Substantial freedom was granted to commerce and manufacture.

The policies of the three leading Italian states differed considerably, for there all traces of French influence were attacked. In the Papal States there was a reformist party, interested in improvements in local administration, but it could make no real headway. French measures, from obligatory vaccination to secular law courts, were rescinded. Political police were supplemented by religious orders that busily reported any subversive elements. As many as three thousand suspects were confined to their homes at any given time in Rome, and the numbers actually in jail were almost as large. In addition, the financial administration was corrupt, burdening the state itself and its subjects.

Further north, the Piedmontese regime was less reactionary; the administration was relatively efficient and the church was under some government control. But the army dominated the country, censorship was severe, and the regime grew progressively more repressive and clerical as time went on. In the South, where the Kingdom of the Two Sicilies embraced three eighths of the peninsula, the king bound himself by a treaty with Austria to introduce no liberal reforms. He abolished a constitution he had promised to observe, restored much church land, and sponsored an extremely brutal police.

Italy, then, lay fully in Metternich's grasp. If the Austrian territories were treated best, they were nonetheless Austrian and subject to rigorous political controls. Other states, including the papal territories, might resent Austrian intrusion and dominance, but they could not resist it. They lacked the military force and they depended on Austria for preservation of their reactionary regimes.

Outside the Austrian system directly, two other states followed an essentially Metternichian policy, in close alliance with Austria. Ferdinand VII reëntered Spain in 1814 amid great popular enthusiasm. He arrested prominent liberals and dissolved the parliament, vowing to disregard the constitution that the liberals had drawn up in 1812. He restored all church property, banned foreign books and papers, and reëstablished the Inquisition. Public services deteriorated and Spain's finances were in constant difficulty. Along with the Kingdom of the Two Sicilies and to an extent Austria, the reaction in Spain was characterized not only by extreme repression, but also by the elaborate support given to church and nobility and by the growing inefficiency of leading government agencies.

Russian Conservatism. The Russian government rivaled Metternich for leadership in defense of order. Alexander I abandoned almost all ideas of reform and allowed brutal suppressions of peasant agitation. His successor, Nicholas I, came to power on the heels of a small but frightening rising of some army officers, in the Decembrist revolt of 1825. The Decembrist riots protested the corruption of the administration, censorship of the press, and control of the university—the leading apparatus of the conservative state. They sought some reform of serfdom, which still virtually enslaved large sections of the Russian peasantry. But their attempted revolt failed and it simply confirmed Nicholas in his quest for repression and avoidance of all change. Nicholas' leading concern proved to be the development of the secret police, the Third Section of the Imperial Chancery—a huge network of uniformed police, spies, and informers. Russian laws were codified and finances temporarily stabilized, but there was no sign of reform in other fields. The landowners determined the Czar's policy toward the serfs; the central bureaucracy grew under Nicholas' autocracy. Educational standards declined, with schools enjoined to stress obedience and Orthodox religion.

DIPLOMACY OF CONSERVATISM

Almost the whole of Europe was locked in a system of rigid, defensive conservatism. Police controls, promotion of religion, defense of the existing social order—these were the leading concerns of governments almost everywhere. And, until 1830 at least, these concerns dominated diplomacy as well.

A series of great-power conferences were held following the Congress of Vienna. The first meetings served to complete the settlement with France. But Alexander, and later Metternich, sought to use the conferences to form an international front against revolution. In 1820, military revolts broke out in both Spain and Naples. Both were motivated by grievances in the armies over growing governmental inefficiency, including low and irregular pay; and the Spanish troops did not want to be sent to repress revolts in Latin America. In both cases, liberal groups supported the risings and established constitutions and parliaments. The conservative powers could not tolerate this affront to their principles. Since in both cases the legitimate monarchs were too weak and unpopular to regain control by themselves, an international intervention was necessary.

In 1820 Alexander called for intervention in Spain by the Quadruple Alliance. Britain refused, stating its willingness to cooperate in preserving peace but its hostility to interference in the internal affairs of other states. Britain could not stomach an effort to support a monarch of Ferdinand's stripe, and it had no desire to open the way to a meddling by great powers that might disturb its economic and diplomatic influence in places like Spain. But British dissent did not stop the movement. In concert with Russia and Prussia, Metternich drew up a memorandum for presentation to the conference at Troppau, in 1820, stating the right of the powers to intervene wherever necessary against revolution. At a subsequent meeting in Laibach, the continental powers authorized Austrian troops to enter Naples, where they restored the king and revoked the constitution. In

1823, the same powers gave France permission to return Ferdinand VII to the Spanish throne.

Changes in Conservative Diplomacy. By 1823 the diplomatic interests of the major powers began to diversify. A conservative alliance of the three eastern powers persisted, although the last formal conference was held in 1822. Eastern and central Europe remained blanketed by conservative diplomacy until the 1850's. Austria intervened against Italian revolutions several times, as in 1831 in the Papal States. Russia and Austria together helped keep order in Germany; as late as 1850 the Czar helped persuade the Prussian king not to disturb the political structure of Germany. Russia sent troops against the Hungarian rebellion of 1848 and 1849. A militant conservative diplomacy remained a vital aspect of the Metternichian system.

However, there were areas that this diplomacy could not reach; and Russia had interests beyond pure conservatism. In 1823 Britain confirmed its separation from the conservative alliance by declaring its protection of Latin American independence—and its own growing trade interests there—against any reimposition of Spanish control. In 1830 not only the New World but also western Europe proved unreachable by the conservative powers. No one marched against the Revolution in Paris; and the new French regime was not interested in even occasional cooperation with the conservative powers to preserve order abroad. Both Russia and Prussia talked of sending troops against the Belgian revolution of the same year. France could not tolerate such intervention so close to its borders, and Britain stepped in to avoid a possible conflict. Aided by Russia's distraction with the Polish revolution, the great powers were able to agree to recognize Belgian independence.

Even before 1830, the conservative alliance had been weakened and divided by the revolution in Greece. Like the Serbs earlier, the Greeks were exasperated by maladministration under Turkish officials; and Greek merchants had acquired a definite nationalist impulse. A rising began in 1821 and continued for eight years. In principle, the conservative powers should have moved against the rebels; but there was a widespread popular enthusiasm for the Greeks, even in Russia, and it was difficult to be as concerned about an attack on the Ottoman Empire as about revolts against Christian princes. Britain again backed the rebels, partly because of public pressure, partly to avoid unilateral Russian intervention in Greece, and partly to annoy Metternich. Furthermore, Russia could not withstand the temptation to ignore the principles of the Holy Alliance and help its coreligionists in Greece. Metternich deplored the violation of legitimate order and the prospect of increased Russian influence in the Balkans, but he was powerless. With Russian, English, and also French help, Greece won its independence in 1830; and by the Treaty of Adrianople, in 1829, Russia gained much new territory along the Black Sea and occupied what is now Rumania. Here was the first significant change in the map of Europe since the Congress of Vienna, and also the first successful challenge to established internal order.

Foreign policy themes. By 1830, despite their ideological differences, Britain and Austria had a clear stake in maintaining the balance of power in Europe. Britain wanted freedom from any European threat to pursue its interests overseas; Austria realized that peace was essential to the preservation of order, and it certainly feared any revival of expansionism on the part of its two allies, Prussia and Russia. France felt a vague desire for greater influence and some suggestion of the glorious policies of the Empire; but its government was far more concerned with winning full acceptance by the other great powers and attending to its domestic problems. The French king after 1830, Louis Philippe, was content to finish some Napoleonic monuments as his gesture toward the glory of the Empire. He sought no involvement abroad and pulled back whenever trouble threatened. Prussia, likewise, was concerned with internal order, save for its tariff initiative in Germany. And Russia was content to probe in the Middle East, attracted by the possibilities that the Treaty of Adrianople and the growing weakness of the Ottoman Empire opened up.

The result was that the only area of significant, competitive diplomatic activity was in the Middle East. Part of the trouble was internal; not only was Greece independent and Serbia largely so, but also a powerful ruler, Mehemet Ali, arose in Egypt to challenge his Ottoman sovereign. Here was a good excuse for great power intervention. Russia, in 1833, sent troops to protect the Sultan and was rewarded by a close alliance. France was also interested in the area; French armies began the conquest of Algeria in 1829 and the French tried their hand at winning influence by supporting Egypt. A renewed Egyptian attack on the Sultan in 1839 brought matters to a head. Austria and Britain, fearful of a further Russian advance in the area, arranged a general guarantee of Turkish independence to replace the Russian protection; and Russia agreed. Faced with this coalition, France, faithful to its policy of avoiding real trouble, backed down. The danger had passed for the time being, though Russian ambition, Turkish weakness, and Britain's desire to prevent any great power gains in the area promised renewed trouble for the future.

The diplomacy of the major powers between 1815 and 1848 remained conservative in two senses. There was the conscious effort to use foreign policy to resist revolution, important particularly early in the period but continuing as a motive for the eastern powers. In a broader sense even British and especially French diplomacy was conservative, anxious to preserve peace in order to attend to problems at home. In both aspects, diplomacy reflected the difficulties of internal order, of defending a regime by force, or of attempting to construct a regime that would win wider acceptance.

CONSERVATISM IN THE WEST

Neither France nor Britain could impose a Metternichian type of conservatism. Both had traditions of parliamentary rule and some freedom of thought that they could not fully renounce. Yet the conservative movement swept both countries after 1815, and it produced many policies that resembled those of the Holy Alliance powers.

In Britain, the monarchy was weakened by the mania of George III and the dandyism of his son; Parliament ruled, representing the wealthiest elements of society. The leaders of Parliament were Tories and conservatives, fearful of disorder at home and eager to repress it by all possible means. The threat of disorder was real, for Britain's war-based prosperity collapsed by 1816 and strikes and riots by the unemployed were frequent. The government saw plots and threats even where none existed. A network of paid informers and spies was developed; in 1817, the Habeas Corpus Act was suspended, allowing imprisonment without trial, and seditious meetings were banned. In 1819, 50,000 people assembled in St. Peter's Field, in Manchester, to hear speeches demanding government reform; the government called in troops, who killed eleven people and injured hundreds in the "Massacre of Peterloo." Following this, the Six Acts restricted public meetings and the circulation of newspapers still further.

The peak of repression ended by 1820, so that Britain's reactionary period was the shortest in Europe. There was still much resistance to reform; only in 1832 could even the middle classes be satisfied with political progress. But a group of younger Tories began to espouse the cause of reform even earlier. Taxes and tariffs were simplified and revised, and many duties were lowered. Robert Peel drafted a simplified and humane criminal code that removed the death penalty from almost 200 types of crimes; and a beginning was made in prison reform. A new police force was developed, both to prevent crime and to preserve order without resort to clumsy military forces. In 1828 the Anglican monopoly on public offices was removed, so that Protestant dissenters could now hold public posts without any restrictions; and limitations on Catholic political activities were lifted in 1829. These various reforms opened the way to further changes, for the slowness and reluctance of most Tories in meeting reform demands could no longer be endured. The long period of Tory rule was coming to an end.

French Conservative Policies. There was no question that the Restoration monarchy in France would be conservative; the only question was, conservative of what? Louis XVIII, though he was brother to the king executed in the revolution, was anxious to reconcile all elements of French society, including the supporters of the Revolution; or perhaps he was just tired of traveling and eager to solidify his throne in the only manner possible. Hence the Charter, which granted a parliament, freedom of religion and thought, and legal equality; hence the lack of major persecution of former revolutionaries and Bonapartists, though there were a few show trials. The King did not try to restore the old regime. Owners of the land seized from emigré aristocrats were assured of possession, though later the nobles were given a million francs in compensation. The church was given new honors and funds, but the Concordat of 1801 remained in force; and as the government supported Catholicism so it expected firm loyalty in return. The press was given substantial liberty. Finances were put in good order, an extraordinary accomplishment after the Napoleonic wars. And, in the first years, the King was careful to choose moderately liberal ministers.

Yet, for all this, the Restoration regime ultimately failed and was easily displaced by the Revolution of 1830. If its conservatism was initially moderate, the policies of its leading supporters were decidedly reactionary. Many churchmen and nobles sought the systems of the old regime; in the South, particularly, the reactionaries killed and terrified many liberals. Though the King on the whole restrained these people, he could not entirely disassociate himself from them. The murder of a member of the royal family, in 1820, prompted even Louis XVIII to take a stronger line. Liberal ministers were replaced by conservatives. The government reconstituted press censorship and restricted freedom from arbitrary arrest; it rewrote electoral laws to give virtual control of parliament to the large landlords and the old nobility. Churchmen were given the leading positions in the educational system. It was in this period that French troops invaded Spain to restore the most reactionary monarch in Europe.

Reaction increased under Charles X, Louis' brother, who came to the throne in 1824. A few rather tentative measures were proposed to restore some of the principles of a manorial economy, and a law was passed decreeing the death penalty for certain kinds of sacrilege. Several history and philosophy courses were suspended at the University of Paris because their professors were suspected of subversion. In all this there was much more talk than action; no one, for example, was executed under the sacrilege law. Charles X seemed bent on creating the image of an old regime monarch, though he did not dare touch the enduring legislation of the Revolution. And certainly the repressive measures were real enough, though even here they failed in practice to prevent attacks from press and rostrum.

Both France and Britain, then, made some gestures toward a Metternichian type of conservatism, but resistance was too widespread and political traditions too opposed to make them stick. In Britain, however, the modifications of conservatism, if gradual, were voluntary; in France, they were brought only by revolution.

CONSERVATIVE PHILOSOPHIES

The conservative reaction after 1815 was not political alone; there was widespread intellectual embrace of conservatism as well. Intellectuals of various types sought some alternative to the rationalist philosophies that seemed responsible for the chaos of the French Revolution. Even fundamentally rationalist theorists, such as Victor Cousin in France, sought a unifying principle above individual reason—some general faith in morality and public order that would prevent excessive experimentation. But the leading proponents of conservatism were part of the rising Romantic Movement, which reached its peak after 1815.

Much in Romanticism remained irrelevant to politics. A new generation of Romantics grew up in the 1820's, devoted to stylistic innovations in literature and art. Heinrich Heine revived the central themes of German Romanticism in his poetry, dwelling on the love of nature, the beauty of old folk tales, and the glorification of the spontaneous emotions of the heart. Everywhere—in Russia, Poland, and Scandinavia—Romantics collected old legends and poems and wrote epics commemorating the soul and history of their people. Painters such as Joseph Turner developed greater freedom in the handling of light, color, and movement; the Gothic revival in architecture reflected the Romantics' interest in history and in nonclassical styles. Innovation was equally striking in music and drama. The central, unifying impulse of the Romantics remained apolitical, the expression of individual and collective emotions through novel artistic forms.

Romanticism and Conservatism. There was much in Romanticism, however, that lent itself to conservatism, as earlier Romantics had already shown. The stress on emotion over reason could easily be converted to a critique of the rationalist approach in politics and a statement that men needed political restraint simply because they were driven by passions. The Romantic search for beauty in history could become a defense of tradition. The Romantics often stressed the organic nature of social development, seeing links constantly between present and past. Most of all, many Romantics sought something higher than man, some guiding force that reason could not grasp. This force could be God, or the state, or the nation, or a bit of all three; man could be seen as part of a collective whole, subject to its guidance, rather than as a free agent in determining his lot.

The specifically conservative philosophers of the period developed many lines of argument, but they agreed on the importance of order, religion, and a strong state. For Joseph de Maistre, the leading reactionary philosopher in France, order depended on absolute authority, authority on Christianity, and Christianity on an absolutely sovereign Pope. Only a church as strong in politics as in religion could defeat the rationalist absurdity of revolution. Men like Savigny in Germany stressed the historical basis of law and institutions; reason could create nothing new; no political principles could be generalized, for political structure evolved in accordance with the character of each people. Haller, in Switzerland, more simply held that a strong state was justified by the very fact that it was strong and that the weak needed the protection of the strong, the sovereign. The stress on authority and the futility of change ran through all the conservative theories. The conservatives opposed reform proposals of all sorts; they abhorred revolution; and they often attacked even earlier movements, such as the Reformation, because such movements had encouraged change and individualism.

Religion and Conservatism. A revival of intellectual interest in religion was closely associated with the elaboration of conservative philosophies. Religion naturally appealed to men who looked to tradition and authority, who sought a higher, unifying principle beyond reason. It was a clear antidote to the human presumption that had brought about revolution. The religion sought was not, of course, that of a rational theology; religion was an inner experience, not a system of thought. So said Schleiermacher, the leading theologican of the nineteenth century. It was the emotional experience, not reason, that brought man to some union with God. In France, Chateaubriand stressed primarily the beauty of Christianity. Christianity at last had found vigorous and diverse intellectual defenders against the corrosive doctrines of rationalism.

The theories of the conservatives and the Christians were not spun in isolation; they had immediate impact. They could easily be cited in defense of conservative politics, and many conservatives wrote on the issues of the day. The work of the Christian intellectuals corresponded, also, with signs of a popular revival of emotional religion. Pietists in Germany and Scandinavia, preaching a hatred of reason and a "religion of the heart," still flourished; Methodism spread to a minority of the lower classes in England, preaching obedience to established authority as well as active religion. Even in France there were signs of renewed popular interest in religion; Catholic revival meetings in the 1820's could rouse a fervent response in peasant villages.

Until the mid-1820's, the forces of order seemed in full command. There had been unrest in several places, but it was easily repressed. The intellectual community gave solid backing to authoritarian regimes. Much of the populace seemed content; the religious revival was a good sign, and many people were clearly attached to the restored regimes. Spanish peasants, for example, tore down revolutionary posters in 1820; Neopolitan peasants remained attached to monarchy and church.

But a storm was brewing. Political agitation had been repressed but not eliminated. The tone of the intellectuals was about to change, partly because of the restrictions conservatives placed on university life and on publications. And the social effects of economic advance proved increasingly difficult to contain within the conservative structure.

INTELLECTUAL DISSENT AND THE ISMS

There were two philosophical approaches that could lead to dissent. The most obvious was rationalism; the leading liberal theorists and many socialists were distinctly in the rational tradition. But Romanticism could lead to dissent as well. The Romantic interest in individual passions could lead to a passionate devotion to individualism and liberty; the Romantic interest in the beauty of popular traditions could lead to a vigorous advocacy of improvement for the people; and the frequent interest in national cultures could lead to a revolutionary nationalism. Furthermore, Romantic styles appealed particularly to the middle classes, who saw beauty in sentiment and who sought a cultural alternative to aristocratic classicism; the middle classes also supported political dissent and believed in the power of reason. So two traditions, opposed in the most formal theory, could unite in political impulse. By 1830 the conservative theorists had virtually disappeared in France, some of them converted to a flaming liberalism. Doctrines of dissent spread widely in England and Italy and penetrated Germany as well.

Liberal theories were developed particularly in Britain and France. Liberal economists, deriving from Adam Smith, produced the most specific intellectual movement. This group, led by men like Ricardo in England and J. B. Say in France, held that economic advance was surest when the economy was left in the hands of private individuals. They believed there was an "invisible hand" guiding economic activity which assured an orderly result from diverse individual effort. Private competition would produce goods of the highest quality and lowest price. State functions should be confined to defense, preservation of internal order and justice, and the construction of a few public works which private groups could not maintain. The classical economists differed widely over certain issues: some held that high birth rates doomed the working class to perpetual subsistence wages, while others felt that advancing prosperity would spread to all. But whatever the mood, it was agreed that the government could not interfere with the natural laws of the economy. According to the pessimists, an effort to protect the workingman would simply prompt him to have more children, which would worsen conditions through the competition of excess workers; or as the optimists held, it would force a nation to raise its prices, hurting its competitive position and ultimately its workers. Businessmen must be free to offer the wages and conditions the state of the market required. And there should be no restrictions on the introduction of new methods, on exports and imports, or on the movement of labor.

Liberalism and Personal Liberty. Political liberals shared many of the assumptions of the economists and usually agreed that government activities in the economy should be minimal. They stressed that each individual was the best defender of his own interests and that governments should do only what individuals were absolutely incapable of doing for themselves. In particular, political liberals defended freedom of thought and expression; they damned religious as well as political restrictions and sought the freest possible exchange of ideas. For, as John Stuart Mill later wrote in *On Liberty*, man's highest achievement is the development of his mind, a development which he alone can, in final analysis, accomplish. The liberals agreed on the definition of the proper boundaries for liberty. Benjamin Constant, a member of the leading liberal group in France in the 1820's, repeated the formula: liberty is "the right to pursue our own ends unimpeded, so long as they do not interfere with the equally legitimate activities of others." The liberals largely abandoned the eighteenth-century defense of liberty, for they could not maintain a belief in natural right, but they stressed that liberty could be fully justified, with equal rationality, by its usefulness to society and the individual.

Liberals sought a political system that would appropriately limit government and represent the interests of at least the substantial elements of the community. They wanted a parliament, with real power to check the monarch, and with real representation of the upper classes. And they wanted a constitution, to define the structure and limits of government. German writers such as Dahlmann took a lead in urging constitutional government, as did liberals elsewhere on the continent.

The basic premises of liberalism are easy enough to define but, even among intellectuals, there were major disagreements over the boundaries of public and private actions and over the structure of the state. The leaders of French liberalism in the 1820's sought a very limited suffrage, and most liberals were hostile to democracy; but liberalism did shade off, as in England, into demands for broad suffrage. Most liberals were constitutional monarchists, but republicanism was not incompatible with liberalism. Some liberals felt that education could remain in private hands, while others, such as Mill, said that governments could compel school attendance. Some liberals held that the government had virtually no role in the economy, but others came to feel that regulation of child labor and other abuses was essential to liberty itself. It is easy to draw overly sharp lines around liberal theory. The basic liberal premise that governments could intervene only where an individual's acts affected others was quite flexible; and though liberals agreed on rough guidelines, in this period, they disagreed on specifics. As with any school of political theory, liberals were most unanimous in what they condemned: restrictions on press and education, authoritarian government, and traditional limitations of economic innovation.

Liberal Christianity. Shading off from liberalism were a variety of related philosophies. There was, first of all, liberal Christianity, which differed from ordinary liberalism only in its corollary stress on religion. It is true that most leading churches and many religious writers supported authority and order and sought to repress the very currents of liberalism. The major Protestant churches in England and Holland, however, were quite latitudinarian, stressing morality over theology and tolerating some of the assumptions of rationalism and science about man's nature and the universe. Within these churches there were many who supported liberalism and actively sought liberty for other sects; an Anglican canon, for example, wrote one of the most vigorous advocacies of full political emancipation for Dissenters and Catholics. Within the Catholic church, also, a liberal movement developed by the late 1820's; liberal Catholics sought a reconciliation of Catholicism and liberalism, a recognition by the church that freedom of thought and expression was not only valid but also could benefit the church itself. The movement was formally condemned by the papacy in 1832 and 1834, but it survived in France, Belgium, and Germany. From this time onward, liberal Catholicism remained an important minority movement in church affairs, albeit overshadowed by papal blasts against all the liberal doctrines.

Radicalism and Socialism. In England and, after 1830, in France, radicalism developed as a clear intellectual movement. The radicals wanted more thoroughgoing reform than did the liberals, though they shared many liberal assumptions. Most of all, they sought democracy and, in France, a republic. They wanted liberties, certainly, but they often suggested some government action in favor of the poor; they wanted parliaments, but they were less concerned than the liberals about their precise powers and far more concerned with their representativeness.

Socialism also developed as an intellectual movement in the period; unlike the other isms, it had almost no popular impact until much later, though a few British union movements were touched by a vague socialism and socialist leadership played a role in Paris in 1848. A major school of socialist thought did develop, however, based particularly in France and characterized by its effort to calculate all social needs rationally. The utopian socialist Charles Fourier condemned all existing social institutions and proposed that society be grouped in small units, each containing 1620 persons, in which every individual would be able to do whatever work suited his natural inclination. Various other small community schemes were proposed, and some were tried out by Europeans and Americans in the United States. More influential were the writings of Louis Blanc, who proposed government sponsorship for cooperative workshops, and of Saint-Simon, who proposed a technocracy, run by industrial experts, with public ownership of capital and public coordination of projects to elevate the poor. Virtually all the utopian socialists assumed that their schemes would spread by example and education, rather than by violence or organizational activity; that is why they were truly utopian, but that is why also they fit so naturally into the intellectual atmosphere of the period, in which so many theorists tried to spin out formal and final plans for society.

Nationalism and Dissent. Along with liberalism, the rise of nationalist theory was the most important intellectual contribution to dissent in the first half of the nineteenth century. Many Romantics, interested in national traditions, were in fact conservative, as we have seen. But insofar as they were nationalists, they suggested political change. In eastern Europe, much intellectual nationalism remained purely on the cultural level. George Lazar began in 1816 to teach, in Rumanian, the distinctiveness of Rumanian history; Vuk Karajich in 1814 published the first Serbian grammar; and the historian Palacky published a history of Bohemia in 1836, the first step in Czech nationalism. None of these actions was directly political, but they gradually created a national consciousness that could easily become politically active.

The leading nationalist writer of the period was Joseph Mazzini, who formulated a second type of nationalism (different from purely cultural) that is conventionally called liberal nationalism. The term is appropriate, for many nationalists were liberals and many liberals nationalists; but it is worth noting, in view of later conflicts between the two impulses, that Mazzini was not really a liberal. He did not believe that the individual could stand alone; a higher entity was needed, and that, of course, was the nation. He did share a liberal faith in a common humanity, stressing that each nation had a special role in the service of mankind; and he certainly disavowed any superiority for his own nation, Italy. But for him, national unity in Italy had to be the foremost goal; nothing could be accomplished before this. From unity would flow the proper amount of liberty, though duty and social justice for the whole citizenry were always more important. To achieve unity, all methods were appropriate, including the revolution to which Mazzini devoted his life.

The flurry of ideologies in the early nineteenth century is indeed astonishing. Conservatives sought to make systematic what never had needed formal statement before the revolutionary attack. The continued impulse toward rational planning, the emotional fervor engendered by Romanticism, and the clear evidence that change was possible induced an even wider variety of theories of dissent and of innovation. Virtually all the principal political movements of the nineteenth and twentieth centuries were suggested in this period: not only formal movements such as liberalism or socialism, but also less formal but equally real political developments such as technocracy. Some of the theories bore practical fruit only later; but liberalism, nationalism, and to a degree radicalism blossomed into diverse political activities quite quickly. In combination with new social grievances, they ended by shaking the conservative order.

SOCIETY ON THE VERGE OF INDUSTRIALIZATION

Eastern Europe was exempt from decisive social change between 1815 and 1848. More and more large estates in Russia and Hungary began producing for western markets, by introducing new agricultural methods and by enforcing the work obligations of their serfs more rigorously. There was an increase in manufacturing as well, largely through the spread of the putting-out system, in which peasants produced textile and metal products in their own homes. A nonaristocratic professional class expanded to fill the growing needs of government bureaucracies. But the basic structure of society remained untouched and largely unchallenged.

British society, under the full impact of industrialization, underwent the most complete change in the period, though the lines of development had been established earlier. Factory industry gained increasing dominance over other forms of manufacturing; by 1850 there were as many factory workers as artisans, and factories accounted for a far greater output. Manufacturing itself gained a predominance over agriculture unprecedented in history. By 1850, half of Britain's population lived in cities, and the value of production derived from manufacturing had well outstripped that derived from agriculture. British agriculture continued to be the most efficient in Europe, and for the estate owners earnings were generally good in the period; but the greater wealth now lay in industry. The repeal of the Corn Laws, in 1846, removing tariff protection from foreign grain imports, both symbolized and encouraged Britain's commitment to favor industry over agriculture.

Within industry, textile manufacturers continued to lead in total employment and production, for mechanical weaving processes now joined mechanical spinning. Partly because of the spread of textile machinery, heavy industries—mining, metallurgy, and machine building—grew rapidly. During the 1820's, the first operating railroad lines were established, facilitating trade generally and creating direct demand for iron and coal. By 1850 most branches of manufacturing and transport had been touched by mechanization and several leading industries were entirely transformed.

Effects on Society. Such rapid economic change naturally had unsettling effects on society. Many individuals profited from economic opportunities, and industrialists and merchants gained substantially in numbers and wealth during the period. But these years also saw the peak of deprivation and unrest in both city and countryside. Some artisans, displaced by machines, tried to destroy their metal rivals. Outbreaks of machine-breaking, known as Luddism, were particularly severe in economically depressed years between 1815 and 1820. Other urban artisans, not threatened by direct displacement, sought new political rights and organized unions and strikes to better their economic lot. They were joined by some factory workers, particularly cotton spinners and coal miners. The result was a significant upsurge of industrial agitation from 1818 to the mid-1830's, aided by a relaxation of the legislation against unions in 1824. Most agitation was for immediate gains, but in the 1830's a number of workers formed a short-lived national organization, the Grand National Consolidated Trades Union, under the socialist impulse of Robert Owen. Certainly, there was plenty to protest in the period. The rapid growth of cities outstripped housing and other physical facilities. Urban death rates rose markedly between 1820 and 1840. Hours of work were long for women and children as well as for men; and though wages varied, they seldom allowed much above subsistence living. There was little help from above. The government regulated the conditions of child labor in 1833 and restricted daily hours of work to ten for women and children in 1847, but the laws were not well enforced. Worker protest efforts almost uniformly failed, but their cry of anguish was unmistakable.

There was unrest in the countryside as well, where rural laborers were pressed by continued enclosures and by the introduction of some agricultural machinery. Major risings took place in 1830 and in 1843. This was a troubled period for British society, and particularly for its lower orders.

Continental Industrialization. Industrialization touched the continent in this period also, through competition with British imports but also through the spread of factories at home. Belgium led the way, aided by British and French capital and its own substantial deposits of coal. New procedures were adopted by some branches of the textile industry in France and by a few big firms in metallurgy. There was significant factory development in the Ruhr and in Saxony, in Germany, and in Switzerland;

and isolated factories were established elsewhere. In the 1830's and 1840's a number of states began to build a railroad system, led by Belgium and the German states, whose governments were particularly active with plans and government aid.

Most of this activity remained rather rudimentary. By 1848 only about a tenth of the French manufacturing labor force worked in factories; half the output of French metallurgy came from old-fashioned forges and foundries. The common impression that the first half of the nineteenth century in France or Germany was shaped by industrialization is erroneous, as is any notion that the disorder of the period was due primarily to the spread of industry. A few men made vast fortunes by adopting the new techniques; a small portion of the labor force was drawn into the factories, and in contrast to their English counterparts they often found conditions rather satisfactory; and the threat of a British-type industrialization clearly disturbed many traditional groups. But the real changes in society were more subtle.

Commerce and domestic and artisanal manufacturing expanded rapidly in western and central Europe, though by the 1840's domestic manufacturing faced serious factory competition. New opportunities brought new men into business groups at every level. Small shops spread in cities and even in villages; at the other extreme, men gained great wealth in new banks, insurance companies, and merchant houses. This was a period of exceptional mobility for the middle classes in western Europe. A great expansion of enrollments in the higher schools supplemented business opportunities and increased the number of professional people.

Cities expanded rapidly, though not at the British pace. Urban artisans almost doubled in number in Germany between 1820 and 1848. At the same time, the forms of artisanal production were changing. The earlier abolition of guilds in western Europe removed much traditional protection of artisanal conditions, and strict laws forbade any significant associations to replace them. The abolition of guilds spread to central Europe in the period, with Prussia taking the step in 1844. Artisan masters increasingly acted like employers of their journeymen, rather than comrades in labor. They expanded the number of men employed and, on the whole, prevented them from rising to the master's position. Traditional mobility was blocked as, in France and Germany, the number of masters remained the same despite the rapid increase in the ranks of journeymen. Many artisans improved their earnings in the period, but they could not ignore the threat to their way of life.

In the countryside, population pressure continued to outstrip available land, particularly in central Europe. There were new opportunities for sale of agricultural produce on the market, but many peasants could not adopt the necessary new methods; and the opportunities brought harsher controls from landlords in large estate areas. Where peasants owned most of the land and were free from manorial restrictions, as in France and the Low Countries, they remained relatively content. But manorialism remained intact in Austria and only modified in Prussia, Spain, and southern Italy; and in several cases landlords increased their exactions and governments tried to extract more tax money from the peasants.

Economic Recessions. Finally, in Britain and on the continent, the period was marked by a series of major economic recessions, in which food was scarce and expensive and unemployment widespread. The most notable crises were in 1818, 1828 and 1829, 1837, and 1846 and 1847, but there were others. Crises disturbed the earnings and expectations of businessmen, and they drove workers and peasants to desperation; at the extreme, death rates always rose during recessions.

The inevitable result of specific disasters and more far-reaching pressures was recurrent disorder on the part of peasants and artisans. There was Luddism, as when Silesian weavers broke into textile factories in the 1840's; there were food riots in the countryside and in towns; there were strikes, by urban artisans particularly; and, on occasion, there was revolution. The deprived or threatened groups were often not attracted by the ideologies of protest in the period, but they frequently joined with groups which were. The combination could be explosive, for it linked ideas of a better future with groups desperately opposed to the established order.

THE RISE OF LIBERALISM AND RADICALISM

As the conservatives realized, liberal movements began to develop very quickly after 1815. In southern Italy the secret society whose members called themselves Carbonari, which had been formed during the Napoleonic period and which contained over 50,000 members by 1820, increasingly stressed liberal demands for individual freedoms and a constitutional, parliamentary monarchy; the society spread to northern Italy and to France. In Germany, though the *Burschenschaften* were suppressed, a liberal sentiment still smoldered in the 1820's, to burst forth again in 1830. Liberalism was represented in eastern Europe by small groups of aristocrats, like the Russian Decembrists or the Hungarian leader Széchenyi, who sought to modernize their countries in western terms and to loosen the grip of absolutist monarchy. Masonic organizations in Spain gave the small Spanish middle class a forum for discussion of liberal ideas, and liberalism won some army leaders. In Spain and in the Kingdom of the Two Sicilies, the revolutions of 1820 followed a clear liberal impulse, by providing constitutions and summoning parliaments, by allowing liberty of the press, and by attacking the power of the church.

The most important liberal movements of the 1820's developed in Belgium, France, and Britain. In Belgium, many businessmen and land-owners resented the heavy hand of Dutch rule, both because it was foreign and because it imposed severe restrictions on university life, the press, and the economy. They were joined, increasingly, by Belgian Catholics, who were out of favor with the Protestant king of Holland.

Liberalism in Britain and France. British liberals were found both in and out of power after 1820. The Tory reformers, in measures such as Catholic emancipation, enacted some aspects of a liberal program. But most liberals wanted more than this. Even before 1820, during the years of repression, they demanded an extension of suffrage and a revision of parliamentary districts; they also sought corresponding municipal reform, to release the cities from the control of closed corporations. In the press, in often massive public meetings, and in petitions the reformers sought to press their points home. When an electoral reform bill was defeated in parliament in 1831, riots and demonstrations broke out throughout the country. Public sentiment was clearly behind the liberals. The abuses of the existing system were glaring, for some new industrial cities had no parliamentary representation and over a third of the seats were controlled by large landed proprietors. The reform movement could not be denied.

In France, liberals were relatively quiet before 1820, partly because of the initially moderate tone of the Restoration government and partly from simple exhaustion after a quarter-century of turbulence. But increasing governmental conservatism brought renewed liberal attack. As in Britain, the liberals did not have to act in secrecy. They could use parliament and the press as their forum; they easily controlled most of the newspapers and, despite the limited suffrage, they won a majority in parliament after 1825. French liberals were headed by a group of intellectuals, the *doctrinaires,* many of whom served in parliament. They sought a drastic reduction of church influence, a moderate extension of the suffrage, more powers for parliament, and protection of freedom of thought and expression.

By the late 1820's, liberals in many areas were a force to be reckoned with. They had organization, in reform groups or secret societies. They were articulate. They represented powerful interests—an element of the aristocracy in eastern Europe, professional people almost everywhere, businessmen and bankers in France, Britain, and Belgium; and in western Europe they had broader popular appeal as well.

Liberalism Defined. Like most isms, liberalism is extraordinarily difficult to define, even for a specific period. There were clear differences between liberalism as a theory and liberalism as an opposition political movement, and further differences between both and liberalism once in power. To complicate matters further, there were differences not only in the power but also in the purposes of liberals in various areas. The liberal impulse was one of the most important currents of the nineteenth century, partly because it was flexible enough to accommodate a variety of interests and ideas.

Liberals believed in progress; they were optimistic about the chances of men, or at least some men, to better their lot and arrange a better social order. They believed in efficiency, in rational arrangements. They sought freedom from irrational restrictions, such as limitations on economic advance. They wanted government tax systems, bureaucracies, and laws to be orderly; they wanted a clear plan, a constitution, stipulating the structure and functions of government; and they wanted a parliament, both to check arbitrary executive power and to give representation to enlightened elements of the community. And certainly, they wanted protection of specific individual freedoms, particularly in thought and religion. This was the common fund of liberal ideas.

Liberals also differed over many matters. While they all agreed on the importance of individual freedom, they also recognized that it might have to be limited in the interests of order; the question was, what limits were proper? Liberals stressed parliaments, but some accepted parliaments with only slight powers and most, in this period, recognized the importance of an effective monarchy. They stressed the need for representation but differed widely on how much representation. Liberals in this period feared the mob and were not democratic, and they insisted on property qualifications for voting (for they believed wealth revealed excellence), but some sought the enfranchisement of an upper-class elite while others wanted to include propertied elements in general.

There was, in liberalism, a certain distrust of the state, though this is clearest in British liberalism. Some liberals sought a government with only minimal functions of police and defense. But if the state were efficient, if liberals had a voice in it, more positive functions could be seen. The German liberal tradition, on the whole, stressed the state as the positive creator of human rights and looked for vigorous state action in a variety of fields. French and even British liberals split on the role of the state in the economy. During the 1830's some French liberals argued that railroad building should be left in private hands, but others, equally liberal, asserted that state action was vital, in the public interest. Similar debates occurred, in many countries, over the role of the state in regulating abuses of labor, particularly child labor; liberals could be found on both sides of the issue. Even in tariff matters there was diversity; British and most German liberals resisted high tariffs as unwarranted government interference in the economy, but few French liberals were anything but protectionist. No liberal sought rigid government control in all or even most fields of activity; but it is impossible to equate liberalism with a thoroughgoing attack on government power. Almost all liberals in politics, unlike some of the British theorists, sought government encouragement to education and certain humanitarian reforms.

There was, in liberalism, an internationalist implication, inherited from the Enlightenment belief in the basic uniformity of human nature. But most liberals, after 1815, were nationalists, believing that their country had a distinctive character and, quite possibly, a superior one. In Germany and Italy, liberals were the leading advocates of national unification. Liberal nationalists did maintain, in theory, that all nations had their rights and that there was a common humanity to which all contributed, albeit in distinctive ways. But by the end of the period it was clear that nationalism could induce a scorn for other nations in clearly liberal movements.

Liberalism is, then, something of a will-o'-the-wisp. It is possible to see all sorts of gaps between liberal theory and practice. French liberals could try to repress the church quite illiberally; German liberals could accept a powerful state and a weak parliament. Did this make them less than liberals? The answer depends on how useful it is to judge an active political movement by theoretical standards, how useful it is to impose largely Anglo-Saxon criteria on liberals in quite diverse situations.

Liberal Agitation. The first important liberal outburst occurred in 1830, with Paris leading the way. In 1829 Charles X filled his ministry with extreme royalists and dissolved the hostile parliament; when the voters returned a liberal chamber, Charles issued four ordinances, suspending the liberty of the press, again dissolving parliament, and excluding all middle-class elements from the electorate. Liberal newspaper editors, led by Adolphe Thiers, placarded Paris against these ordinances, and a crowd of artisans and some students gathered. Clumsy police work led to the construction of barricades, and the revolution of July 1830 had begun. Charles left the country, after no real effort at resistance, and the liberals arranged for a new monarchy—called the July Monarchy because of the month of origin—under the Duc d'Orléans, Louis Philippe.

Following news of the Paris rising, agitation developed in many other areas. The Belgian revolution was successful in gaining national independence, with diplomatic help from Britain and France, and in establishing a parliamentary monarchy with protection for civil and religious liberties. A Polish rising, led by liberal, nationalist aristocrats, was beaten by Russian troops; and Austrian troops put down an important revolt in the Papal States in 1831. There were disturbances elsewhere in Italy and in Germany; liberal movements in several German states forced constitutional concessions.

In the Reform Bill of 1832, the British reform movement finally bore fruit. About 150 parliamentary seats were taken from areas with sparse population and given to more populous districts, including the industrial towns; and property qualifications were lowered, so that in England and Wales 20 per cent of the adult male population could vote.

The results of the developments of 1830 to 1832 divided western Europe from the bulk of the continent, in politics, more than ever before. The governments of Germany and Italy continued to clamp down on agitation, and a few states, such as Piedmont, became even more clerical and conservative. But the liberal-nationalist movements, though as yet unsuccessful, grew now in strength and organization. In Italy the somewhat archaic rituals of the Carbonari were replaced by more directly revolutionary groups, notably the Young Italy movement launched by Mazzini; and there were periodic risings, particularly in the Papal States. In Germany, the *Burschenschaften* spread once again, and business groups and other reform organizations worked for political change. In Spain, liberals actually seized control of the government in the mid-1830's, again backed by the army; their chief accomplishment was the seizure of all church lands. Liberalism spread in Austria, and in Hungary the lower gentry, about one sixth of the population, turned to an anti-Austrian nationalism under Louis Kossuth. Even in the Russia of Nicholas I, a growing number of university-trained intellectuals developed an interest in political and social reform. Most of Europe remained locked in conservatism, but resistance was clearly growing.

In Britain and France, where real political changes had taken place, most liberals were largely satisfied with the new order. They still sought some changes; in Britain, there was important agitation against the Corn Law by advocates of free trade and the industrialist interest, until its repeal. But most liberals were pleased with the suffrage extension and subsequent reforms, which included abolition of slavery in the colonies, the first child labor law, and a new Poor Law which sought to reduce the tax burden necessary for relief and to force paupers into harsh workhouses — the latter requirement designed to discourage dependence on state aid. Liberals had less reason for satisfaction in France. Charles X's ordinances were of course abandoned, and the powers of parliament were strengthened somewhat, though the king could still name his own ministers. The influence of the church was curtailed, and suffrage was extended by lowering property qualifications, but the change only doubled the electorate to a mere 200,000 people.

Agitation Against Liberals. Both in Britain and in France, the 1830's and 1840's saw renewed agitation — agitation now directed against liberals themselves. The British trade union movement, until it declined in the later 1830's, sought radical social reforms. The Chartist movement began in 1836, demanding universal suffrage and, through this, a number of social reforms. Backed by artisans and workers, the Chartists on three occasions sent massive petitions to parliament and threatened violence. They expressed the discontent of the lower classes at exclusion from politics and at the harshness of the new Poor Law.

Many artisans and intellectuals in Paris were bitterly disappointed by the July Monarchy. The limited suffrage, the almost complete neglect of social problems, the pompous satisfaction of many liberals — all this drove many groups into opposition quite quickly. A variety of republican societies were formed; their membership was not large, but the groups were designed for agitation and did help induce periodic rioting. And there were major strikes and riots due to economic grievances alone. The government, in response, submitted all associations to police surveillance, arrested many leaders, and tightened restrictions on the press — and these measures were sponsored by men who had led the liberal resistance to the Restoration. In France, a moderate liberalism stressing public order, economic individualism, and parliamentary monarchy now became a kind of conservatism. Arrayed against it were more radical liberals, republican-democrats, socialist theorists, and discontented artisans generally.

Agitation in Britain was kept in bounds relatively easily, without resort to harsh repression. The opponents of the existing order were almost exclusively from the lower classes, and the lower classes still lacked the education and resources to form enduring resistance organizations. The Chartists could pose a periodic threat, particularly if spurred by an economic crisis, but in the intervals their numbers dwindled sharply. The fact was that British liberals, even if not fully content, could now work within the system; they had the vote and, increasingly, they had an organized liberal party, formed from former Whigs and Radicals, to represent them.

This was not the case in France. Added to lower-class grievances was a real liberal objection to the government. Government repression did manage to reduce disorder after 1834; but the lull induced King Louis Philippe and his ministers to limit the liberal features of the regime, in the interests of preserving order and enhancing the new dynasty. After 1840, with François Guizot as prime minister, the government controlled the parliamentary elections and created, by well-placed bribes, a largely docile body. Here was something that even most liberals could not tolerate, and a reform movement developed which called for a more independent parliament and a further extension of suffrage. This movement was far from revolutionary but it induced, somewhat ironically, the last wave of liberal revolutions in Europe.

CONCLUSION

Europe on the eve of the revolutions of 1848 was still conservative in many ways, which was why the revolutions themselves were such a shock. Even in western Europe, the habits of many people, businessmen as well as peasants, had not changed much; and many were still attached to the existing order. Most actively religious people were conservative, for they respected authority and were urged by religious leaders to resist new ideas. Many people who suffered from the economic changes of the period were still guided by respect for tradition and did not blame their troubles on their government; many who benefited from the changes, as businessmen or workers, were content with their gains.

The number of dedicated conservatives, however, was rather small. Most people were still politically unaware or apathetic, rather than positively committed to the existing order. That is, they respected their monarch, but their attachment was remote; they would not attack the government, nor would they defend it spontaneously. The peasant, for example — and peasants still constituted over three quarters of Europe's population — was rarely interested in the government. He would obey orders if he was conscripted into the army, and so might help repress agitation, but he had little general sense of loyalty to the state.

Aristocrats and churchmen, particularly Catholics and Lutherans, were quite consciously attached to a conservative state in western and central Europe; only in Poland and Hungary did aristocrats risk an attack on the government. For most aristocrats, the French Revolution had proved that defense of church and monarchy was essential to the preservation of aristocratic privileges and economic power. Though their numbers were small, these conservatives brought wealth and great political influence to the protection of the state.

Opponents of conservatism undoubtedly outnumbered politically conscious conservatives, though their number, too, was small. Outside England, professional people—lawyers, doctors, journalists, even some bureaucrats—were most responsible for political protest, whether liberal, nationalist, radical, or even socialist. These were men who read what liberal and radical intellectuals wrote and had contact with intellectuals in the schools. Repressive tactics of conservative regimes affected them directly, from their student days onward. In some cases, concern for their own future may have prompted political unrest, for it is possible that some professions were becoming overpopulated by the 1840's. In any case, many professional people wanted a taste of political power. They were the ones who filled the secret societies in central Europe and who backed political opposition movements during the July Monarchy in France. However, their numbers were rather small, though they expanded as educational opportunities increased. Only about 3 per cent of the population even of highly urbanized Britain were professional people. And by no means all professionals supported political opposition, for some were attached to conservative regimes by their jobs or expectations in the bureaucracy. Even if they had had a taste for violence, professional people alone posed little threat to a strong conservative government.

Other elements of the middle class shared some of the professionals' political interests, particularly in a moderate liberalism. Businessmen in Italy, for example, though they shunned the radical Young Italy movement, did support demands for economic modernization that could have a political tinge in an area where many governments were backward and inefficient. It is very difficult to say how intense the political concern of businessmen was. In England before 1832, many manufacturers took a lead in demanding political rights, but once they received them they did not use them actively, for the personnel and policies of the British government did not change quickly after the Reform Bill. Outside England, political interest was rarer still. In central Europe, many businessmen were able to gain support for their economic demands even from conservative regimes. Generally, businessmen might acquiesce in political opposition if others led it, and in so doing could give an important sense of support to active liberals, but they played little direct role in the major movements of the period. Their attention was largely confined to the very difficult task of economic innovation.

Beyond the middle classes, political interests of any sort had developed only in western Europe, primarily among urban artisans. Many Parisian artisans were republicans. Chartist petitions for democracy in Britain collected over a million signatures; if some signatories, particularly among industrial workers, were expressing mainly nonpolitical grievances, at least there was growing exposure to political possibilities.

With these important exceptions, however, agitation among the lower classes had no real political focus. Peasant and artisanal unrest did provide the force for the revolutions of the period, including those of 1848, but the rioters themselves meant to attack economic injustice, not governments.

Neither conservatives nor liberals, then, had the positive support of the bulk of the people of Europe in 1848. Liberals had the strength of ideas and enthusiasm, not of numbers; hence they so seldom won their revolutions. Conservatives benefited from widespread indifference to politics, but this was inadequate to prevent recurrent revolution and nonpolitical protest. The revolutions of 1848 forced both conservatives and liberals to rethink their relationship with the masses and to contemplate the extension of political rights and interests. The revolutions also helped determine which side the various lower classes would choose as they gradually gained political consciousness.

SUGGESTED READING

For political history see E. Halévy, *The Growth of Philosophic Radicalism** (3 vols., 1901-1904) and G. M. Trevelyan, *Lord Grey of the Reform Bill* (1929), on England; F. B. Artz, *France Under the Bourbon Restoration, 1814-1830* (1931); and J. Plamenatz, *The Revolutionary Movement in France, 1815-1871* (1952).

The crucial issues in the period revolve around the rise of the various "isms," yet much remains to be done to grasp their nature. Liberalism really lacks a good treatment: see T. P. Neill, *The Rise and Decline of Liberalism* (1953), G. deRuggiero, *The History of European Liberalism** (1927), and H. J. Laski, *The Rise of European Liberalism** (1947), for three efforts. E. L. Woodward, *Three Studies in European Conservatism: Metternich, Guizot, and the Catholic Church in the 19th Century* (1930), is excellent; nationalism is studied in B. C. Shafer, *Nationalism: Myth and Reality** (1955) and E. H. Carr, *Nationalism and After* (1944). For early socialism, see G. D. H. Cole, *Socialist Thought: The Forerunners, 1789-1850* (1935). Romanticism is excellently treated by J. Barzun, *Romanticism and the Modern Ego** (1943), and H. Marcuse, *Reason and Revolution: Hegel and the Rise of Social Theory** (1941); see also C. C. Gillispie, *Genesis and Geology, A Study in the Relation of Scientific Thought, Natural Theology, and Social Opinion in Great Britain, 1790-1850* (1951).

For diplomatic history: A. J. May, *The Age of Metternich, 1814-1848** (1933) is a fine introduction. H. C. Schenk, *The Aftermath of the Napoleonic Wars: The Concert of Europe — an Experiment* (1947) deals with basic concepts of diplomacy in the period.

*Available in a paperback edition.

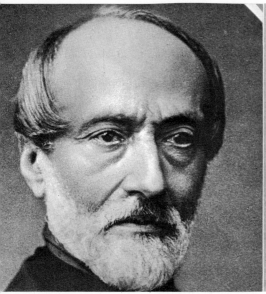

Mazzini: The Bettmann Archive   Kossuth: Historical Pictures Service

MAZZINI AND KOSSUTH

The rise of Romantic nationalism was one of the key developments of the first half of the nineteenth century. It was produced by individuals of high ideals and a passionate devotion to their cause. Many of the Romantic nationalists were intellectuals only, content to study their nation and its culture. But some were political agitators as well as theorists; of these, Guiseppe Mazzini (1805-1872) was the archetype. Others were revolutionary organizers above all, such as Lajos Kossuth (1802-1894). The blend of nationalist theory and revolutionary impulse was particularly heady in Italy and eastern Europe, from this point well into the twentieth century. The combination of past greatness and current weakness and foreign domination, plus excitable personal temperament, helped produce men like Mazzini and Kossuth, who in turn set the tone for nationalist fervor later on.

Mazzini was born in Genoa and educated to be a lawyer; but his profession early became the advocacy of Italian freedom and unity. Shocked at Austrian domination of northern Italy and at the backwardness of all the Italian states, he organized, in 1831, the Young Italy movement, one of the first specifically national-ist organizations in Europe. From this time onward, Mazzini sought to rouse the common people of Italy to the national cause. Ironically, he was himself seldom able to be in Italy, for his radicalism forced him into exile to avoid arrest. He did participate in the Roman revolution of 1849, inspiring the people by his enthusiasm and his anxiety to improve the lot of the masses. But for the most part he urged nationalism on from afar, mainly from England. He had the charisma of a true leader: a striking appearance, a magnetic personality, infectious enthusiasm. But the countless movements he tried to form were small and usually short-lived. Even in the 1860's, when he attempted to organize a labor movement in Italy, he quickly lost out to anarchists and Marxists.

Mazzini's clearest achievement was his political philosophy, which formulated the doctrines of liberal nationalism. Mazzini was not, in a strict sense, a liberal. He wanted individuals to be as free as possible, but he looked to the collectivity — the nation — not to the individual as the basis of the social order, and he saw duty to the nation overriding liberty. But his nationalism was not the narrow sort of later decades; he saw the nation as a subdivision of a common humanity; he did not vaunt one nation over others, but asserted the rights of all; and he looked forward to much the same sort of moral and material progress that the liberals did. National freedom was, for Mazzini, the precondition for man's contribution to mankind. Nations had been divinely established to provide the unity of sentiment and character necessary for the fulfillment of any individual. From national freedom would flow democracy, social justice, and a new morality, even a new religion.

Lojos Kossuth lacked Mazzini's broad philosophy, but his dedication to the cause of the Hungarian nation was as intense as Mazzini's to Italy. Kossuth came from a poor noble family. He was a Slovak, but he saw that Magyar nationalism was the only real cultural force in Hungary and it was for this that he worked. Kossuth was a magnificent orator, a magnetic personality, and a good organizer. While serving as a delegate at the Hungarian Diet, he founded the first newspaper in Hungary, an act for which he was imprisoned. In 1841 he edited another paper, with a revolutionary tone. In 1847 he was elected to the Diet and on March 3, 1848, he made a fervent speech urging a constitution for Hungary, a speech that in a real sense launched the revolution of 1848 throughout the Hapsburg monarchy. When the emperor yielded, Kossuth served in the new Hungarian cabinet and then led the military campaign against Austrian repression, and with great ability. After the revolution was crushed, he campaigned for the Hungarian cause in Britain and the United States.

Like Mazzini, Kossuth saw national freedom as more than an end in itself. He advocated social justice through the abolition of feudalism and other reforms. Like Mazzini, he was open to national claims other than his own, though he championed Magyar interests over others in Hungary. By the end of his life, for example, he urged freedom for all the major national groupings along the Danube, followed by a confederation for mutual protection.

Mazzini and Kossuth both lived to see some fruits of their endeavors, and both were bitterly disappointed in what they saw. Kossuth blasted the *Ausgleich* of 1867, because it fell short of full independence; he claimed that it would fail, but saw also that it would postpone national freedom beyond his lifetime. Mazzini lamented that Italy united under the banners of monarchy and social conservatism. In practical politics, Mazzini and Kossuth played vital but brief roles, and they failed. In the longer run, they helped inspire a national sentiment that endured, but they could not direct this sentiment. Nationalism proved easily separable from the broader idealism of men like Mazzini and Kossuth. It could be used for purely diplomatic purposes; it could be used to defend a conservative social order. The liberal nationalists are historically important because they launched and supported one of the leading secular loyalties of the modern world. They are fascinating because their vision was greater than this and because they could not carry it through, either by their own agitation or by the inspiration of later movements. ∎

FORCES OF ORDER AND OF DISORDER

Despite the variety of political systems across the face of Europe, a recurrent confrontation between conservatives and advocates of change was common to almost all areas between 1789 and the mid nineteenth century. The forces of change, drawing on many social groups and sets of ideas, wanted to restructure the existing system and were, on occasion, willing to risk physical disorder to achieve their goals. Their efforts produced some of the most dramatic scenes in European history during the revolutionary era. Less easy to picture, but surely as important, were the forces of order: most established military organizations; the aristocracy and allied groups; and large numbers of common people who were either content or at least psychologically unprepared to risk disorder. Each side, then, had real strength, and each won some important victories.

The concept of forces of order and of disorder is certainly general. The nature of each "side" varied with the country and changed over time. Many types of people, even a single individual, might have switched from one to the other as the specific issues changed. But even contemporaries saw a basic battle between progress (or destructive innovation, depending on which side one was on) and stability, that overrode specific clashes. Indeed, something of the same conflict spread into the arts and industry, as self-conscious innovators—whether Romantics or pioneers of mechanization—faced determined conservatives. Never before had the idea of change been so widely or confidently asserted. Many people welcomed this. Others—and this was perhaps the most interesting and decisive group —feared it but believed it was inevitable. Even conservatives sometimes gave the impression that they were only holding the line for as long as possible, against an inevitable tide.

The French revolution launched the conflict between order and disorder in modern Europe. For decades after the revolution, and far beyond the borders of France, the clearest distinction between the two sides was the attitude each took toward the revolution and its heritage. Conservatives condemned, the advocates of change deplored many aspects of the revolution and hoped to avoid its excesses, but in the final analysis they believed that it had been a

The execution of Louis XVI was among the events which opened the door to a century of social upheaval. *Source: Musée Carnavalet, Paris.*

This cartoon, entitled "The Leveling of France," ridicules the new ideology of equality for all Frenchmen after the revolution. *Source: Giraudon.*

good thing. The revolution represented disorder in two senses. It showed the possibility and, to some, the joy of violence for a political cause. For friends and foes alike, it provided enduring symbols of its destructive power, most notably in the execution of Louis XVI. But the violence was meant to have a purpose; the revolutionaries hoped to replace the whole existing social order with a society based on new principles, the leading principle being equality among men. This principle could be lampooned, the degree to which it was carried out even in the radical phase of the revolution challenged; but it remained basic to the subsequent attacks on the *status quo.*

The forces of order, increasingly alert as they realized the magnitude of the threat to their values, had many weapons. Diplomacy was quickly transformed into a defense of order. The Holy Alliance, the most explicit expression of the new spirit of diplomacy, maintained some appeal for the rulers of central and eastern Europe even after the 1870s. For a more limited time, particularly in the early 1820s, leading philosophers and political theorists expounded the con-

The monarchy developed new defenses against the threat of disruption by forming the "Holy Alliance." The leaders of this anti-Napoleonic league were Francis I of Austria-Hungary, Frederick William III of Prussia, and Alexander I of Russia. *Source: Historical Pictures Service.*

Pastoral serenity among the farming classes, 1851. *Source: Historical Pictures Service.*

The aristocrats still enjoyed the "season" in Paris, 1866. *Source: Historical Pictures Service.*

The allegiance of a Russian serf to the landowner was not yet broken. *Source: Historical Pictures Service.*

A meeting of the Society of Protestant Missions, in London, appealed to the idea of limited social change through missionary reforms. *Source: Historical Pictures Service.*

THE REASONING SPIRIT OF REFORM

The "dark politics of reform" which menaced the wealthy establishment is chided in a conservative illustration from the *British Constitution Triumphant*, published c. 1820. *Source: Newberry Library, Chicago.*

" When naval traffic ploughs the main,
Who shares not in the merchant's gain?
'T is that supports the regal state,
And makes the farmer's heart elate;
The num'rous flocks that clothe the land,
Can scarce supply the loom's demand;
Prolific culture glads the fields,
And the bare heath a harvest yields."

———

THIS IS

THE WEALTH,

That supports the LAWS OF ENGLAND.

"Calm thinking villians, whom no faith can fix,
Of crooked counsels and dark politics."

———

THESE ARE

THE SCOUNDRELS

That would plunder
the WEALTH,
That supports the
LAWS OF ENGLAND.

servative cause. But the enduring strength of conservatism rested in the broad groups of the population that felt a stake in things as they were. The aristocracy, which blossomed again in Paris after 1815, and which everywhere constituted real "high society," resisted political change most explicitly. But many common people, particularly the better-established peasants and artisans, were largely content too. If it is important not to exaggerate the beneficence of traditional agricultural or craft labor, it is equally important to realize that many ordinary people were content with their work and their communal life. Still others were unaware of any alternatives; many could not imagine the destruction of a social hierarchy that counted them as inferiors, perhaps, but which gave them a definite place in the social order and, at least under the more charitable masters, some active protection as well. For all levels of society, religion was a solace and its pastors vigorous defenders of the *status quo*. In terms of church building, missions, and intellectual activity, the nineteenth century was one of the great religious centuries, though ironically it was also the century in which religion lost its hold over many people. Religion, a secure place in society, apathy, and for some people also rising wealth—here were an abundance of reasons for the persistence of the conservative defense and for bitter resentment against the proponents of changes big and small. Military force capped the conservative structure and was often decisive, in England fully as much as in more obviously repressive countries like Russia, but it often had the backing of many elements in European society.

Against the conservatives, the advocates of change had many weapons. Where censorship was not too severe, they controlled most of the press, and generally saw the advantages of an active press more clearly than the conservatives; hence, among other things, most of the effective lampoons

A protest against the violent abuse of the poor is shown in a cartoon of the Massacre at St. Peters. *Source: Published by George Cruickshank, 1819.*

CONTINENTAL UNREST

IN BOHEMIA:

The Revolution of 1848 in Prague, June 16. 1848. *Source: Historical Pictures Service.*

IN FRANCE:

The attack on the Palais Royal, Paris, 1848. *Source: The Granger Collection.*

IN GERMANY: (opposite)

Students assemble at Eisenach to march to Wartburg to demand the establishment of a democratic regime. *Source: The Bettmann Archive.*

IN ENGLAND:

The Chartists stage a street protest meeting in a march toward Kensington, April 10, 1848. *Source: The Bettmann Archive.*

of the period attacked the conservative cause. Though advocates of change seldom won the bulk of the population to their side, they were inspired by their principles to mobilize what mass support they had more effectively than the conservatives could. Chartist petitions and demonstrations in Britain were the clearest forerunners of a democratic politics aside from outright revolution. Even on the continent, assembly was frequently used to promote reform. Because of the strength and obstinacy of the conservatives, however, revolution was the most important and effective expression of the desire for political change. Revolution grouped many types of people, students and artisans most notably but, in Paris, even the uniformed National Guards on occasion. Knowledge of the methods of revolution spread widely, and by 1848 all sorts of people knew the importance and effectiveness of barricades. Only the most brutal repression could defeat a revolution at its peak, and few rulers were willing to sponsor such bloodshed at first. From Paris and Brussels to Prague and Budapest, revolutionaries in 1830 or 1848 managed to defend themselves and even to attack military posts and public buildings. But revolutions were not made by force alone. After the streets were won, there had to be planning for the new regime. Groups of students, craftsmen, professional people met and discussed methods. There was an explosion of ideas and schemes. But, all too often, the schemes contradicted each other and an effective government could not be

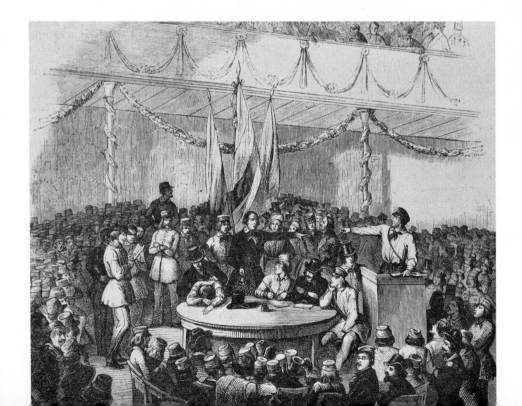

formed. Still, it was difficult for any but the most devoted revolutionaries—and these were rare types—to maintain the pitch of enthusiasm that had sent them into battle in the first glorious days. So disputes, inexperience, and emotional letdown weakened most revolutions steadily. Often, as in Germany in 1848, the troops that had been successfully repelled in the first days found it easy, within a year or so, to close down the main revolutionary institutions. In Berlin control of the streets returned to the military as early as October, 1848. Even where the old rulers did not return, as in France, the new regimes quickly turned to the defense of an established order that had not changed much from prerevolutionary days.

In the aftermath of 1848, the opposition between the forces of order and of disorder changed, if it did not entirely disappear. For at least a generation, the leading advocates of change abandoned even vague appeals to violence; they were willing to accept what they could get by peaceful compromise. For their part, rulers in central and western Europe, or at least their chief ministers, had absorbed some of the medicine of political change. They no longer resisted all reform and they provided channels through which further change might be promoted. For every country, this double transformation of previously bitterly opposing forces raises the question of who, if anyone, had won. Was imperial Germany, by the 1870's, largely a victory for the conservatives, as most historians have claimed, despite major institutional changes? At the other extreme was nearly democratic England or republican France, by 1880, as clear a triumph for the advocates of change as institutions of politics seemed to imply? All that was entirely clear is that the old lines of battle had disappeared.

Soldiers halt street fighting in Berlin, October 16, 1848. *Source: Organization and Revolution: Working Class Associations in the German Revolution of 1848–1849.* P. Noyes (Princeton University Press, 1966).

IN THE AFTERMATH OF 1848, THE FORCES OF ORDER HAD MADE SOME CONCESSIONS BUT THEY SELDOM HAD TO SURRENDER POWER.

(Top) Prussian soldiers break up the Democratic Constitutional Convention in Berlin, November 14, 1848. *Source: The Bettmann Archive.*

(Bottom) Monarchies were forced to swallow the pills of constitutional reform. Cushioned from the mass uprisings and popular feeling, the rulers were awakened after almost a half-century of protest. *Source: Historical Pictures Service.*

Chapter 4

A Period of Transition
1848 – 1870

The revolutions of 1848 can be seen either as an end or as a beginning. They marked the end of liberalism as a revolutionary force in western and central Europe, the end of the long period of artisanal agitation, the last series of revolutions countenanced by the middle class, the final peasant rising in western or central Europe, the last revolution inspired by Romantic enthusiasm. Clearly, with the revolutions, a sixty-year period of political turmoil drew to a close. But by the same token the revolutions launched a new period in which old grievances were either satisfied, given legal channels of expression, or turned in new directions. Though the revolutions failed in a formal sense, they were not without immediate result: political and social structures changed in France, the Hapsburg monarchy, Prussia, and Piedmont. In their broader impact, the revolutions forced changes both in liberalism and in conservatism; and they helped end the utopian period of socialism as well

The effects were not confined to politics. The failure of the revolutions turned intellectuals to new directions. Formal Romanticism was dead, partly because its ideals had been shown unrealistic in the revolutions. Some intellectuals consciously sought a new toughness of mind, others turned to a more sweeping condemnation of modern life than the Romantics had ever developed, still others devoted themselves to stylistic innovations of unprecedented daring; the intellectual climate, still diverse, was definitely changing. The impact of the revolutions on diplomacy was even more direct: a regime was created in France which actively sought diplomatic reforms; and there is a straight line between the revolutions and Italian unification, and from both to German unification. In other words, most of the leading developments of the next two decades were directly or indirectly produced by the revolutions. Along with the full advent of industrialization on the continent, the revolutions created the issues of modern Europe: the social question, the problem of Germany, the linkage of diplomacy with nationalism, the challenge to liberal values from right and left, the growing power of state and private organizations. The two decades after the revolutions saw, in a real sense, the birth of a nearly contemporary Europe. The old regimes were now dead, and attention was turned to newer problems.

EVENTS OF 1848

The sweep of revolutions across the continent was an astonishing development. From Sicily to Denmark, from France to Hungary, the wave of revolution flowed. A common liberal impulse looked to France for guidance, though it covered diverse interests. There was also a common economic crisis, based on potato disease and poor grain crops, that goaded the lower classes from France through Prussia; even in Britain, 1848 saw the last Chartist effort.

Revolution in France. The first major uprising occurred in Paris, in February 1848, when artisans and students gathered in the streets to protest the government's prohibition of a meeting on the suffrage. Like his predecessor, Louis Philippe fled to England without much resistance, and a new provisional government was installed under the Romantic poet, Alphonse Lamartine. The government wanted a republican, democratic regime, but it also wished to preserve order and avoid social reform. Nevertheless, it was under constant pressure from artisan crowds and radical organizations. Actually, the government yielded little; two working-class representatives were allowed to investigate labor conditions, and the National Workshops were set up to relieve the unemployed. But the investigation, while thorough, produced little legislation and the Workshops served to control and regiment the destitute, rather than to provide a new, socialist form of business organization as many artisans and socialist leaders had hoped. Numerous protests against government policy were put down without difficulty. In April, a new legislature was elected to draw up a constitution for the republic; but it was chosen democratically, giving conservative peasants a predominant voice. The result was a marginally republican assembly, opposed to social reform. One of its first acts was the dissolution of the Workshops, in June, which provoked three days of bloody fighting between 50,000 workers and artisans and the regular army. These June Days effectively ended the revolution, for the conservative assembly was now unchallenged; order was further solidified in December when Louis Napoleon, nephew of the great Emperor and as such a symbol of authority, was elected president of the Second Republic.

Revolution Spreads. Revolution broke out in Vienna soon after news of the Paris rising arrived. Petitions were circulated in business and intellectual groups, demanding an end to censorship, economic reform, and an effective parliament; but the government rejected them all. Student demonstrations led to fighting with the army, in which artisans joined; and at this point the Emperor did back down, dismissing Metternich and summoning a united diet to draw up a new constitution. The Vienna agitation stirred other parts of the Empire. Under Louis Kossuth, the Hungarian Diet demanded and won a new constitution establishing civil liberties, the abolition of serfdom, a parliament based on wide suffrage, and autonomous Hungarian ministries within the Empire. Czech nationalists from Prague demanded the same sort of local autonomy, civil liberties, and a Czech parliament. Finally, in April, the government abolished serfdom in the entire Empire; this was the main accomplishment of the revolution, but it also helped defeat the revolution by satisfying the peasantry and turning them into a conservative force.

The revolution was also badly weakened by other divisions. Wealthy middle-class elements in Vienna were quickly satisfied by the government's concessions, even though most of the apparatus of the old system, including the army, remained intact; and they were terrified at the prospect of further lower-class disorder. The various national movements could not cooperate. In Vienna, many of the revolutionaries, themselves Germans, actually applauded repression of agitation in Bohemia, Hungary, and Italy. The government was able to pick off the revolutions one by one. The Czechs were put down in June 1848; the Italian revolutions were attacked in July, though final suppression occurred only in August 1849; in October 1848, the army bombarded Vienna into submission; and in 1849, with the aid of Russian troops, the Hungarian rebels were defeated. The Constitutional Assembly continued its work into 1849, drawing up an admirable document that granted substantial autonomy to provinces and towns to relieve the nationalities problem and provided for a parliamentary, liberal monarchy for the Empire as a whole. The government, now victorious and reactionary, simply ignored this effort.

Revolutions in Germany followed much the same pattern as in Austria. There was a usual, quick middle-class fear of lower-class agitation; and the problems of nationalism distracted the revolutionaries from purely internal reforms. Demonstrations in March 1848 prompted many states to grant various constitutional changes and to call in moderate liberal ministries. In Berlin, demonstrations led to typically clumsy military intervention and this, in turn, to the erection of barricades by artisans and some students. The Prussian king called the army off, convoked a Prussian parliament, and summoned liberal business and professional people to office. In most German states, then, liberal ministries and parliaments grappled with problems of drafting effective constitutions and preserving order by establishing some sort of civilian guard.

In addition, nationalists in southern Germany called a national assembly in Frankfurt, to create a real German unity. The Frankfurt parliament, which met in May 1848, spent about eight months discussing abstract issues involved in drawing up a national constitution. The end product called for a federal Germany, from which Austria would be excluded, under the Prussian king; and it established civil liberties for all

Germans and laid down rules for parliamentary governments in the individual states.

Middle-class revolutionaries alienated the lower classes with extraordinary thoroughness in Germany. With the artisans, little could be done perhaps, for their leading demand was for restoration of the guilds, which liberals could not accept. But the peasants were also rebuffed; peasants had risen in several areas, demanding a complete end to serfdom, but the politicians in Frankfurt held that manorial rights were property, and property of course had to be protected. Many in the lower classes simply abandoned the revolution; others tried renewed disorder, which frightened the middle classes still further. The Prussian king was able to return the troops to Berlin, to preserve order, in November 1848, and to suppress the parliament; and in 1849 he put down risings elsewhere in Germany—in some cases, ironically, at the request of the Frankfurt assembly. The assembly had already recognized the power of Prussia by authorizing Prussian armies to attack Denmark in order to defend territory held by the Danish king that it regarded as German, and by inviting the Prussian king to become hereditary ruler of the united Germany. When Frederick William IV turned this offer down, the Frankfurt assembly dissolved in disarray.

In Italy, the fourth major center of unrest, most agitation pointed to a war of national liberation against Austria and for unity, rather than a real, internal revolution. An uprising in Sicily did win constitutional concessions and, in 1849, the Roman revolution forced the Pope to flee and introduced not only a republic but also some social reforms. But the center of the revolution was in the North, where middle-class nationalists sought the expulsion of Austria above all. Insurrections in Milan and Venice were aided by volunteers from other areas and by the armies of Piedmont, whose ruler—far from a revolutionary—sought to profit from the situation. The armies were defeated without great difficulty by the Austrian troops, first in July 1848, and again in 1849; and with greater difficulty the rebellious cities were subdued, Venice by Austrian troops and Rome by the newly conservative French government.

The Revolutions Summarized. The revolutions of 1848 had both goals and weaknesses in common. Certainly, the most articulate revolutionaries everywhere enunciated the doctrines of liberalism and, usually, nationalism. Yet almost nowhere did liberals initiate revolutionary rioting. Many historians have seen 1848 as a crucial watershed in the history of liberalism, as the point at which liberalism became pragmatic and mildly reformist instead of idealistic and revolutionary. There is certainly much truth in this, and liberals did abandon any thought of revolution in most areas after 1848. But even before 1848, liberals preferred reform to revolution, and even during 1848 liberals petitioned and assembled in parliaments, rather than organizing the forces of revolution. Liberal doctrines were held by men of substance, who feared excessive disorder. The liberal impulse was opposed to the firm, even authoritarian, leadership that any successful revolution requires. And in many cases, liberals already had much of what they sought: they had parliaments and constitutions in France and several of the German states; they had an efficient bureaucracy, strong local governments, and substantial economic freedom in Prussia. They wanted further improvements in all this, but not a complete upheaval; and always they had before them the example of the French Revolution of 1789 which was launched on liberal principles but whose excesses turned against basic liberal values. It was important not to let revolution go too far. Hence liberals in Vienna and in the German states did not displace existing government structures, including the monarchies and the armies; hence liberals in France, though countenancing the change in regime, sought to limit any changes beyond this. The liberal politicians who controlled the revolutions of 1848 acted timidly not in spite of their liberalism, but because of it.

Liberal leadership in the revolutions was complicated by conflicts with other movements involved. Most clearly, lower-class elements, who provided most of the muscle for the revolutions, were not attracted to purely liberal goals and so quickly frightened the liberals themselves. In Paris and to an extent elsewhere, the lower classes sought democracy; and they were joined in this by radical liberals themselves. Many liberal leaders in France, Germany, and Italy were now willing to accept democracy, but some fears of it remained; in France, for example, the parliament of the Second Republic tried to disenfranchise all people—and they were mainly the poor—who had not maintained the same residence for three years. More important was the liberal refusal to meet the social demands of the lower classes. Liberals could not accept the vague socialism of Parisian artisans or the reactionary demands for guilds by German craftsmen. The clash between liberal principles and lower-class interests became clear very quickly and led to renewed disorder; and in almost every revolution, this caused liberals to accept the imposition of order by force, even where, as in Germany and Austria, the force was the army of the old regime.

The divisions within revolutionary ranks clearly doomed most of the revolutionary efforts; in several major cases, a more subtle split between liberal and nationalist causes weakened the revolutions also. Except in France, nationalism at the very least demanded time and attention that might otherwise have been available for consolidating internal reforms; in the northern Italian cities, indeed, the revolution was little more than a national war. Aside from this, in Italy, Bohemia, and Hungary, liberal and nationalist interests coincided, for these were all cases in which foreign rule had to be excluded or modified, and it was quite logical to seek a liberal as well as a national regime in its stead. But in Germany and Austria, the situation was more complicated. Here too, most nationalists were liberals. But there was no foreign rule to attack. The national interest seemed to demand a strong state—to unify Germany and protect German nationals against foreign powers, such as Denmark, or to protect German Austrians against other racial groups. The Germans in Frankfurt who offered a crown to the Prussian king, the Austrian liberals who cheered the army's victory in Prague, were making a choice: the national goals were more important than the liberal ones. The choice, necessary for the first time, hampered the liberal aspect of the revolutions; and it would be confirmed later, in Germany and Austria particularly but also elsewhere.

One final question must be asked about the revolutions: did they fail? There were a few enduring gains of real importance, notably the abolition of serfdom in Austria and Prussia and the establishment of universal suffrage in France. Certainly, the revolutions were put down and sternly conservative regimes were installed. Yet within two decades most of the leading demands of the revolutions had been achieved. By 1871 Germany and Italy were unified and Hungary had substantial autonomy; parliaments with some real powers had been established in Germany, Austria, Italy, and France; and France was a republic once more. If the revolutions failed in the immediate sense, they helped set in motion forces that quickly gained victory. Partly this was because liberals and nationalists set about to achieve their goals by more practical means. The year 1848 is often cited as the end of Romantic idealism and the dawn of a tough-minded pragmatism. This is not really true, as we shall see; idealism persisted, but it turned in new directions, leaving liberalism and nationalism freer to make the accommodations necessary to success. And at the same time, the defenders of the established order changed their tactics. The fall of Metternich was more than symbolic; it opened the way to a conservatism that would not resist all change, but would seek to control and channel innovations that now seemed inevitable.

Certainly, the revolutions of 1848 brought an end to the age of revolutions in western and central Europe. Partly this was because established regimes found new weapons against agitation; police units were expanded and trained in riot control, and new weapons such as the repeating rifle soon gave a decisive advantage to the forces of order. Partly it was because the middle class now turned firmly against disorder, feeling that revolution's threats to property and middle-class economic position were too great to endure, for any cause. Beyond this, the middle class and the peasantry were now largely satisfied. Peasants in central Europe were freed from serfdom and, as their French counterparts had done before, they now turned to a defense of the established order. The middle class, if not immediately at least by the 1860's, had favorable economic legislation, parliaments, and reasonably well-protected civil liberties. Of the large social groupings often involved in protest during the previous half-century, this left only the artisans. But the artisans began to decline in numbers between 1850 and 1870. Many journeymen entered the factory labor force, and many masters rose into the ranks of small employers. Artisans in all categories benefited from the prosperity of the 1850's and 1860's; and many found calmer methods of expressing any grievances they might feel, through pacific unions and cooperatives. The year 1848 saw the last of the great preindustrial protests of western and central Europe. After it, in part because of it, peasants were able to adapt to, and often to profit from, market agriculture; the middle class became increasingly dominated by businessmen who certainly profited from industry; and the urban labor force, itself increasingly prosperous, changed in character and only gradually developed appropriate — and largely nonrevolutionary — methods of protest.

ECONOMY AND SOCIETY

Western and central Europe enjoyed an almost uninterrupted boom between 1850 and 1870. There was a short, sharp depression in 1857 and 1858 and troubles in some industries during the 1860's, but nothing to compare with crises before or after this period. Industrialization gained ground in France and Germany and began to reach Italy and Austria as well, while British prosperity continued to mount. In addition to the rise of factory production, there were several other general inducements to growing prosperity. The increase in population, though still great, began to moderate in the industrial countries; almost the whole population rise in Germany, Britain, and France could be accommodated in the cities. Now that population gains were matched by new opportunities for productive work, the increase in market potential was even greater than before. Discoveries of massive new sources of gold in California and Australia tended to raise prices or at least moderate price declines, and so again spurred interest in augmenting production. Finally, these were the decades when railroad building began to influence the whole economy. France quadrupled its railroad mileage, and the basic system of trunk lines was complete all over western Europe by the 1860's. Again this opened new market possibilities, and the construction process itself, spurred by government investment in most cases, created vast needs for heavy industrial goods.

Agriculture as well as industry responded to new opportunities, provided particularly by the growth of cities and the improvements in transport. The abolition of serfdom in central Europe allowed peasant landowners to devote more attention to market production and created a large force of landless laborers to work on the big estates. Most governments stepped up their programs of technical education and began to provide loans at reasonable rates for agricultural improvements. There were a number of important technical changes, particularly on large estates: the use of chemical fertilizers and of mechanical threshers were the key gains. There was growing specialization in cash crops, mostly grains still but dairy and meat products in a few areas, notably Denmark. And everywhere, production increased. French agricultural production rose 20 per cent between 1845 and 1855, rose a full 40 per cent from 1855 to 1864, and then slowed to a 15 per cent increase in the next decade. This was the golden period of agricultural production in western and central Europe. The production increases were essential for industrial growth; and the earnings they

RAILROAD CONSTRUCTION IN EUROPE: 1870—1910.

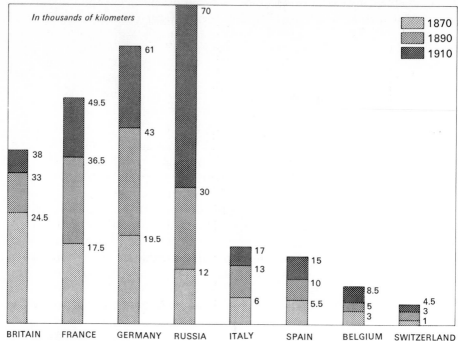

In thousands of kilometers

1870
1890
1910

	1870	1890	1910
BRITAIN	24.5	33	38
FRANCE	17.5	36.5	49.5
GERMANY	19.5	43	61
RUSSIA	12	30	70
ITALY	6	13	17
SPAIN	5.5	10	15
BELGIUM	3	5	8.5
SWITZERLAND	1	3	4.5

Note: This graph does not show the density of railroads within each country.
A smaller country naturally had a closer network of rails.

brought helped satisfy aristocratic and peasant landholders. Not only the absence of peasant protest, but also the willingness of many aristocrats to tolerate political changes owed much to rural prosperity.

Industrial Strength Increases. The gains of factory industry over-shadowed the important developments in agriculture. Germany now acquired great industrial strength, surpassing France in heavy industry by 1870. German coal and iron production rose 600 per cent in the period. Though the French lagged, their heavy industrial production tripled during the Second Empire. In all industrial countries, the period saw a second wave of industrial inventions. Particularly important were the new methods in heavy industry, for the Bessemer process allowed a massive increase in metallurgical production and a growing reliance on steel instead of iron. But many light industries could now be mechanized as well, as the sewing machine spread a factory system to the manufacture of shoes and clothing. Finally, new business forms were developed, which by facilitating industrial investment contributed greatly to the advance in production. The corporate form spread rapidly, aided by the liberalization of laws on the establishment of corporations in Britain, France, and Germany. Corporate banks were introduced, with large resources for industrial investment; a number of such banks were formed, with govern-ment encouragement, in France, Germany, and Austria. Most business units even in factory industry remained fairly small and familial, but innovations in business structure and the rise of heavy industry, which demanded large units, clearly heralded the advent of "big business."

Both workers and businessmen gained from the industrial advance of the period. The working class continued to grow rapidly, drawing on the population increase and the displacement of many traditional artisans. By the 1870's there were over three million factory workers in Germany. On the whole, conditions for the workers improved. Wages rose by at least 25 per cent in France; in Britain, real wages increased a full 50 per cent as the benefits of a relatively mature industrial structure began to spread. Workers were able to buy better food and clothing, and their health improved. New welfare programs in the cities aided them as well. City railways and, in London, a subway relieved some urban congestion. The French government cleared slums and built new parks in Paris and Marseilles. Cities in the Ruhr tightened inspection of housing and wholesale markets. Finally, national governments improved admittedly rudimentary systems of factory inspection; this improvement, along with the growing sophistication of machinery, helped reduce industrial accidents and the employment of small children.

Because living conditions were less burdensome, and perhaps because

GROWTH OF POPULATION AND URBANIZATION IN EUROPE: 1850—1910.

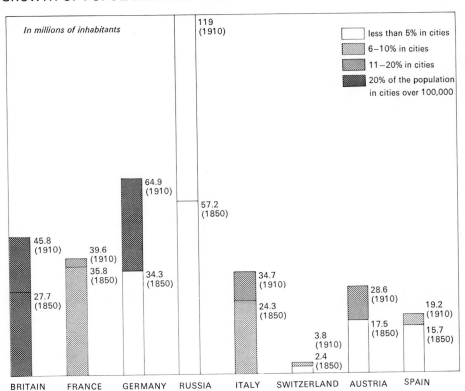

so many workers were new to their jobs, there was little industrial protest during the period. Few workers yet displayed a distinctive political consciousness, though in France most were voting republican by the 1860's. The major gains in unionization were still among artisans. In Britain, a conservative New Model Unionism spread among skilled workers, seeking gains from mutual aid, quiet bargaining, and a general aura of respectability. There were, of course, more radical movements, some of them linked to the First International, which Karl Marx helped to found in the 1860's. In Germany, the socialist Ferdinand Lassalle formed a Universal Workingman's association in 1863, and the Marxists established the Social Democratic party in 1869; in France the International organized a few thousand workers in the late 1860's. The 1860's also saw the first important industrial agitation in Belgium, the first union in Italy, the first factory strike in Russia. But all these movements were small and tentative. They held promise—or threat—for the future, but had little influence on the period itself.

Middle-class Gains. The group that most clearly benefited from the prosperity of the period was the middle class. Profits rose far more rapidly than wages did, partly due to the growing sophistication of business forms. For the first time, even in Britain, the middle class gained control of the majority of capital wealth. And the class grew with new opportunities in business, in government, and in the professions. In Britain, professional groups alone rose from 2.5 per cent to 4.5 per cent of the total population, and the whole middle class constituted nearly a fifth of Britain's people by 1870. There was new mobility for many levels of the middle class, through new business firms and through the expansion of secondary education facilities, whose enrollments increased over 100 per cent in both France and Germany during the period.

The middle class gained, then, new wealth, new numbers, new educational levels—and a new confidence. Members of the middle class became dominant patrons of theater and the arts. Their tastes were often somewhat showy and they sought a culture that would bring clear prestige, preferring older styles in art and architecture because the social value of classical pillars or Gothic arches was well established. Middle-class culture alienated many leading artists, whom the class in turn tended to regard as dangerously Bohemian. But the new resources and interests of the middle class helped expand opera houses and symphonies, supported the restoration of many architectural monuments, and contributed to the introduction of science, modern languages, and history into the curricula of the upper schools.

The new power and awareness of the middle class inevitably influenced politics. The age of middle-class revolutions passed not only because the class became more fearful of disorder, but because its interests now could not be ignored by any government, no matter how conservative, in western and central Europe. Revolution was simply unnecessary. Positions in bureaucracy and army were increasingly open to the middle class, particularly after a wave of civil service reforms began in the late 1860's. And the spread of parliaments and liberal parties allowed increasing expression of middle-class interests. These decades constituted, in many ways, a peak period of middle-class power: the economic boom, the advance of middle-class culture, the absence of challenge from below all contributed to the steady advance of middle-class interests.

This was the age of Samuel Smiles and the Crystal Palace Exhibition in Britain, both of which expressed middle-class confidence in the power of the individual to better himself and in the progress of society through industrial advance and humanitarian legislation. Magazines like the *Gartenlaube,* in Germany, reached increasing thousands of middle-class homes with its praise of the ethic of hard work and self-restraint. As middle-class ascendancy grew, many workers and aristocrats were converted to its values. Groups like the leading British artisans, for example, were less likely to protest after 1848 because they were busy working to improve themselves and their position in the economy. At the same time, middle-class propaganda helped spread an interest in moderate political reform and national loyalty, which could absorb some types of discontent.

Conditions in the East and South. The social structure of eastern and southern Europe remained far different from that of the North and West. The same period that saw an end to many traditional social conflicts in the West witnessed the first of many decades of troubles in the rest of Europe. There was still little industrial progress in Russia, the Balkans, Spain, and southern Italy; only a few isolated factories were established, only a few short railroad lines. There was almost no business middle class. Small professional groups existed (although in Russia even these came largely from the gentry), but they held little power. At most, as in Bohemia or Rumania, they contributed to a small but rising sense of nationalism.

The foundations of society in these areas remained agricultural, yet rural conditions were becoming increasingly difficult for many people. A few regions took advantage of market opportunities in the West, but the absence of railroad systems and the lack of technical education and capital limited such efforts. At the same time, a major population rise began around 1860, greatly increasing the pressure on the land; and legal changes, particularly outside Russia, weakened the position of the peasantry still further.

Serfdom was abolished throughout eastern and southern Europe during this period, but seldom were peasants allowed to retain much land. In Spain, an 1855 law that allowed peasants to buy and sell land was used by landlords in the south and west to gobble up peasant holdings; the same trend emerged in Sicily, when serfdom was fully abolished in the 1860's. The result in both cases was the spread of a sharecropping system, in which most peasants gave up half their produce to the owners of the large estates. In Hungary, serfdom was essentially abolished during the revolution of 1848, but over 90 per cent of the land remained in large holdings, owned by Magyar nobles but often tilled by South Slavic peasants. The abolition of serfdom in Rumania, in 1868, deprived peasants of almost all the land; the Rumanian landlords produced increasingly for export, but this did not benefit the agricultural laborers, who were kept in careful subjection.

Only in Russia was the abolition of serfdom accompanied by some effort to protect the peasantry, and even here aristocratic interests dominated the terms of the Emancipation. The Emancipation occurred for a number of reasons. Many bureaucrats and some landlords saw that serfdom inhibited the modernization of the Russian economy. There were widespread fears of peasant rebellion as well. Russia's losses in the Crimean War brought these feelings to a head, by increasing the possibilities of unrest and by showing clearly how far Russia lagged behind the other great powers. In 1861, serfdom was abolished, and peasants were given most of the land in Russia. Two interests, however, qualified the Emancipation. The government sought new powers over the peasantry, now that aristocratic controls were largely removed, and so established firm regional and village government. Peasants were not allowed to move or to sell land without village permission; and village acts were supervised by regional councils, the *zemstvos,* in which local aristocrats had the predominant voice. Aristocratic interests were furthered by the huge redemption payments demanded of peasants for their new freedom, payments often far in excess of the value of the land received, and by continued aristocratic ownership of much of the most fertile land. The economic power of the aristocracy declined rapidly after Emancipation, but the opportunities for the peasantry remained limited.

The Emancipation, along with population pressure, clearly increased peasant discontent in Russia. The government had raised hopes which it simply did not fulfill. In Russia, then, as for more obvious reasons in most of the rest of eastern and southern Europe, the 1860's saw the beginnings of a rural unrest that continued sporadically through World War I and beyond. Governments had abolished the old legal order, but had not given peasants the means to take advantage of the new system. Peasant risings in Spain in 1850 and 1861; the increase of peasant banditry in southern Italy; the 2000 risings that greeted Emancipation in Russia in 1861 — all these were clear signs of mounting unrest.

NEW AND OLD STYLES OF CONSERVATISM

A few governments reacted to the revolutions of 1848 and to subsequent changes in politics and society by maintaining a vigorously traditional conservative stance. The papacy, most notably, tried to align Catholics in a policy of total resistance to change. Pius IX had assumed the papal office in 1846 as a liberal, and had introduced some reforms in the Papal States; but the indignity of being driven from Rome by revolutionaries, in 1849, turned him into a staunch conservative. Repressive policies were restored to the Papal States in the 1850's, and the Pope sought alliances with other conservative powers. Concordats were signed with Spain and Austria, giving the church economic support and control over educational systems and censorship. The church backed the repressive policies of Napoleon III, in France, in return for protection of Rome by French troops and an important role in the French educational system. Except in Spain, the papal policy failed rather quickly, for few governments could retain a traditionally conservative stance and few cared to grant large privileges to the church. But Pius IX refused to alter his policies. Robbed of his states by the unification of Italy, he responded, in 1864, with the Syllabus of Errors, which condemned liberalism, socialism, science, and any idea that the church should recognize change. Finally, in 1870, papal infallibility was proclaimed by the First Vatican Council. It was of course important to strengthen church government in a period when governments were withdrawing much of their support, but this proclamation seemed to represent another defiance of modern times, in a period when limitations on authoritarian rule were gaining increasing recognition.

By no means all European Catholics shared the papal view. A minority of the French church disagreed with the Syllabus of Errors; many German Catholics, particularly in the Rhineland, believed in religious liberty and parliamentary government. And there was substantial resistance to the proclamation of papal infallibility. Catholicism, then, should not be equated with traditional conservatism. But it was true that movements of opposition to papal policies were mostly put down and that a large number of Catholic politicians hoped for nothing more than a full restoration of traditional social and political structures. This was not a new Catholic position, though it was now more vigorously stated. It had much in common with the conservatism of the previous period. But times had changed, and papal politics were now not conservative, but reactionary.

At the other extreme, the government of Piedmont reacted to the revolution of 1848 by turning to a moderate liberalism. It granted a constitution and a parliament. It proclaimed equality under the law and, after a bitter battle, abolished the church courts. Under the leadership of Count Cavour, a policy of economic modernization was adopted that stressed lower tariffs and railroad construction. Links were also established with liberal groups in other areas of Italy. The Piedmontese government had decided to assume leadership in Italy and realized that its goals depended on a liberal policy; and this policy was maintained in the united Italy of the 1860's. The liberalism resembled that of the July Monarchy in France, with somewhat greater stress on economic advance. A parliament existed but the ministers of government were responsible to the king; the church was attacked as necessary to establish religious freedom, but there was no desire to destroy the Catholic position; suffrage was extremely limited. Here, as in France earlier, was a liberalism very close to conservatism.

A New Conservatism Arises. The most important political development of the period, not completely dissimilar to Piedmontese policies, was the rise of a new conservatism. This conservatism sought to preserve the essentials of the old order: a strong government, capable of suppressing unrest; a monarch with real power, aided by an extensive bureaucracy; a social hierarchy, including a hereditary aristocracy; some elements of traditional religion. But to preserve the essentials, the new conservatism recognized that some change was necessary. First, while repressive policies remained, they had to be made more flexible and above all more efficient. Second, economic modernization had to be encouraged, to maintain the diplomatic position of the state and to prevent middle-class and lower-class discontent. Third, some protection had to be offered the lower classes, again to prevent discontent and to win the lower classes away from cooperation with middle-class elements; new conservatives for the first time sought direct contact with the masses, to win positive loyalty to the state. Finally, and this was the element of new conservatism that emerged most slowly and incompletely, the state had to accommodate itself to aspects of middle-class liberalism and nationalism, so that these movements would turn away from protest and so their gains could be properly controlled by conservatives themselves. A new generation of conservative leaders came to power in this period, men born in the nineteenth century and aware of the character of their age.

A new conservatism first became evident in France, for Louis Napoleon had no restraining ties with a traditional monarchy or aristocracy. Eager to establish a Bonapartist dynasty, he saw that novel policies were essential to command support. The repressive aspect of his regime appeared quickly. Barred by the constitution from succeeding himself as President of the Second Republic, opposed by a largely monarchist parliament, Napoleon seized full powers by a *coup d'état* in 1851. He disbanded parliament and had its leaders arrested or driven into exile. Radical papers were suppressed and 27,000 potential dissidents were seized. Following this, the government established a rigorous censorship, expanded the police force, and widened the major streets of Paris to facilitate the movement of troops against riots. A rubber stamp parliament was created, with an appointive upper house and an almost functionless lower house; official candidates were nominated for election to the lower house, and government agents actively inhibited political opposition.

From the first, repression was supplemented by other policies. Napoleon sought an active and fruitful contact with the masses. He retained universal suffrage for the lower house of the legislature and held several plebiscites to confirm his rule. His officials helped control the vote, to be sure, and the voters were seldom offered many alternatives; but Napoleon also campaigned for public support. He relied on the backing of prominent interest groups, naturally — the Catholics, the landowners, the businessmen. But he also tried to persuade the lower classes, particularly the peasants, to vote for his policies for their own sake, and he had considerable success. To win general support and to strengthen his France, Napoleon embarked on an active policy of economic expansion. He created new investment banks for industry and agriculture; he speeded up railroad and port development; he lowered tariffs, after 1860, to spur French industry.

He greatly expanded public works to better urban facilities and provide employment, and he improved waste lands and spread technical information for the benefit of agriculture. Napoleon claimed at times that he was a socialist, which was nonsense; but he was a conservative anxious to advance the economy for the general benefit.

Napoleon III constantly sought an active and glorious foreign policy, to enhance his regime, to add to French territory, and somehow to create a better Europe. Though he was too interested in his dynasty and in Latin peoples generally to be a real French nationalist, he certainly tried to appeal to nationalist sentiment, which in France traditionally urged not only national expansion but also French leadership in the liberation of Europe. Napoleon's sponsorship of Italian unification, particularly, appealed to this distinctive nationalist sentiment. Finally, after 1860, Napoleon even wooed liberals directly. He was to a degree forced to this by growing Catholic opposition and, by the mid-1860's, by foreign policy reverses. But he claimed he always intended to restore liberty after order was firmly established and his liberal reforms were not allowed to interfere with the bases of his regime. During the 1860's he increased the powers of parliament, by giving it some controls over the choice of ministers and the imperial budget. He reduced Catholic influence in education and, in 1870, even chose a liberal prime minister. In this, as in most of his measures, he retained the support of his people. In May 1870, a final plebiscite was held to approve the liberal reforms, and the Emperor received the approval of 7,336,000 citizens, against 1,572,000 opponents.

Prussia After 1848. Without sharing the innovating tone of many of Napoleon's actions, Prussian politics after 1848 took on some similar characteristics. There was, certainly, a similar stress on authority, and the Prussian government did not make as many concessions to liberalism as Napoleon did in the 1860's. There also remained in Prussia, as among Catholics and monarchists in France, important conservative groups that resented the political changes of the period.

The Prussian government had long supported industrial development and agricultural modernization, and these policies were continued in the backing given to railroads and industrial investment banks. Soon after the revolution of 1848, the Prussian government showed signs of accommodation with other forces of the modern world. There was, in 1849, an abortive effort to link Prussia with German nationalism, both to advance Prussian interests and to calm the nationalist impulse. Frederick William IV proposed a union of German princes under Prussian leadership, with Austria excluded. Austria, with Russian backing, forced Prussia to abandon this scheme in 1850, but a precedent had been set for Prussian policy. More important, the government issued a constitution, revised in 1850, that guaranteed certain liberties to the Prussian people and established a bicameral legislature that would meet annually. The upper house was composed of hereditary members, all aristocrats; the lower chamber was elected by universal manhood suffrage, but through a class system of voting in which each of three groups, defined by the taxes they paid, elected the same number of delegates to a district convention, which then chose the parliamentary representatives. This meant that 15 per cent of the population controlled two thirds of the seats. Here was a conservative parliament indeed, but it was a parliament and as such went some way toward meeting liberal demands. It proved to be one of the cleverest devices of Prussian conservatism until 1918. Finally, the government moved toward some social reforms, to content the lower classes and draw them away from social radicalism. The abolition of serfdom was maintained and supplemented by limited measures to aid small landholders. The guilds were restored, which confirmed most artisans in their support of conservatism. In addition factory legislation was passed to limit abuses of child labor. By the mid-1850's Prussia had the most advanced and best-administered factory legislation in Europe, a lead that it maintained well into the twentieth century.

During most of the 1850's, Prussia took no further initiatives in domestic or foreign policy. A rigid censorship was maintained and the police kept careful watch over suspected subversives. The reform measures were not rescinded, but a traditional conservatism seemed to overlay them. Then, in the early 1860's, even the limited parliament that had been granted was attacked. The new king, William I, sought to expand the army and increase its budget. Parliamentary liberals resisted such gains for the conservative Prussian military and refused to grant further funds to the government unless the army reforms were withdrawn. In this impasse, in 1862, the king appointed Otto von Bismarck as his chief minister.

Bismarck resisted the temptation, urged by traditional conservatives, to abolish parliament outright. But he did ignore parliament and collected funds without its approval; and he went ahead with the army expansion. His main goal was defense of monarchy, of army, of aristocracy, of state. He did not hesitate to use forceful means to achieve this goal. But again, he was no traditional conservative; he clearly accepted the new means to achieve his ends.

Bismarck's principal device to end the constitutional impasse was a successful foreign policy leading toward German unification. His successive victories were the inducement by which liberals, who were also nationalists, were won to his side. By 1866, when a North German Confederation had been established under Prussian leadership, Bismarck was able to obtain a Bill of Indemnity from parliament which legitimized the state's expenditures since 1862. By linking his conservatism with nationalism, Bismarck won clear sanction for his defense of a strong king and a strong state.

Bismarck did not rely on nationalism alone, however. He sought some direct contact with the masses. He had vague sympathy for socialist ideas, insofar as social reforms might aid and content the poor without disturbing the basic social hierarchy. His interests in this area emerged more clearly later, but even in this period he had several discussions with Lassalle about the abuses of capitalism. Most important, in the parliament of the North German Confederation and later in that of the united German

Empire, Bismarck granted universal suffrage for the lower house, and without the class voting system that distorted this suffrage for the Prussian parliament. To be sure, he checked the lower house by an upper chamber appointed by state governments, with Prussia in control; and he retained the class voting system in Prussia. But he also had real hopes that the German masses could be persuaded to vote conservatively—could be directly used to support the established order.

Finally, Bismarck made concessions to the liberals. If the Indemnity Bill was a major victory, Bismarck had to admit that it was illegal to expend money without parliamentary consent. He established a parliament for the North German Confederation. Parliamentary powers were carefully limited, for Prussia had a veto over all acts and controlled the military; and ministers were responsible to the Prussian king, not to parliament. But in 1867 Bismarck expanded parliament's power over the budget and in the following years agreed to much liberal economic legislation, including the abolition of guilds in Prussia. With liberalism as with democracy, Bismarck made some real concessions, enough to assure widespread support; with both, he carefully hedged the concessions to guarantee the preservation of the Prussian political and social structure. Here was a new conservatism triumphant.

Conservatism in Other Areas. A new conservatism emerged to some degree in the other major states of Europe, though on the whole it was less clearly marked. In Britain, some of the essentials of a new conservatism had been established before. Conservatives had long supported parliament, and many of them had backed limited social reforms. Yet party structure was by no means clear in the 1850's. Whigs and Tories alike included both conservatives and liberals, and neither party could formulate clear programs. During the 1860's, Benjamin Disraeli assumed the leadership of the Conservative party and began to seek real issues that could gain popular support. Like new conservatives on the continent, Disraeli sought to use nationalism and a positive contact with the masses to benefit his cause. His foreign policy interests emerged only later, but his search for a popular basis led him, in 1867, to push through a major suffrage extension, which had originally been proposed by the Liberals. By this act, most urban workers were given the vote, and though the Conservatives lost the elections of 1868, Disraeli was convinced that a well-organized and alert Conservative party could prosper in a substantially democratic system.

In the Hapsburg monarchy, a new conservatism emerged far more tentatively. Governmental policies in the 1850's were in many ways simply reactionary. Guided by his forceful minister, Prince Felix Schwarzenberg, the Emperor granted an illiberal charter to his subjects and then abrogated even this in 1852. Yet the pre-1848 regime was not restored intact. Under Alexander Bach, a former liberal, the bureaucratic structure was greatly extended and its efficiency increased. This allowed, of course, far more extensive repression, for local police and administrators were now under central control. But the greater efficiency of the system encouraged many Austrian liberals, as did the increased official support for economic development. And the Bach system represented not only centralization, but also Germanization, for regional autonomies were eliminated and the new officials were self-consciously German. Here, then, was a staunch conservatism that could appeal to some elements of the Austrian liberal mentality. And, if few measures were taken directly to attract the common people, at least there was no effort to reverse the abolition of serfdom; indeed, the Bach system was partly necessary to compensate for the gaps in local government which this abolition entailed.

After Austria's defeat in Italy, in 1859, even these modifications of conservatism were not enough. New concessions had to be made to the liberals, while the non-German nationalities demanded some recognition. The provincial diets were revived and a two-chamber parliament was established for the whole Empire. For the next six years, the government repeatedly promised a further conversion to a constitutional and federal structure. All of this was complicated by the Emperor's reluctance to abandon bureaucratic controls. Also, concessions to nationalism and to liberalism posed grave difficulties even for the most flexible conservatism in Austria, for the nationalism of German Austrians, which sought dominance in the whole Empire, conflicted directly with the demands of Magyars and Czechs, and the leading liberals were also German nationalists.

Austria's defeat by Prussia forced further concessions. In the Ausgleich of 1867, a dual monarchy was created, giving Austria and Hungary substantially autonomous governments, including separate parliaments. The Germans retained predominance in Austria, but the Magyars now ruled Hungary; the claims of other nationalities in both kingdoms were ignored, except for those of the Poles in Galicia. The parliaments of Hungary and Austria were strengthened, but suffrage was very limited and districts were gerrymandered to assure respective Magyar and German control. Finally, the government granted guarantees for civil liberties; it virtually abolished the Concordat with the church; it gave full legal equality to the Jews; and it admitted liberal ministers to the Austrian government. The Hapsburg monarchy had come to terms with liberalism and with two nationalisms, even if it had not met the demands of all the national groups.

Even Russia shared to some extent, if only temporarily, in the new flexibility of conservative policies. Alexander II, who came to power in 1855, was not interested in reform for its own sake, but he did see the necessity for the emancipation of the serfs. The establishment of regional *zemstvos,* elected by property holders divided into three categories, and a reform of the judicial system that brought more uniform procedures and greater equality before the law, represented further efforts at political modernization. Clearly, the concessions were more limited in Russia than elsewhere, for there was no national representative body and restrictions on the serfs continued; and here, conservative flexibility did not endure.

In western and central Europe, the transformation of conservatism was considerable by 1870. There remained important traditionally conservative groups: Catholics in Spain, Italy, and to an extent elsewhere; monarchists in France, who were about to have their final fling; the Conservative party in Germany, which stayed aloof from Bismarck and his new political structure for another decade. But conservative leaders and governments in most countries had made real concessions to nationalism, to liberalism, and often to democracy. They had not surrendered; they remained conservative of state authority and a social hierarchy; but they had made peace with novel political and economic forces.

The new conservative policies brought many people into greater contact with governments than ever before. In 1870, governments were still primarily tax collectors and military recruiters, and both activities were expanding. But governments were increasingly involved in the education and regulatory protection of ordinary people; and sometimes the common man now voted. The advent of political democracy in France and Germany was a decisive development. It allowed many people, particularly in the countryside, who respected authority and were basically satisfied with their lot, to vote conservatively and develop a positive attachment to the state. It allowed others, gradually, to express an opposition to the existing system, but to express it legally, within that very system. And it put middle-class liberals on the spot, for outside Britain they had not been the leading advocates of democracy and it was not clear that they had much to offer the common people.

The Liberal Dilemma. The continued pressure of liberalism and nationalism was the basic cause of the alterations in conservative policy. These alterations, in turn, forced changes in both movements. For the historian, the interpretive problem is clear: did liberalism surrender its basic principles to the twin temptation of conservative compromises and nationalist success? The liberal dilemma was most acute in Austria and Germany, but liberals in France and Italy faced it as well.

These were the years when liberalism turned clearly into a pragmatic political movement. Little liberal theory was now being produced. Many previously liberal intellectuals modified or abandoned their liberalism. Some, like the historian Heinrich von Treitschke in Germany, turned to an aggressive nationalism led by an authoritarian state; others, like John Stuart Mill, moved increasingly toward socialism. Liberalism no longer represented the vanguard of political theory. But liberal parties were formed all over western and central Europe, and the constituency of liberalism expanded significantly. The support of new businessmen and others strengthened liberalism in many ways, but it also encouraged liberal leaders to accept workable compromises with other groups, compromises that might not fully accord with liberal theory but that provided definite gains for the backers of liberal parties.

The liberal movement was relatively muted during the early 1850's. The shock of the 1848 revolutions, their failure, and the impact of postrevolutionary repression discouraged liberal activity. Liberals in England were free to act, of course, but they suffered from the confusion of Britain's party system and from the concentration of Palmerston, the Whig leader, on foreign affairs, to the exclusion of an interest in further domestic reform.

Liberalism revived fairly quickly in Italy, in association with the policies of the Piedmontese government. And here, liberal leaders made a conscious sacrifice: they recognized that national unity was the first goal, and that this could come only under Piedmontese sponsorship. Admittedly, Piedmont, even with its reforms, was a far from perfect liberal state; its parliament had only limited powers and was based on a very restricted suffrage. But most liberals felt they could accept this for the sake of national unity; even radicals like Giuseppe Garibaldi ultimately bowed to the Piedmontese system. After unification, throughout the 1860's, the Italian parliament was filled with men of the moderate-liberal stripe, who accepted the qualified parliamentary system fully and who, for the sake of completing national unity, countenanced a variety of repressive measures against dissent in southern Italy. In return, they received not only a united nation, but also liberal economic legislation and the reduction of church power.

By the late 1850's liberalism revived in Germany, and liberal representatives gained ground in most state parliaments, including that of Prussia. As the fight over the military budget took shape in Prussia, a Progressive party was formed to defend the rights of parliament; despite the Prussian suffrage system, the party won a hundred seats in 1861 and its successor emerged as the most powerful political group by 1867. In the interim, the liberals fought vigorously for parliamentary power, though they confined their efforts to legal channels. But with the success of Bismarck's foreign policy, the Progressive party split, in 1866. A minority refused to endorse Bismarck's measures, but the majority formed the National Liberal party and voted to legitimize Bismarck's expenditures. In so doing, they accepted a parliamentary system that reserved important military, financial, and ministerial authority for the Prussian king. Was this, as has often been argued, a liberal surrender? Certainly it produced only a highly qualified parliamentary structure; but even before 1848, the demands of many German liberals had been quite modest. If by surrender one means a decisive change in German liberal views, rather than a failure to adhere to some abstract standard of liberal purity, the validity of the judgment can be questioned. Indeed, in terms of traditional liberal interests, there were many gains in the late 1860's. Some parliamentary power over the budget was recognized, and liberals managed to extend the rights of parliament in 1867 and to gain a guarantee of regular parliamentary meetings. The government reduced police controls, abolished guilds, extended legal equality to the Jews, liberalized laws on the formation of unions and corporations, and enacted various economic reforms. And, above all, there was the steady progress toward national unity.

THE UNIFICATION OF ITALY, 1859-1870

Austrian liberals were less vigorous in the period than their German counterparts—particularly because they lacked any parliamentary outlet until the 1860's—but they followed a somewhat similar evolution. Like the Germans, they accepted concessions that were limited and that came from above, from the monarchy, rather than being seized from below; like the Germans, their satisfaction with national gains, in this case the protection

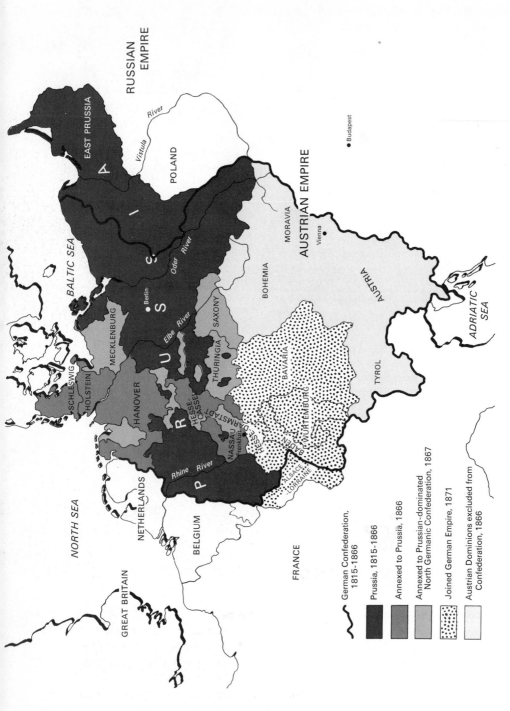

THE UNIFICATION OF GERMANY, 1815-1871

RUSSIAN EMPIRE

EAST PRUSSIA

Vistula River

POLAND

Budapest

AUSTRIAN EMPIRE

MORAVIA

Vienna

BOHEMIA

AUSTRIA

BALTIC SEA

Berlin

Oder River

P   R   U   S   S   I   A

Elbe River

SAXONY

THURINGIA

MECKLENBURG

SCHLESWIG

HOLSTEIN

HANOVER

HESSE-CASSEL

NASSAU

Frankfurt

HESSE-DARMSTADT

BAVARIA

WÜRTEMBURG

BADEN

ALSACE

LORRAINE

TYROL

ADRIATIC SEA

Rhine River

NORTH SEA

NETHERLANDS

BELGIUM

FRANCE

GREAT BRITAIN

German Confederation, 1815-1866

Prussia, 1815-1866

Annexed to Prussia, 1866

Annexed to Prussian-dominated North Germanic Confederation, 1867

Joined German Empire, 1871

Austrian Dominions excluded from Confederation, 1866

of Germans in Austria, increased their willingness to tolerate limitations on the power of parliament. But like the Germans also, they made some major strides. They received a parliament and a constitution, guaranteeing equality under the law and freedom of expression and of movement; the church was put under the control of the secular state; and the system was completed by Count Beust, a minister devoted to the interests of the Empire but undeniably a moderate liberal.

In all three central European countries, Austria, Germany, and Italy, liberalism advanced significantly in the 1860's. The gains were greatest in the field of economic and civil liberties, and of course in the protection of national interests. Freedoms of press, of education, and of association were rather fully guaranteed; barriers to economic activity, such as cumbersome tax laws and restrictions on corporate formation, were largely removed. But in the parliamentary sphere, liberal gains were incomplete. Parliaments existed, but they did not control the bases of political power. Here was where the liberals compromised, though they continued to work for parliamentary gains; and in compromising, particularly in failing to achieve ministerial responsibility to parliament, the liberals forfeited the assurance that their other gains could be preserved. The 1860's and 1870's were the high-water mark of liberalism in central Europe, but they can also be seen as the years of liberal failure.

Liberals counted on continued and increasing electoral support, such as they received in the 1860's, to push further reforms through. This was a reasonable expectation and helps explain the compromises of the period; but it did not turn out to be correct. Liberals in Italy continued to win most of the votes, but with a limited franchise they represented a mere 2 per cent of the population; they did not try to appeal to the masses and so they could not win their support. German liberals accepted democracy, but they could not flourish with it. Peasants had no reason to vote for the liberals, who had given them nothing in 1848 and who stood for secular, urban interests; artisans were hostile, for liberals had abolished their guilds and promoted the factory industry that threatened artisanal life; industrial workers might be briefly attracted, but soon turned against the party that represented their employers.

In western Europe, liberals not only accepted democracy but also found new bases of support. French liberals faced many problems and temptations in Napoleon's Empire. As elsewhere, most liberal leaders were of a new generation, convinced that revolution was unworkable; but distinctively, French liberals in this period became republicans, having learned that neither monarchies nor empires could protect liberal values. To be sure, as Napoleon III granted greater powers to parliament in the 1860's, a minority of republicans accepted his system and one, Émile Ollivier, consented to serve as prime minister in 1870. But in contrast to German liberals, the majority of the French republican group refused this compromise and continued to advocate a change of regime. And they won increasing popular support, particularly in the cities. By 1870, a powerful and reasonably well-organized republican group existed. It had learned three lessons from Napoleon's regime, and these were to be applied in the following decades: first, to distrust executive authority and insist on a powerful parliament; second, to distrust the church as an inherently conservative body; and third, to build a popular base, to accept democracy and use it to support a republic.

In Britain, as on the continent, a modern liberal party was formed in the 1860's. Under William Gladstone and John Bright, liberals established a firm party structure, which accepted substantial democracy and worked for a political base in the now-dominant cities. In his first ministry, 1868 to 1874, Gladstone completed the liberal structure of Britain by opening the civil service to competitive examinations, rather than to privilege, and by extending educational facilities. Here, uniquely, there was no question of liberal compromise.

NATIONALISM AND DIPLOMACY

The most obvious and important changes in Europe between 1850 and 1870 occurred in diplomacy. In 1850, the Vienna settlement remained almost intact; by 1870, it was in shreds. Austria and France had been diminished, Italy and Germany unified and added to the list of great powers. The new conservative leaders consistently pushed for diplomatic change, led initially by Napoleon III who, ironically, was to lose his empire through diplomatic follies. Revived liberalism and nationalism pressed for territorial adjustments also, and many states sought to moderate internal political stress by successes abroad.

It is easy to see the main diplomatic changes of the period as a triumph of nationalism. German and Italian unifications fulfilled long-standing nationalist demands. Nationalist intellectuals in Rumania, thwarted in an abortive rising in 1848, won satisfaction ten years later when their country was united and granted autonomy in the Ottoman Empire. Moderate Hungarian nationalists, who sought autonomy rather than independence, triumphed in the *Ausgleich* of 1867. Nationalist intellectuals tried increasingly to preach a practical and forceful diplomacy, instead of stressing liberal and cultural methods. Walter Bagehot, in England, taught that only strong nations could prevail and that those that survived were best. A conservative nationalism in Russia stressed Russia's mission against the liberal West. And in Germany and Italy, nationalists increasingly urged diplomatic and military methods. The Italian National Society, formed in 1856, sought unity under Piedmont. In imitation, the German *National Verein,* established in 1859, stressed Prussian leadership for Germany. South Slavic nationalists looked increasingly to Russia and, to an extent, to Serbia for support. There can be no question that nationalism was becoming increasingly and consciously intertwined with diplomacy.

Three qualifications must be introduced, however, to any notion of an overwhelming and triumphant nationalism. First, nationalism remained a minority movement, confined to elements of the middle class, and, especially in eastern Europe, to landholders chafing under foreign rule. This meant that where nationalism triumphed, it did so against the apathy and sometimes the outright hostility of much of the population. This was clearest in Italy, where nationalism was upheld by professional people in the northern cities almost exclusively. Garibaldi's famous march through the south was a march of northern volunteers supported by northern funds; and soon after unification, antinational risings in the south had to be put down by force. Catholics in Germany as in Italy remained antinationalist in the period, and the proclamation of papal infallibility was easily seen as a declaration of traditional, supranational loyalties.

Second, the nationalisms that succeeded in the period were balanced by the rise of new nationalisms long doomed to failure. Partly because of the obvious national successes, partly because of the continued spread of an interest in ancient cultures, derived ultimately from the Romantic tradition, nationalism gained intellectual support in a variety of new areas in the period. There were hints of national aspirations in Bulgaria and Albania; the Czech national movement gained ground among intellectuals and landowners; in Russia, Finnish, Ukrainian, and Lithuanian movements began; and there was a rise of Catalonian separatist sentiment in Spain and of a Provençal movement in France. Ironically, perhaps, the period of the great national unifications saw the bases laid for the next era of nationalist agitation, which would seek to tear down existing states and particularly the multinational empires.

Third, and most important, the diplomats who achieved the national success were not nationalists. Cavour, though he had a nationalist background, worked primarily for the advancement of Piedmont. Bismarck certainly sought to protect Prussian interests above all and never even contemplated the unification of all racial Germans. Napoleon III, if a nationalist, was an international one, working for Italy or Rumania fully as much as for France. All of these men understood nationalism and could use it and even foment it, but they were not its creatures. A diplomacy activated and controlled by nationalist enthusiasms arose in the following period, and even then only incompletely.

During the early 1850's, there was little diplomatic activity. Cavour was building a Piedmontese state with an eye to diplomatic advance, but he was not yet ready. Prussia had abandoned its initiatives in Germany, and Austria seemed once again in control of central Europe, though its harsh hand annoyed many Prussians, including Bismarck. Napoleon III was consolidating his regime and Britain, as usual, was content with the status quo on the continent.

The Crimean War. The first change in this situation, and in some ways the key to all the others, came in the Near East. Nicholas I was, as always, interested in gaining influence in the Ottoman Empire, particularly by claiming protection over the Orthodox Christians there. Britain was as anxious as ever to maintain Ottoman integrity, to avoid any great power influence near its routes to India. The new element came from

Napoleon III, who saw a chance to begin his program of a glorious diplomacy, to enhance his prestige, and to undo the Vienna settlement which he regarded as an insult to France and to the Bonapartes. He allied with Britain, in 1854, to protect the Ottoman Empire against Russian interference and with Britain blundered into the Crimean War against Russia, which ended in allied victory in 1856.

The Crimean War was the first conflict among major European powers in forty years, and it was bound to have important repercussions. It temporarily weakened Russia, forcing attention to internal reforms, and certainly increased Russian grievances against the western powers. Most important, it drove a wedge between Russia and Austria. Russia expected Austrian support, in return for Russia's assistance in Hungary in 1849 and out of respect for the Holy Alliance tradition. But Austria, long fearful of Russian influence in the Near East, remained officially neutral, though Austrian troops occupied Moldavia and Wallachia, which had been under Russian protection. Austria gained no sympathy from Britain and France by its hesitancies, and it certainly alienated Russia; this contributed powerfully to the lack of support for Austria in the difficulties of the following decade.

The Congress of Paris, in 1856, settled the Crimean War by granting autonomy to Moldavia and Wallachia (united two years later as Rumania), giving Russian Bessarabia to the Ottoman Empire, and neutralizing the Black Sea. In theory, the Congress revived collective discussion among the great powers on European issues; Cavour, for example, was allowed to raise the Italian question. But the appearance of European unity was illusory. Cavour gained nothing and decided on independent action. Russian frustration, Austrian isolation, and even new jealousies between France and Britain prevented significant collective action in the great events of the next decade. Napoleon III was anxious for a revision of Europe by great power discussion, but he wanted this on his own terms, and soon decided that he, too, must take forceful action by himself.

Napoleon had long been attracted by the Italian cause, partly because he had spent much time in Italy. He resented Austrian influence in the peninsula and hoped for an expanded Piedmont in the north, linked in federation with the Papal States and Naples. In 1858, he allied with Cavour against Austria; war broke out the following year. France was unable to drive Austria out of Italy, but Austria, fearful of disorder at home, ceded Lombardy to Piedmont. Following this, Cavour helped foment risings in central Italy, including much of the Papal States, and annexed these territories after plebiscites indicated popular enthusiasm for Piedmont. In 1860, Garibaldi and a small band of volunteers, aided by Piedmontese funds and weapons, moved through the kingdom of Naples and then, under some pressure by Piedmontese troops, joined southern Italy with the north. A united Italy had been achieved.

Napoleon III had not gained much from his Italian venture. He did annex Savoy and Nice to France as a reward for his help, but his interference and incomplete military success angered the Italians. France had a new state on its southern border, and by no means a friendly one. French troops remained in Rome, to guard the Pope against an Italian take-over and to conciliate Catholic opinion at home. The new Italy, despite its great success, was aggrieved by the failure to gain Rome and Venetia. Austria was weakened. And most important, German nationalists developed a new interest in imitating Italy's achievement.

Bismarck, coming to power in 1862, was convinced that a unification of at least part of Germany, under Prussia, was essential. He had long felt that Austrian influence in Germany was detrimental to Prussia and had to be expelled. He recognized the power of nationalism and wished to make certain that it abetted rather than opposed Prussian interests. In leading the unification of Germany, Prussia had many advantages that Piedmont had lacked. Its economic power was great, rivaling that of France by the 1860's. Its military was well trained, well equipped, and highly mobile; and Prussia alone of the great powers had retained widespread conscription. In Bismarck, Prussia had a leader of great diplomatic skill, adept at seizing any opportunity but equally able to restrain his ambitions to avoid needless difficulties.

Prussia benefited also from the distraction of the three powers really capable of opposing it. Russia was indebted to Prussia for assistance in putting down a Polish rising in 1863 and was indisposed toward foreign adventures. France was distracted by an effort to conquer Mexico and by Napoleon's vague feeling that perhaps German nationalism was as justified as Italian. Britain, a sea power anyway, continued to fear French ambitions. All three powers failed to appreciate Prussia's strength and constantly expected it to bog down to their advantage. The result was that Prussia not only met no real interference from the great powers, but even received some assistance on occasion.

Prussia at War. In 1864, Prussia went to war against Denmark over the old issue of Danish possession of the presumably German territories of Schleswig-Holstein. Austria, fearful of Prussian gains, obtained the administration of one of the duchies, with Prussia administering the other. During the next year, Bismarck raised a number of objections to Austrian policies in Holstein. He also met with Napoleon III to obtain French neutrality in case of a war with Austria, in return for vague promises of French gains in the Rhineland, and Napoleon helped arrange a Prussian-Italian alliance, with Italy to gain Venetia as a reward for a new war on Austria. Finally, Bismarck suggested a revision of the Germanic confederation, through the addition of a national assembly elected by universal suffrage; if he did not win over German opinion by this proposal, he at least confused it.

Prussia's victory over Austria in the Seven Weeks' War of 1866, in which most of the other German states joined Austria, was swift and decisive. Bismarck wisely refrained from any territorial demands on Austria, thus reducing the possibility of later friction. Instead, he united all German states north of the Main river into the North German Confederation, under Prussian leadership.

There remained two threats to Bismarck's goals. France had gained nothing from its support of Prussia, and French opinion grew increasingly restive; and Bismarck felt that France's power and traditions of intervention in Germany had to be decisively broken. Further, the south German states were still free, and though they formed military alliances with the new Confederation, they were traditionally anti-Prussian and pro-French. Whether Bismarck had long planned a full German unification or whether he simply pressed for it now that it seemed feasible and necessary cannot be known. What is certain is that after 1866 he worked for a war with France to complete German unity.

Napoleon III was now aging and ill, increasingly distracted by liberal opposition. Partly because of the liberals, he was unable to improve France's armies as he knew was necessary. Moreover, he could not form alliances: Russia still remembered the Crimean War; Britain still feared French ambitions, spurred by Bismarck's revelation of French interest in the Low Countries; Italy was angered by French presence in Rome; Austria, though interested, resisted any formal alliance at least until its government could see that a French victory was probable. Yet, despite its weakness and Napoleon's better judgment, France declared war on Prussia in 1870. Bismarck turned French protests over a proposal to give a Prussian prince the newly vacant throne of Spain into an apparent insult to Prussia, and Prussia, in the French view, seemed to insult France in turn.

The Franco-Prussian War of 1870 to 1871 was ended in the rapid defeat of France, though Paris long resisted a siege. The results of the war spread through the whole of Europe. Italy marched into Rome; Russia unilaterally abrogated the neutrality of the Black Sea; the French, after Napoleon was captured by the Prussians, proclaimed a new republic. Bismarck obtained a large indemnity from France and took over Alsace and most of Lorraine, both because they were inhabited by racial Germans and because his military advisers insisted on a more easily defended border with France. The south German states had joined the war on the Prussian side and now agreed to a united Germany. In January 1871, in the Palace of Versailles, William I of Prussia became Emperor of Germany.

A NEW REALISM?

It is easy to see the period from 1850 to 1870 as a triumph of force over ideals. Burgeoning industry created a background of material power. Liberals accepted and many nationalists urged the use of force to obtain their goals. Bismarck spoke of a diplomacy based on "blood and iron." A forceful diplomacy was clearly successful, not only for Germany but also for Italy. Consultations among European powers gave way to unilateral acts and military conquest.

In intellectual life itself, a new, tough-minded tone seemed to be developing. Many novelists sought realistic portrayals of society and the sufferings of the oppressed, to replace Romantic flights of fancy. On the stage, scenery became more realistic and actors cultivated a "natural style" of rendering their lines. In science, new discoveries in the principles of electricity and electromagnetism confirmed the advances possible in purely material investigations—and they had important applications in industrial technology. A new wave of attacks on religion, based on historical investigations of the Bible, showed in yet another field the power of a realistic approach.

The two leading intellectual developments of the period, the Darwinian theory of evolution and the Marxist theory of socialism, bolstered the attack on traditional ideals. Darwin, in his *Origin of Species* (1859), showed that the evolution of all living species was determined by the survival of the fittest. He underlined the struggle for existence and demonstrated that man derived from purely animal origins. Very quickly, a Social Darwinism developed that stressed the importance of struggle among nations or among social classes; and of course the challenge of evolutionary theory to traditional Christianity was quickly taken up, particularly in Germany.

Marx, dedicating the first volume of *Das Kapital* to Darwin, felt that his socialism had a firmly materialistic and scientific basis. It rested on a view that all human activity was fundamentally determined by the means of production, and that all history—all aspects of human endeavor—were based on a constant struggle among social classes whose character was defined by their relationship to the means of production. In capitalist society, the propertied bourgeoisie was driven to create an ever larger and more desperate proletariat; economic crises showed that capitalists themselves could not control the results of industrial technology. A socialist society was inevitable, but only after revolution and a transitional proletarian dictatorship. Marx poured scorn on socialists who ignored the laws of history and the necessity of class war.

The new and varied delight in realism did not monopolize intellectual activity, however. The realists themselves were not lacking in ideals. Many realistic novelists felt that their portrayals would lead to social reforms. Marx predicted a future society little short of utopian, for all his scientific socialism; the past laws of history and of class struggle would end with proletarian victory, governments would wither away, and men would live in harmony, producing what they could and taking what they needed.

Most important, the period saw a conscious withdrawal of many intellectuals from realism and rationalistic materialism. Led by Édouard Manet, an Impressionist school began in painting which defied traditional standards and sought to portray the truth of nature by capturing impressions of light and color. This was realism, to be sure, but it did not rely on a literal representation of the subject. In poetry, Charles Baudelaire in France and some of the pre-Raphaelites in Britain sought personalized styles that would convey their emotional strivings. They vaunted art for art's sake, disgusted with the materialism of their society. In their personal lives as in their writing, they defied conventions and tried, by symbolic images, to pour forth their souls. There was a clear link with Romanticism in these efforts, but the stylistic innovations were far greater now, as many writers tried to portray their revulsion against industrial society and their sense of man's need to glorify his emotions and his sorrows. In the arts and ultimately in philosophy, this new aesthetic impulse was to have consequences fully as important as the more obvious realism of the period.

In a broader sense, can the character of this period be described as unusually tough-minded, unusually devoid of interest in goals beyond material power? Certainly there was a new thirst for wealth at various levels of society. More and more people were developing a desire to improve their material standards, rather than devoting themselves to a maintenance of traditional levels; but whether this led to greater materialism is hard to say. If many nationalists became more pragmatic, nationalists in the outlying areas of Europe remained as starry-eyed as ever. If liberals turned to a greater practicality, there were the new missionaries of socialism, devoted to what still seemed a most idealistic purpose. If Bismarck talked of blood and iron, was he somehow more realistic, less gentle, than diplomats of the preceding era? These are problems that are difficult to solve, perhaps impossible to solve historically. In politics, in diplomacy, in all aspects of social activity, much was developing in this period that is recognizably modern. In all fields there were major departures from the past. The interpretation of the period inevitably reflects one's evaluation of contemporary life.

SUGGESTED READING

The revolutions of 1848 have been sketchily treated in English. A general account, quite weak in many respects, is P. Robertson, *Revolutions of 1848: A Social History** (1952). An interesting interpretation is F. Fejto, *The Opening of an Era: 1848, An Historical Symposium* (1948). On specific countries, see V. Valentin, *1848: Chapters of German History* (1940); T. Hamerow, *Restoration, Revolution, Reaction: Economics and Politics in Germany, 1815-1871** (1958); J. Blum, *Noble Landowners and Agriculture in Austria, 1815-1848: A Study in the Origins of the Peasant Emancipation of 1848* (1948); R. J. Rath, *The Viennese Revolution of 1848* (1957); D. C. McKay, *The National Workshops: A Study in the French Revolution of 1848* (1933).

Intellectual developments in this transitional period are excellently suggested by J. Barzun, *Darwin, Marx, Wagner: Critique of a Heritage** (1941). See also I. Berlin, *Karl Marx: His Life and Environment** (1948), and H. J. Laski, *The Communist Manifesto, Socialist Landmark: A*

*Available in a paperback edition.

*New Appreciation Written for the Labour Party** (1948). On Darwin's impact, see P. B. Sears, *Charles Darwin: The Naturalist a Cultural Force* (1950).

For general diplomatic and political history of this period and beyond, A. J. P. Taylor, *The Struggle for Mastery in Europe, 1848-1918* (1954), is excellent. Political history for the period generally has a biographical emphasis: see J. M. Thompson, *Louis Napoleon and the Second Empire** (1954); T. Zeldin, *The Political Systems of Napoleon III* (1958); D. Mack-Smith, *Cavour and Garibaldi* (1954); A. J. P. Taylor, *Bismarck* (1955); E. Eyck, *Bismarck and the German Empire** (1950). For Russia, on the main development of the period, G. T. Robinson, *Rural Russia under the Old Regime: A History of the Landlord-Peasant World and a Prologue to the Peasant Revolution of 1917** (1949).

Bismarck: The Granger Collection   Cavour: Alinari

BISMARCK AND CAVOUR

The most obvious biographical pairing in the nineteenth century is that of Otto Eduard Leopold, Prinz von Bismarck (1815-1898) and Camille Benso di Cavour (1810-1861). Their achievements are manifestly comparable. They unified their nations by a careful combination of diplomacy and force and by rallying diverse political groupings. It was Bismarck who proclaimed the policy of blood and iron, but Cavour showed no less willingness to use what military power he had and to practice a secret, often deceptive, and always selfish diplomacy. Both men, also, knew where to stop; when their major goals were achieved they were content to work for stabilization by a combination of conciliation and force.

The similarities of achievement between Bismarck and Cavour are all the more striking in view of the different political backgrounds of the two. Cavour was the younger son of a Piedmontese noble family, and was easily won to liberalism. He read widely in Bentham, Adam Smith, Rousseau, and other liberal or democratic writers. He was hostile to the church's political power; he wanted economic progress through free trade. Travels in France and England confirmed his liberal orientation. The French Revolution of 1830 showed him the compatibility of liberty and monarchy; and he greatly admired the individualism of the English, their political institutions, and their economic system. Cavour was a man of great wealth, which he steadily increased. Between 1835 and 1848 he led in the introduction of scientific farming in Piedmont; he was also active in banking, chemical production, and the development of steamboats, and he organized the first railroad in Italy. In 1847 he established a nationalist newspaper to support Italian unification; and in the revolution of 1848 he persuaded the king to introduce constitutional government to Piedmont. His full entry into politics came in 1851, when he was named Prime Minister. Again he worked along liberal lines for economic development, tax reform, and free trade, and he was associated with other aspects of Piedmontese liberalization, notably the attack on the church's political privileges.

Bismarck was also an aristocrat, from an old Prussian family. A diplomat by profession, his first fame resulted from his ardent conservatism in opposition to the revolution of 1848. He condemned democracy and parliamentary rule; he vigorously asserted, then and later, the need for a strong monarchy. As a secretary to the Prussian delegation at the German Diet in Frankfurt, he denounced the upstart Frankfurt assembly and ostentatiously refused to have anything to do with it. His stance was regarded as excessive even by the Prussian government, but it helped win royal favor and his appointment as chief delegate to the German Diet in 1851; various ambassadorial posts followed, and when, in 1862, William I needed a champion to withstand parliament, it was to Bismarck that he turned.

Differences in background certainly showed in later policies. Bismarck never had Cavour's explicit interest in economic advance, though he accepted it. Cavour had a real concern for a workable if very limited parliament, whereas Bismarck used parliament mainly as a sop to the liberals. Yet the similarities outweighed the differences. Both men were disdainful of opposition and could be brutal in suppressing it. Cavour's repression of protests against unification in southern Italy and his rigging of parliament to avoid a party system can be compared to Bismarck's treatment of Poles, Catholics, and socialists and his own manipulation of parliament. Yet both men were opportunists, committed to no set line of internal policy. Cavour could work with royalists, liberals, and radicals and he even tried to conciliate Catholic sentiment; Bismarck could appeal in some degree to every major political force in Germany. Both men, finally, were devoted to their kings and their countries. Bismarck's impulse to the unification of Germany sprang from his desire for increased Prussian power. Cavour, despite some theoretical interest in Italian nationalism, worked for Piedmontese aggrandizement above all.

Cavour and Bismarck can both be taken, then, to illustrate the current of tough-mindedness that has been cited as characteristic of the decades after 1848. The very fact that men of such different political orientations acted so similarly can be taken as a sign of the decreasing importance of political principles. More clearly, the two men themselves set the tone which historians have attributed to the whole period. They had a similar desire to serve their states by using the major political currents of the period; and they were personalities of similar force and vigor. The changes in the political currents after 1848 and the new opportunities in diplomacy created great possibilities for individuals to make their mark. At no other time in the nineteenth century, after 1815 at least, were "great men" so important in European history, for they could lead the accommodation of old and new political forces. Cavour and Bismarck created two new countries. More than this, the success of their methods and the political systems they devised contributed to the enduring political character of Italy and Germany. ∎

INDUSTRIAL EUROPE, PROGRESS OR DECLINE?

Industrialization brought massive changes in European life, in material conditions most obviously, but not only there. For most people, the visible environment changed dramatically, as increasing numbers moved into the cities and the cities themselves took on a new aspect under the chimneys of the new factories. From the very beginnings of industrialization, people asked themselves about the value of these changes, about whether the progress was good or bad. The debate continues today, in a way that makes historical judgment difficult; for we still must take a stand on many aspects of the quality of life in industrial society. Many of the basic problems we still discuss were recognized very early. Well before 1850, people were worried about growing materialism and the boredom and stultifying quality of life in factories and tenements. Even the aesthetics of industrialization provoked argument from the first: one could find the new factories ugly, as many traditionalists did; or ugly but useful for other reasons; or representative of a new kind of beauty. And it was not merely formal theorists who tried to judge industrial society. Ordinary people, faced with unprecedented change, had at

New factories, like those in the Krupp establishment in Germany, made drastic changes in the countryside. *Source: Historical Pictures Service.*

Fig. 38. Krupp's Etablissement in Essen.

ast implicitly to decide whether their new life in factory ities was better or worse than their old, usually rural xistence.

Both now and during the nineteenth century, a number of actors complicated a judgment about the direction of industrial society. Detailed arguments are possible about recise conditions during early industrialization, and concientous historians have disagreed over these. More important, with what are we to compare industrial society? During early industrialization and since, many people have xaggerated the beauties of pre-industrial life. The problems of rapid urbanization quickly created a bucolic sentiment that praised rural and artisanal life beyond all bounds. On a purely factual basis, then, an accurate historical judg-

New industrial processes, such as the Bessemer method of steel production, created new jobs and new products. *Source: Historical Pictures Service.*

The invention of electricity enhanced the appearance of some parts of the city. Here, a Parisian street scene of 1880 shows the use of electric lights. *Source: Historical Pictures Service.*

ment requires careful examination of the sort of world industrialization displaced. Above all, however, the evaluation of industrialization depends on one's own standards. If one feels that material advance and related acquisitiveness are good things, then surely many aspects of industrialization must be deemed worthy; but it is possible to condemn industrialization on these very grounds. Is it the historian's function to make such judgments, or should he be content to seek out the facts as accurately as possible?

The material gains of industrialization were quite quickly apparent. New manufacturing processes made some work easier and produced new quantities of goods. The Bessemer process opened up a true steel age; and on the unprecedented volume of steel production rested the expansion of railroads and machine tools, which transformed every area of the economy. New products, as well as increased production, were part of industrialization from the first; Europeans became acquainted with novelties as diverse as the bicycle and electric

Industrialization and its products were popularized in the great trade fairs of the second half of the century. This is a scene from the Great Exposition in London, 1851. *Source: The Granger Collection.*

Huge schools, such as the London School of Technical Education, were built to provide training for the new industrialized society. *Source: Historical Pictures Service.*

lighting. And although inequalities of wealth remained great and may indeed have increased, industrialization in the long run brought material gains to most groups; so the new products were not playthings of the rich alone. By 1900 less than a third of the population in industrial countries lived on the margins of subsistence, the first time in human history that a majority of people had not been poor; and the definition of subsistence itself had been broadened.

Rather early, industrialization created a new mentality to accompany its economic forms. Prepared by the values of the eighteenth-century Enlightenment, an admiration of material achievement and progress spread with machines themselves. This mentality was not adopted overnight. Religion, traditional resignation, or a positive dislike of the new economy could delay its spread, and a current of rejection of industrial life lasted

New attitudes toward social welfare developed as shown by a ward in a London hospital with an attendant nurse, 1888. *Source: Historical Pictures Service.*

The physical suffering of many workers is shown in the inhumane working conditions of a step-mill. *Source: Historical Pictures Service.*

Foul conditions were not confined to the mills and factories as home work conditions proved equally as bad. *Source: Historical Pictures Service.*

well into the twentieth century, influencing movements as diverse as fascism and socialism. But without doubt, the new mentality gained steadily. An early expression was the London Crystal Palace Exhibition of 1851. Here for the first time, millions of people were able to see the range of products typical of the new economy and the machines that created them, displayed in a steel and glass building that was itself a monument of modernity. Publicists and ordinary visitors were properly awed by man's, or rather the Englishman's, achievement.

The hymn to progress was not, however, crassly materialist. Publicists pointed not just to new products but to new institutions designed to alleviate suffering and improve men's minds. At its fullest, the mentality that grew up with industry was humanitarian rather than merely materialist. And the proliferation of hospitals and schools was a rather direct product of industrialization, facilitated by its new techniques and the wealth it created, demanded by the social problems of its cities. Without question, health and educational levels improved vastly in the first industrial century. These developments could be seen as proof that industrial society itself healed the worst moral and physical problems of its first years.

On the debit side, in the earliest decades of industrialization, was the great physical suffering of many workers. It is important not to exaggerate here. Step-mills, for example, were rare; and new inventions, particularly the steam engine, rapidly displaced them. Workers in many factories benefited from the first, as machines lightened their labor and increased their earnings. One can, of course, question the

Problems were not limited to the cities, for even the peasant sometimes envied the comfortable life of the pig. *Source: Historical Pictures Service.*

values of a society that allowed even a minority of its workers to suffer as some of them, women and children as well as men, did. But the more persistent material suffering in industrial society occurred outside the factories, contrary to common impressions. Competition caused by machines and simple population growth forced many artisans and domestic producers to work increasingly long hours for low pay. Many peasants were similarly squeezed. Here one could find real misery, in some cases increased misery, in 1900 and beyond. Other traditional producers were able to adapt somewhat better, like the peasants who began raising livestock for commercial markets, but the adaptation was painful and risky. For common people in the cities, whether employed in factories or in more traditional production, the problems of adaptation to novelty were even greater. Did a factory worker find higher earnings adequate compensation for an increased pace of work and the constant din of machines? Not at first, surely, for there is evidence that many workers did not know what to do with their extra pay and at the same time regretted the loss of an outdoor life and greater flexibility in their work schedule. By the later nineteenth century subsequent generations of workers had been converted to an extent at least; here again one can talk of a new mentality. Enjoyment and expectations of rising pay and the benefits it would bring in terms of better clothes and more expensive recreation had at least modified the older longing for the countryside and for a more traditional family life. But this adaptation itself can be seen as yet another, if more subtle, evil of industrialization. And though cities overcame their worst physical inadequacies during the later nineteenth century, they remained dirty and ugly. Here again, an array of questions for the historian-judge: did the ordinary person encounter more

The wonders of mechanization were so far-reaching and individually felt that many people did not know how far the process would go. *Source: Historical Pictures Service.*

"London by Rail," an engraving by Gustave Dore, shows the crowded and dirty conditions of urban life. *Source: The Granger Collection.*

Slums grew up on the outskirts of cities as well as in their centers, particularly in fast-growing capitals like Berlin. *Source: Historical Pictures Service.*

153

ugliness in the late nineteenth century than in, say, the late eighteenth? If he did, did he realize it; that is, was ugliness seen as a problem? To the extent that it was not, is this because of a blunting of the aesthetic sense due to industrialization? In short, how is the historian to interpret the effects or even the nature of the drabness conveyed by pictures of the poorer quarters of nineteenth-century cities?

Finally, the moral if not the physical problems of

REPERCUSSIONS OF NEW INDUSTRIAL WEALTH: MILITARISM AND IMPERIALISM

The Emperor inspects munitions at the Paris Exposition of 1867. *Source: The Granger Collection.*

England presses for coin as the African colonies are subdued by Anglican religion and English ale. *Source: The Bettmann Archive.*

industrial society were not confined to the common people. Indeed, some of the most persuasive critics of industrialization have focused on the damage done to the elite of society, as it became influenced by the general materialism and desire for personal gain. The dynamic of industrial production and the new valuation placed on material objects and on energy undoubtedly extended beyond the realm of the economy. Producers and admirers of machines were often producers and admirers of new types of armaments as well. It is obvious that World War I and all modern wars depended on the technology of industrialization; did they also result from a new rapaciousness that industrialism fostered? Here, as in other questions, one must try to decide if industrialization created new vices or if it rather gave old vices, such as a thirst for conquest, new toys to play with. Imperialism, like increased militarism, depended on industrial technology and was motivated in part by material acquisitiveness. But again, its motives were certainly not entirely new, perhaps not new at all; and in this case it brought some benefits to many native populations as well.

Louis Napoleon, as warmonger, wears a coat of weapons in this German cartoon. Source: *Der Weltkrieg in Der Karikatur.* Edvard Fuchs (Munich, 1916).

Industrialization can, then, be blamed for changing the nature of ordinary people or of the ruling elites, for the worse. Without going so far, it can be blamed for creating situations of novel temptation. It is hard to see the leaders of the later nineteenth century, starting with Louis Napoleon or even Bismarck, as bloodthirsty militarist types. Yet the leaders were surrounded by increasingly elaborate military hardware, which incidentally made direct military leaders more influential if only because their services rose so rapidly in cost; they were influenced also by business leaders anxious to sell such equipment and a general public which may have been led toward greater militarism by the frustrations of industrial life.

One is tempted to say that industrialization has brought benefits to those people, happily the majority to date, who have lived through industrial wars. This, admittedly, involves judgment of the twentieth century as well as the nineteenth. Whatever his final verdict, the historian of the first industrial century must deal with the difficult combination of circumstances: material gains, unprecedentedly bloody wars, and changes in human values difficult to state accurately, much less to evaluate. A satisfactory, comprehensive judgment is probably impossible, but hopefully this will not discourage the attempts.

Chapter 5

Years of Consolidation
1870 – 1900

In domestic politics and in diplomacy, 1870 and 1871 marked an obvious transition from the previous two decades. Four states had new or reasonably new constitutional structures: Germany, France, Italy, and Austria-Hungary. British politics were also altered by the recent suffrage change. The way was now open to solve many of the disputes about political structure that had raged intermittently, and not only in France, since the French Revolution. Conservatives and liberals did not merge, and in France they were about to wage a final battle, but they now drew increasingly close. The national unifications settled longstanding foreign policy issues; with the exception of France, the leading nationalisms of Europe were now largely satisfied. As in domestic politics, there was a period of adjustment to novelty in the 1870's, but diplomats soon turned to new, and on the whole peaceful, paths.

The 1870's also saw the inception of more disturbing developments, developments that ultimately shook the equilibrium so painfully acquired in the political field. Economic growth continued, but it took on increasingly novel forms; the crudeness and rapidity of industrialization alienated more and more intellectuals, while economic novelty disturbed many established groups. And economic growth was now often interrupted, for recessions in every decade affected many elements of society. New types of social discontent arose. Most notably, socialism raised a new wave of political protest. The period opened with the formation of the Marxist Social Democratic party in Germany in 1869, and with the bitter social strife of the Paris Commune in 1871. But new grievances arose among conservatives as well, spurred by disgruntlement at the political compromises of the new regimes and by serious strains in the economy. Finally, in somewhat different forms, massive social protest burst forth in eastern and southern Europe, comparable in some ways to the agitation of western Europe earlier in the century, but heightened by less flexible social systems and by the doctrines of protest that could be imported from the West.

Confidence in Europe's Future. The undercurrents of renewed protest developed only slowly, however. A mood of confidence in Europe's future reached a peak in 1900. Further changes were expected, of course, but western Europe was attuned to progress and there seemed no reason to expect anything but peaceful and gradual improvement. It is difficult to say how widely this mood was held, and certainly it had little support in eastern Europe. In the West, the middle class remained most optimistic, but other elements of society shared some of the same feelings.

The great achievement of the last three decades of the nineteenth century was the integration of vast segments of the population into the body politic. Essentially universal male suffrage covered western Europe by 1900 — some Scandinavian countries were about to allow women to vote too — and there were significant extensions of the vote in Austria and Italy. The result naturally put a strain on existing political parties, which had to offer programs that had wide appeal if they wanted to survive. New political rights undeniably encouraged new expectations. Socialism could not have risen so fast nor won such wide support without the political consciousness that older parties helped to spread. Socialist politics, however, tested and in some ways confirmed the new system, for the major socialist movements, even when revolutionary, did not directly defy the legal order. They frightened many people even so and they gave their constituents more persistent influence in politics than violent protest had ever achieved for the lower classes, but they undoubtedly helped turn working class discontent, which would have arisen even without political rights, into peaceful channels.

The political system did not satisfy everyone. Many people, particularly in the countryside, still saw no reason to participate in politics. Sometimes these people were content, but there were many aggrieved elements of society for whom politics was not relevant. Even some workers rejected the political path that socialists pointed out, in favor of more direct action.

Rise of Mass Nationalism. The most widespread new political interests in the period were nationalistic. Nationalism spread to all social classes and to all political persuasions; even socialists were not immune. As politicians and governments turned to the common people for direct support, they had to teach them to be loyal. New schools, military training, and newspapers preached nationalism with unprecedented intensity. Many people remained primarily attached to their church or locality; many felt only a moderate national feeling. We cannot claim to know exactly what most people felt. Undeniably, however, nationalism spread and it was often vigorously held.

The destruction of old loyalties undoubtedly helped the rise of mass nationalism. National school systems tore down local differences while they weakened religious feeling. Urbanization continued to break down old attachments, even to customary family units. Traditional respect for authority and for the upper classes, who were urging nationalism now, aided the conversion; even churchmen often preached nationalism after 1870. Many people were coming into new contact with foreigners and outsiders, as workers from countries like Italy took jobs in France and

Germany and as new cities, particularly in central Europe, mingled many races. Old hates and new could develop in this situation, and could be translated into nationalism. New contact with the state, through welfare programs as well as through education, made national loyalty seem increasingly logical. Beyond these factors, nationalism made many people feel important and gave more meaning to their lives; this has been the most enduring effect of nationalist feeling.

During the period, conservatives became the most vigorous advocates of nationalism, for nationalist issues were popular and they could, obviously, attach people to the existing order. But nationalism was not a conservative force in the true sense. It spread far more widely than did real devotion to existing institutions. It served as a respectable cover for intensely felt grievances. It was preached not by conservatives alone, but by intellectuals and rabble rousers who wanted change and disorder. More important, in foreign policy nationalism was not meant to be conservative. It was exciting and meaningful precisely because it promised at least vicarious adventure abroad. The period from 1870 to 1900 was one of great strain, because the effects of mature industrialization were being felt for the first time. Nationalism helped preserve a superficial calm, but it increasingly projected the anxieties of at least a minority of the population into diplomacy. Aristocrats and bureaucrats who flocked to the banners of imperialism, as well as shopkeepers who rioted against Jews, had found an outlet for violent feelings.

The leading themes of these three decades must be stability and consolidation, however. There were no revolutions, no major diplomatic changes within Europe. In western and central Europe, at least, the main lines of economic development had already been set. Yet there were undercurrents of disturbance. Most of them developed only slowly: social protest in eastern Europe, socialism in the West became major factors only in the 1890's. A mood of confidence seemed at its height by 1900. Yet this mood was a fragile one. Few intellectuals shared it, many workers disputed its bases, and in eastern and southern Europe it had almost no hold. The collapse of the nineteenth-century order came only in the next period, when internal stresses were translated into diplomatic tension. But in these decades, when the issues of liberalism, nationalism, and early industrialization seemed largely resolved, new forces arose to challenge the settlements that had been attained.

POLITICAL CONSOLIDATION

The new regimes, forged during the 1860's and 1870's, were still open to question by liberals and conservatives alike. Catholics almost everywhere still feared political change. Liberals chafed under the limitations of the parliamentary systems in central Europe. Many national groups in

Austria-Hungary remained unappeased. Conservatives of many types doubted the wisdom of concessions made to liberalism. Yet by 1890, many of the leading issues were resolved. The church abandoned most of its resistance to the new regimes. Liberals and conservatives drew together, without merging, partly because of the new threat of socialism but also because of the satisfaction which both movements could take in the new regimes. In France and Italy, there were no major disputes at the political level, for a moderate, opportunistic liberalism seemed to dominate almost everyone in political life. Even in Austria-Hungary, there was hope that political stability could be achieved. These were golden years for the political manipulator: Count Eduard Taaffe in Austria; Bismarck; Agostino Depretis in Italy. Politics seemed dominated by deals rather than ideals, but this is simply another way of saying that the political systems were widely accepted.

The New French Government. France emerged from the war of 1870 and 1871 with no clear regime at all. With Napoleon deposed, an assembly was elected in 1871, and it was monarchist in majority. Peasants and others who were upset by the war and anxious to end it voted for monarchist notables instead of republican unknowns, who had little base in the countryside and who advocated continuing the war to the bitter end. The monarchist majority was itself divided between supporters of the Bourbons (legitimists) and supporters of the Orleans dynasty, and their disagreements over who should be king helped prevent the actual restoration of any monarchy. Furthermore, the government was headed by Adolphe Thiers, a former Orleanist but now a conservative republican. Thiers showed that the regime, though it was neither monarchy nor empire, was capable of forceful action in defense of order and property. In 1871 a bitter revolt broke out in Paris, as a consequence of the hardships suffered during the siege and disappointment over the humiliating peace with Germany. The new Parisian government, the Commune, hoped at least to isolate itself from the rest of France and rule in the spirit of the Great Revolution. Socialists took an active part in the Commune, though few social reforms were actually put into effect. Thiers, after assembling a sufficient armed force, put down the Commune with great brutality. This set back the radical and socialist movement in France, but helped consolidate a moderate republic.

By 1875, the anomaly of a royalist assembly without a king was becoming ridiculous; and active republican campaigners were converting much of France to their cause. Their leader, Léon Gambetta, talked of the necessity of winning a new social level, beneath the monarchist upper middle class, to political interest and power. Here was the first major liberal appeal to the masses. Gambetta and his followers talked mainly to landowning peasants and small-town shopkeepers, people of substance who wanted to defend their property, but people also who were open to an interest in political rights and who were not vigorously religious. France was the only country in Europe with a large social group of this sort, and so France alone saw liberal politics so well established. The republicans argued that their cause was conservative, both because a republic already existed in fact and because it would carefully preserve private property and the existing social order. The republicans gained increasing ground in by-elections. In 1875, the Assembly agreed to establish a definite presidency, chosen by parliament; by one vote, an amendment was passed designating this office the presidency of the republic.

During the following four years, the republican institutions were further defined, though a formal constitution was never drawn up. The royalists were still powerful and hoped to control the presidency until a king could be chosen. But in the meantime, a two-house parliament was established, in which the Senate was intended to be a conservative body and was at first partly appointed by the Assembly, while the Chamber of Deputies was elected by direct, universal suffrage. The president was given almost monarchical powers, to direct the military, to name the ministers, and in case of dispute to dismiss parliament; the first president was a royalist. But parliament was becoming increasingly republican, and in 1877 it forced the president's resignation and established in fact the responsibility of ministers to parliament and the impotence of presidents to dismiss that body.

By 1880, then, France was a republic with a weak executive and an effectively sovereign parliament, and large numbers of Frenchmen had been converted to the support of this regime. Though France had the most radical political system of any major power, its politics, because of the new small-town support for the republic, were among the most conservative socially. In the old liberal tradition, republicans were reluctant to intervene in economic and social matters. Freedom to unionize was granted in 1884, inspection of factory conditions was tightened somewhat, and in the 1890's a few voluntary social insurance plans were enacted, but this was all. By 1900 France was one of the most backward industrial nations in the field of social welfare. The conservatism of the regime was heightened by the power of the bureaucracy, which remained highly centralized and which continued to recruit its members through a standardized program of education and, largely, from the upper classes. Parliament, for all its great power, was unwilling to tamper with bureaucratic initiatives in most cases, and the instability of ministries prevented any consistent control over professional, conservative administrators.

Goals of the New Republic. The new regime had two principal concerns. First, it sought to strengthen France's military and diplomatic position, after the crushing defeat the country had suffered. The government extended conscription, modernized French armaments, and undertook several diplomatic initiatives particularly in the imperial field. Second, it attacked the position of the Catholic Church. Catholics had long been regarded as the natural enemies of liberal republicanism, and their support first of the Empire, then of the monarchist parties confirmed this view. The leading political issue of the 1880's was the proper relationship of church and state. Under Jules Ferry, the government expelled the Jesuits, required state authorization for all teaching orders, and reëstablished provisions for divorce. Most important, it created a system of free and compulsory primary education to compete with the church schools; and it severely limited the use of clergymen in public schools. The result was a rapid reduction of illiteracy and also a growing secularization of popular attitudes.

There were challengers to the new republic. Monarchists did not give up easily. Many nationalists, often former republicans, were distressed at the republic's failure to deal forcefully with Germany. The frequent changes of ministries, already becoming a stereotype of French politics, and a number of financial scandals involving politicians angered many Frenchmen. This varied discontent found a focus, in the late 1880's, in the cause of General Boulanger, a popular if weak leader in whom nationalists saw a vigorous enemy of Germany, some republicans and radicals a refreshing reformer, and monarchists and Catholics a means of defeating the hated republic. Boulanger's popularity was great, both in elections and in street demonstrations, but in 1889, when the government accused him of conspiracy, the general fled and his movement dissolved.

The Boulanger crisis was an important indication that the republic had not converted all its enemies, but the failure of the challenge strengthened the regime. The crucial point was that the enemies of the republic were too divided and too reluctant to engage in the dirty game of politics to form a coherent opposition movement. In parliament, then, there was little dissent, aside from a segment of the small socialist movement. Most deputies agreed that the system worked well, and though they formed factions to dispute specific measures or, most often, the control of the ministries, no serious issues divided them. The mood of pragmatic consensus in French politics was heightened, in the 1890's, by a movement of Catholics toward support of the regime. Led by Pope Leo XIII, who realized that the republic, however undesirable in form and policy, was here to stay, a *ralliement* was proclaimed to induce Catholics to accept the regime and work for gains within it. By no means all Catholics heeded this call, but many did, and the more conservative republicans made concessions in their turn. During the 1890's the harsher measures against the church's educational role were relaxed.

The Dreyfus Affair. The republic was to face one final, passionate crisis before World War I. The Dreyfus case, which came to public attention in 1898, forced republicans to choose between defense of state and army and the defense of justice and individual rights. Captain Alfred Dreyfus, a Jewish army officer, was framed and falsely condemned for treason. Despite growing doubts of his guilt the army resisted any retrial. Leading politicians and intellectuals were divided. Liberal and radical republicans urged fair treatment for Dreyfus. Army men, most Catholics, and conservatives generally insisted that the honor of the army be defended. Some of the anti-Dreyfusards were against the republic altogether, seeing this case as another opportunity to protest it, but many had no animus against the regime so long as it remained conservative.

One of the leading results of the affair was the formation of two separate republican parties, the Radicals and the Independents (conservatives). Both parties were loosely organized, so the frequent realignments of French politics continued to a degree. But their division was important. It reflected the fact that acceptance of the republic was now sufficiently widespread that conservative-liberal disputes could occur within the framework of the regime.

The Dreyfus affair also led to a final attack, by the Radicals, on the church. The supporters of Dreyfus captured the government in 1899 and sought to reform the institutions that had led to the crisis. Efforts were made to republicanize the army and, between 1902 and 1905, religious orders were subjected to increasing regulation. Finally, in 1905, the Radicals took the unprecedented step of separating church and state. No longer would the church receive state financial support and no longer would the state nominate Catholic prelates. Many Catholics were disgruntled by this measure, but on the whole it was accepted and removed a perennially disruptive problem from French politics.

By the early twentieth century, then, the republic was firmly established. It had gained wide support in French society. It commanded the allegiance not only of liberals, but also of moderate conservatives. Conservatives of the Orleanist type, particularly, found it possible to accept the republican framework. Even many legitimists and Catholics abandoned their political traditions in favor of a restrained republicanism. Most socialists supported the regime. The republic had settled the leading political issues of the nineteenth century: the structure of government and the relationship of church and state were no longer in serious dispute. The crises of the late nineteenth century should not obscure the growing harmony among the major political traditions in France, and the relative ease of their resolution consolidated the republic still further.

Structure of Italian Government. In Italy, the stabilization of the regime was less complete, but the character of Italian politics, before 1890, resembled the French in some respects. Governmental structure was, to be sure, far more conservative, for the monarch retained substantial powers independent of parliament and suffrage was quite restricted. But most politicians accepted the regime. There was no clear formation of political parties, reflecting, as in France, a wide agreement about government policies. In the 1870's, there was some division of parliament between Left and Right. The Right, in the moderate liberal tradition of Cavour, stood for gentle treatment of the church, avoidance of social reform, and a moderate foreign policy. The Left, under Depretis, was more radically liberal, urging educational reforms, more public works, a more vigorous and nationalistic diplomacy, and a harsher policy toward the church. The Left won out, in 1876, and did extend state education, restrict religious orders, and expand the suffrage (to about 7 per cent of the adult male population). But clearly, the differences between Right and Left were not great. Italian politics was dominated by a process of "transformism," in which deputies, no matter what their campaign promises, were transformed once in Rome to full support of the existing system. Political leaders, like Depretis, easily controlled the parliament by offering favors and outright bribes to their fellow legislators. Ministries changed hands often and there were intense factional fights over offices, but there were no fundamental policy disputes within the system.

The problem was, of course, that the political system embraced such a small part of Italy. The lower classes were excluded altogether, which retarded the growth of real political protest but meant that radicalism, when it did arise, would be hostile to the regime. And the Catholic Church, which accepted new regimes elsewhere, continued to refuse allegiance to the Italian state. The Pope still forbade Catholics to vote or to hold political office. All of this facilitated the consensus within the political system, for neither radicalism nor conservatism found expression in it, but it made this consensus far less real than in France. And in the 1890's, the fragility of the government was revealed by attacks from outside the narrow political structure.

In France and Italy, the degree of political harmony that existed rested primarily on a liberal basis. The concessions to this harmony, particularly important in France, came largely from the conservative side. In Germany and Austria, a partial reconciliation of diverse political traditions occurred also, but mainly on conservative terms. And in Austria, as in Italy, the reconciliation ultimately proved unsuccessful, for too many elements were omitted from the political system altogether.

Bismarck's Germany. The structure of the German state changed little after 1871. A number of state parliaments adopted universal suffrage by the 1880's, but Prussia continued to rely on its class voting system. The national Reichstag was democratically elected, but it was restrained by the Prussian-dominated upper house, and the powers of parliament as a whole remained limited. Able to initiate only certain types of legislation, it relied mainly on submission of proposals by the government. The chancellor and his ministers were responsible only to the emperor. Still, a parliament did exist and the government did need to arrange a parliamentary majority to approve such vital matters as the military budget. To this extent, liberals could take genuine comfort.

During the 1870's, the central support for the new regime came, in fact, from the National Liberal party. This group still stood for constitutional government, an efficient and united German state, secularization of German life, and material progress without social reform. On its left were two smaller groups, both of which were critical of the existing regime. One was the socialist party, the other the liberal Progressives, a radical-liberal party that continued to insist on fully parliamentary government. On the right, the Conservative party represented Prussian landlords and continued to be suspicious of the liberal trappings of Bismarck's state. Finally, a Catholic Center party also stood aloof from the state, though it favored moderate constitutional government, because it feared an attack on the church from the Protestant, Prussian-led regime. Bismarck, backed by the National Liberals, at first enlarged the scope of political controversy by attacking the Catholic Church from 1872 to 1877. Liberals feared the conservatism of the church, while Bismarck suspected Catholics of separatist impulses and disloyalty to united Germany. In the resultant struggle, called the *Kulturkampf*, or battle for civilization, the government expelled the Jesuits, increased state regulation of clerical education, and made public education more secular. This alienated the Center party, of course, but also concerned Protestant Conservatives, who feared an attack on all organized religion. In its first decade, then, Bismarck's Germany seemed far from winning general political support.

By the late 1870's, however, the situation began to change. Bismarck realized that his essentially conservative government structure could not rely on liberal support alone, for even the National Liberals were demanding concessions. The conservatives began to turn to the new regime, for they realized that it was not really hostile to their interests. They could accept a parliament and even universal suffrage. They found that, by appealing to peasants in the name of rural solidarity and by using nationalist arguments, they could win considerable support at the polls. Nationalism was a new force for conservatives, who had been attached to older states such as Prussia, to the Lutheran Church, and to the monarchy, but now it penetrated conservative ranks. Further, Prussian landlords were forced to turn to the state for assistance in the agricultural crisis of the 1870's, and Bismarck responded, in 1879, by introducing a high tariff on imports of food. And, the Catholic Church, under the new Pope Leo XIII, made clear its acceptance of a united Germany, in return for a substantial relaxation of the harsher measures of the *Kulturkampf*. Finally, all three major parties—the Liberals, the Center, and the Conservatives—agreed on the need for action to fend off the new threat of socialism.

From 1879 onward, then, the German government relied primarily on a coalition of conservatives and Catholics, both now reconciled to the novel features of Bismarck's system. The National Liberals accepted the system also—though they disagreed on some specific measures—in return for the government's protection of business interests and the degree of parliamentary power that had been achieved. And, trapped between resurgent conservatism and socialism, liberal strength in Germany began to dwindle rapidly. As in most of western and central Europe, the range of dispute between conservatism and liberalism was now greatly reduced, but here liberalism itself was a declining force. It was this fact, as well as the new degree of political harmony, that allowed Bismarck to reverse the partially liberal trend of the previous decade. The conciliation of the Catholics and the new tariff law already contradicted liberal wishes. In 1878, against liberal opposition, an antisocialist law was passed that forbade all associations and publications with socialist tendencies. During the 1880's, three major social insurance laws were passed, covering accidents, illness, and old age. Bismarck intended these primarily to win workers away from socialism, but they also appealed to the paternalistic social consciousness of many conservatives and Catholics. Here was another blow to traditional liberal principles of a free economy, but the liberals were powerless to object. By 1890, all the major political tendencies, aside from the new socialist movement, had been drawn to support of the regime, and Bismarck had proved that the government could rely on various party coalitions and, on certain vital issues, could command almost universal party support.

Austria's Coalition Government. In Austria, as in Germany, the dominant political force of the 1870's was a liberal party, anxious to increase the limited powers of parliament but willing to work fully within the existing framework for any reforms. A number of the usual measures were taken in the field of church-state relations, including a secularization of the school system and the introduction of civil marriage. Several reforms were enacted in the judicial system, in the army, and in economic legislation. But in 1879, the emperor broke with the Liberals and entrusted the government to the talented Count Eduard Taaffe, who ruled until 1893. Taaffe managed to assemble a supporting coalition composed of Catholics, German conservatives, Slavs, Poles, and Czechs. The minority nationalities were wooed by local concessions, such as granting the Czechs a majority in the Bohemian diet and a Czech section of the University of Prague. Liberals were excluded from the coalition and resisted many of Taaffe's specific measures, but as in Germany their power now began to wane. For a limited time, Taaffe's policies won support for the government from almost all politically conscious elements. Even the Czechs, who had been bitterly disappointed by their failure to win a status equal to the Hungarians, abandoned their abstention from parliamentary participation.

The base of the regime remained quite narrow, to be sure. A highly limited suffrage excluded the lower classes, though there was a partial extension of the franchise in the 1880's. More important, even Taaffe could not mend the divisions among nationalities. His concessions to the Slavs angered the Germans yet failed to conciliate a new generation of more aggressive Slav nationalists. The peace among the nationalities was only relative even at the political level and did not extend to many groups that were not represented; and it did not last. Still, relative peace there was, and combined with the calming of liberal-conservative conflict it provided a period of some stability in which the government was able to introduce improvements in administrative structure, in education, and in social welfare.

Political Satisfaction in Britain. In Britain, of course, liberals and conservatives had long been committed to the existing regime; the terms of political debate remained in many ways quite different from those of the continent. There was a further extension of the suffrage in 1884, making it almost universal for males, but this was not a major change. The Conservative party continued to adjust to a democratic order. Under Disraeli, the Conservative government of 1874 to 1880 liberalized trade union laws and introduced government inspection of housing and public health. Increasingly, however, the party sought popular support by an active policy in foreign affairs, under the banners of a vigorous nationalism. The Liberal party was even less interested in internal reforms, for with the new suffrage measures and some further improvement in the educational system (primary education was made compulsory in 1880), their goals seemed almost entirely achieved. Despite the distinctiveness of the English political system and political traditions, then, English conservatives and liberals shared with their continental counterparts a growing satisfaction with the *status quo*. A few changes were necessary to accommodate to a democratic system and a few minor reforms were still sought, but an acceptable order had been achieved.

New Political Harmony. For all the important national differences, then, certain common political forces were at work in western and central Europe. Traditional arguments about the nature of the regime were gone or muted, as conservatives accepted some form of parliamentary power and, usually, some degree of democracy. In this, they accepted policy lines that had been suggested by conservative leaders in the previous period. The conservative conversion was aided by the new flexibility of the Catholic Church, outside of Italy, which proved willing to tolerate not only partially liberal political systems but also a reduction of the political power and the rights in education, marriage laws, and censorship that the church had traditionally enjoyed. As part of their conversion to a more modern outlook, conservative groups in many areas accepted nationalism, which had previously been associated almost exclusively with liberalism. Nationalism allowed conservative politicians to win widespread popular support, essential in a democratic age. Under its banners, they could defend the power of state and army and protect the interests of industrialists and landlords with national tariffs. With its new outlook conservatism won the support of many peasants and many members of the middle class, including big businessmen; no longer was it simply the tool of a traditional aristocracy. This new support confirmed the changes in the conservative approach, but also converted large groups to a defense of older conservative interests, including a resistance to further change. Conservatives opposed additional political reform. They resisted the growing agitation of the urban lower classes, particularly the socialists; efforts by conservatives in Germany and Britain to introduce some social reforms gave way increasingly to a sullen opposition to socialist demands. Conservatives demanded and received protection for the army, the bastion of order and discipline in society. They at least modified attacks on religion. Save in France, they maintained their devotion to a monarchy. And uniformly they defended property, particularly holdings in land.

In many ways, the evolution of liberalism was more startling than that of conservatism. By 1890, liberals had achieved many of their basic goals. Governments now firmly protected business interests; equality under the law was fully established; religious freedom was complete and the power of the churches severely limited; and other individual liberties were protected (though a strong police apparatus was maintained on the continent and often, with liberal consent, used against labor agitators). Parliaments existed everywhere, though liberals often had to accept, with varying degrees of reluctance, limitations on their activities. Largely satisfied now with the existing order, liberals turned increasingly to its defense, against recalcitrant conservatives certainly, but primarily against socialists. They could join conservatives to resist further change and to protect property. In central Europe, liberalism itself dwindled as its former supporters turned either to an outright conservatism or, if they remained unsatisfied, to the new socialist left. Where a strong liberalism survived, as in Britain and France, it did so either by maintaining a sense of conservative threat, as the French Radicals did with their war against the church, or by developing a new interest in social reform. Everywhere, traditional liberalism seemed to have shot its bolt.

Growing political harmony was, then, an overriding trend in the period. Statesmen like Bismarck could move back and forth from liberal to conservative support. Liberals and conservatives directly cooperated on many issues and in some cases, such as France, there were for a time no formal party lines between them. Both movements were largely content with a pragmatic politics, for the great ideals had been realized or abandoned. Much was accomplished within this harmonious framework toward improving the parliamentary system, extending the suffrage, and providing rudimentary social welfare, particularly state-supported education. Yet the new framework was not fully satisfactory. Too many groups were effectively excluded from it; too many interests, including the taste for political ideals, remained unappeased. An undercurrent of protest developed everywhere, forcing the established political movements increasingly to the defensive. Precisely because they had been so successful in resolving older political problems, the politicians opened the way for new issues to dominate the scene, issues which they were by tradition and training ill-equipped to handle.

DIPLOMACY: EUROPEAN STABILITY AND WORLD EMPIRE

The unification and increasing power of Germany opened a new chapter in European diplomatic history. In the long run, the addition of this great power to the European roster was profoundly disturbing, when Germany yearned for status commensurate with its might and when the older powers resisted its pretentions. But until 1890 at least, and to some degree beyond, the diplomatic situation seemed unusually stable in Europe. The most logical explosion, between Germany and a vengeful France, simply did not occur, though there was a war scare in 1875.

There were a number of reasons for diplomatic calm. The need for internal stabilization was one factor. The leading diplomats themselves, notably Bismarck, were relatively free from political pressures and restrained in their ambitions; and this quality permeated the lower ranks of diplomatic personnel, who were still drawn largely from the aristocracy and who possessed both experience and flexibility in negotiations. Unquestionably, the recent changes in the European map made diplomatic tensions more dangerous, and this was widely recognized. The unification of Italy and Germany eliminated two major power vacuums on the continent, where a great power could satisfy its ambitions without immediately encountering another power. Probes within Europe, then, were less easy. Finally, the reorientation of diplomatic interest toward world empire helped modify tensions within Europe. Imperial gains could satisfy very real aggressive impulses without threatening major war. Imperial interests added so many new dimensions to foreign policy that the alignment of diplomatic friendships and hostilities became very confused. One of the leading causes of the European peace was the welter of enmities which tended to cancel each other out. A brief glance at the interests of the major powers should make this clear.

Britain and Germany. Britain maintained its traditional desire to prevent a single great power from dominating the continent, and particularly the Low Countries. Even in the 1870's this led to some fear of the new Germany, but so long as the Germans followed Bismarck's policy of conciliating England there was no intense disquiet; and at least at the popular level, traditional hostility toward France balanced the attention to Germany. More important to Britain, so long as the continent was calm, were imperial interests in Asia and Africa. Here the principal opponents were Russia, as had long been the case in the Near and Far East, and now France in Africa.

Germany's main enemy was of course France, for there was a widespread feeling that France would, sooner or later, try to regain Alsace-Lorraine. Under Bismarck, Germany professed to be a satiated power, uninterested in further gains, and on the whole it behaved as such; only later did a sense of unfulfilled destiny begin to arise. A modest German imperialism began in the 1880's, in Africa, which conflicted with British interests to a degree; there was some fear of Russia, without any specific quarrels, simply because of the vastness and nearness of that country. Germany could and did concentrate on preserving what it had gained, particularly against possible French objection.

Basically, then, the two greatest powers in Europe were firmly committed to a European *status quo.* Germany maintained its army superiority, despite efforts by other states to imitate its conscription, armaments, and trained general staff. Germany's growing population and expanding industry, which stressed heavy industries obviously relevant to war, could only increase its diplomatic influence. Britain was unquestionably declining in a relative sense, but it preserved the world's leading navy, one of the three most advanced industrial economies, and financial resources that were in themselves a powerful diplomatic tool.

Other European Powers. France, the traditional continental great power, had clearly lost status, not only because of its defeat but also because of the relative stagnancy of its industry and its population size. France had important cards still, including a much improved army and, after 1890, a rapidly growing heavy industrial sector; its financial resources were second only to Britain's. But on the whole France was now in the second rank of great powers and its leaders sensibly recognized this. Hence, while its obvious enemy was Germany, nothing was done to aggravate the enmity. And growing imperial ambitions created new and distracting conflicts with Italy and Britain.

Russia remained an expansionist power throughout the period. Great size and the beginnings of industrialization made Russia an obvious diplomatic force, though it is important to note that its effective strength was consistently overrated by other states. Throughout most of the period its attention was focused on the Far East, and its traditional interest in the Balkans and the Ottoman Empire was muted as a result. Hence, though there was potential friction with Austria in the Balkans, Russia's main opponent was Britain.

Austria, clearly now a fading power, maintained a largely defensive foreign policy. It abandoned any thought of recouping its losses in Germany, thus eliminating a potential source of friction, and in fact clung to Germany as one of the main props of its diplomacy. Austria's potential enemies were Russia and Italy, both of which had interests in the Balkans. Austrian policy, though not aggressive, itself turned increasingly to the Balkans. Here was the only area in which Austria could hope to advance, for it lacked the resources and navy for overseas empire. Here was the area, certainly, which had to be protected from any incursion by another great power.

Italy was only on the margins of great power status, and this fact, sensed and resented by Italian nationalists, contributed to a perpetually aggressive Italian diplomacy. Yet Italy lacked the military and industrial strength to become, by itself, a really disturbing force. Its ambitions took two general directions. There was *Italia irredenta,* unredeemed Italy, areas which had once been Italian and which still had some Italian population, mainly around the Adriatic. Here, Italy's main opponent, a traditional one, was Austria. There was a newer interest in North Africa, where Italy might gain prestige and territory to which its excess population could be sent, and where it might revive the memory of Roman imperial holdings. Here the opponent was France.

Continental Alliances. Out of this maze of interests and hostilities, an alliance system was forged by 1882. Bismarck was able to play on the diversity of interests to align most major powers with Germany; and since Germany's policy was pacific, this was in itself a prime factor in preserving the peace. But except for the link between Germany and Austria, all the alliances were somewhat tentative, because the allies themselves had conflicting goals. Defensive alliances could be concluded, but offensive pacts could not; and no one, certainly not Bismarck, could count on support for aggression. This, too, helped preserve the peace.

The key to the alliance system was renewed trouble in the Balkans, in 1875. Insurrections against Turkish rule broke out in Bosnia and Herzegovina, northwest of Serbia, and spread to Bulgaria. Serbia and Montenegro declared war on Turkey, and Russia joined them in 1877. After winning a rather painful victory, Russia claimed large Ottoman holdings on the

Black Sea and set up an extensive Bulgarian state, capable of dominating the Balkans and designed to serve as a vehicle for Russian influence. Neither Austria-Hungary nor Britain could accept this, and in
1878 Bismarck, anxious for peace, called the Congress of Berlin to settle
the issue. The Congress accepted a smaller Bulgaria, and balanced this by
giving new territories to Serbia and by granting full independence to
Serbia, Montenegro, and Rumania; Britain gained Cyprus, to counterbalance Russia in the area; and Austria won the right to administer Bosnia-
Herzegovina. France, finally, was encouraged to take over Tunisia, on the
principle that every great power should gain something.

The Congress of Berlin had several clear results. In the Balkans, it contented almost no one. Greeks resented British control of Cyprus, Bulgari-
ans resented their diminished territories, Serbs resented Austrian control
of Bosnia. Ultimately, these diverse grievances were to explode. But in the
short run, a measure of peace was restored to the area. A fear of Bulgaria
helped distract Serbia from hatred of Austria, and the two countries even
allied defensively in the 1880's. Most important, the great powers worked
for order in the Balkans and turned their expansionist interests elsewhere;
and so long as this was the case, no amount of purely Balkan unrest could
disturb European harmony.

Bismarck, rightly concerned about Russia's anger at its losses in the
Berlin Congress, now concluded the Dual Alliance with Austria, guaranteeing mutual protection against attack by Russia and benevolent neutrality in case of attack by France. Here was a diplomatic novelty: an
enduring alliance, whose terms were secret, concluded in peacetime. It
foreshadowed many similar efforts. The Russians feared this new alliance,
and Bismarck sought to avoid involvement in any of Austria's troubles in
the Balkans. So in 1881 the Three Emperors pledged their neutrality in
case of war with an outside power and provided for consultation in Balkan
affairs. Russia and Austria, natural enemies, were turned by Bismarck
and by their own sense of weakness into uneasy friends; and a lid was
clamped on the Balkans, the source of their discord. Finally, in 1882, Italy
joined the Austro-German alliance, forming the Triple Alliance, out of
resentment at the French acquisition of Tunis. The whole of European
diplomacy now revolved around Germany; of the two outside powers,
Britain was friendly and actually had a loose naval agreement with Italy
and Austria, Germany's allies; and France, carefully isolated, was powerless to disturb the European peace.

Collapse of Bismarck's System. Bismarck's complex system came
tumbling down in 1890, when the Chancellor himself was forced out of
power. The new Emperor, William II, wanted to be his own master; in
addition, there was resentment against Bismarck's antisocialist repression
and against the very complexity of his diplomacy. Specifically, Bismarck's
opponents felt that Germany should drop the Russian alliance, as it
conflicted with German obligations to Austria; and they won out. Germany
was left with the Triple Alliance alone. Russia, now a free agent, was
assiduously wooed by France, who saw a chance to end its isolation and

who could offer Russia funds for industrial investment and protection against the German-Austrian alliance. In 1893 the Franco-Russian alliance, a loose agreement of mutual defense, was concluded. A new balance of power, a confrontation of new alliance systems, was in the making.

For the time being, however, European tension did not increase. France had no desire to incite Russia against Austria, and Russia had no wish to encourage France against Germany. Both were primarily concerned with imperial ventures in which their alliance did no good at all. And there remained one power uncommitted to the alliance system; Britain could still intervene on either side to prevent war. Germany had clearly lost ground in the diplomatic reshuffling, but even its statesmen saw no reason for anxiety.

Imperialism. For all the powers except Austria-Hungary, diplomatic fulfillment in this period came increasingly from imperial conquests. The very stability of European diplomacy allowed states to turn their attention to the many parts of the world where weak political structures and technical backwardness allowed easy gains. Britain already had a vast empire and had gradually added to it during the nineteenth century; Russia, too, had a long tradition of advance in Asia. Thwarted in the Balkans and desperately anxious for diplomatic success to counterbalance internal agitation, Russia increased its thrust for empire in the 1880's. Equally important, other powers entered the competition. France, not an absolute newcomer to empire, saw imperial acquisitions as a balm to national pride after 1871. Italy and, increasingly, Germany viewed empire as a natural attribute of great-power status. The United States and Japan added their own imperial ambitions. All these ambitions reinforced one another. One gain pushed other powers to similar gains, to preserve their prestige and, often, to protect existing holdings from outside threat. As a result, many states gained their empires without being clearly imperialist. British liberals and, later, French radicals opposed empires in theory, but in practice they could not resist the competitive pressure. There was enthusiasm for empire, to be sure, but part of the process was a reflex action.

Small groups and individuals played a major role in triggering imperial expansion, particularly in the 1880's. Karl Peters, intensely nationalist, went to East Africa and began negotiating with native chiefs in Germany's name. Through nationalist groups and business organizations at home, he pressed for German recognition of his holdings, and ultimately Bismarck yielded, without great interest. Missionaries, adventurers, nationalists, profiteers — and combinations of these, often in the same person — staked out countless claims or at least fell into situations from which only intervention by their government could rescue them. Only gradually and incompletely did imperial expansion become a matter of formal state policy and conscious planning.

Despite its somewhat haphazard aspect, the drive for empire quickly penetrated all the available areas of the world. Only the Near East was not fully carved up, because its proximity to Europe raised the danger of war if any power advanced too far; but outside the Ottoman Empire,

Britain took Kuwait and other East Arab territories, and Britain and Russia competed for influence in Persia.

New Empires in Asia and Africa. The Far East was more completely partitioned. At first, attention was focused on the peripheries. Russia expanded into central Asia and competed with Britain for control of Afghanistan. France began building its power in Asia by completing a take-over of Indochina in the 1880's; and Britain, always anxious to protect India, acquired Burma as a buffer state in 1886. France, Britain, Germany, and the United States all vied for the Pacific Oceania; Germany and the United States divided control of Samoa, and France developed its Polynesian holding.

In the 1890's, imperialist pressure began to touch China itself. Russia started work on the trans-Siberian railway and coveted part of Manchuria to shorten the route. Japan sought influence and territory in China to counter Russian pressure. In 1894 Japan defeated China in the Sino-Japanese War and gained Formosa; at about the same time, Russia acquired railroad concessions in Manchuria. The scramble was on. The great powers did not win territories outright, but gained 99-year leases from the Chinese government and in effect controlled the territory completely. Russia leased Port Arthur in 1897; Britain gained Weihaiwei in 1898; Germany leased Kiaochow in 1896; and France leased Kwangchowan in 1899. Only Italy asked for territory and was refused. At the very end of the period, Russia occupied Manchuria without the formality of a lease. The full partition of China seemed only a matter of time.

The other area of primary imperial pressure was in Africa. Portugal, with British protection, increased its control of Angola and Mozambique. Belgium gained the Congo, Germany won Tanganyika and Southwest Africa, and Italy won part of Somaliland. The main empires, however, were British and French. France's holdings ran from east to west, including most of West Africa, the Sahara, Algeria and Tunisia, and part of Somaliland. British holdings, except for a large pocket in West Africa, ran north-south, from South Africa through Rhodesia, Uganda, Kenya, the Sudan, and Egypt. The two paths crossed in 1898, when French and British expeditionary forces met at Fashoda. The French backed down, amid great excitement, but they retained a vast empire. By 1900, only Ethiopia remained fully independent of European empire, while Liberia, Morocco, and Tripoli were partially so.

Causes of Imperialism. The outlines of imperial expansion can be briefly summarized, but the magnitude of the venture remains truly staggering. Between 1880 and 1900, most of the world not already essentially European was gobbled up. Certainly, this was a massive assertion of Europe's confidence and sense of superiority. A number of factors cooperated to produce the imperial drive. Relative calm at home, obvious technical superiority, the adventurism of individuals, and particularly the constant rivalry among imperial states — all this contributed, but there were other influences. A sense of mission developed among many advocates of empire. White men had a peculiar burden, an obligation to help

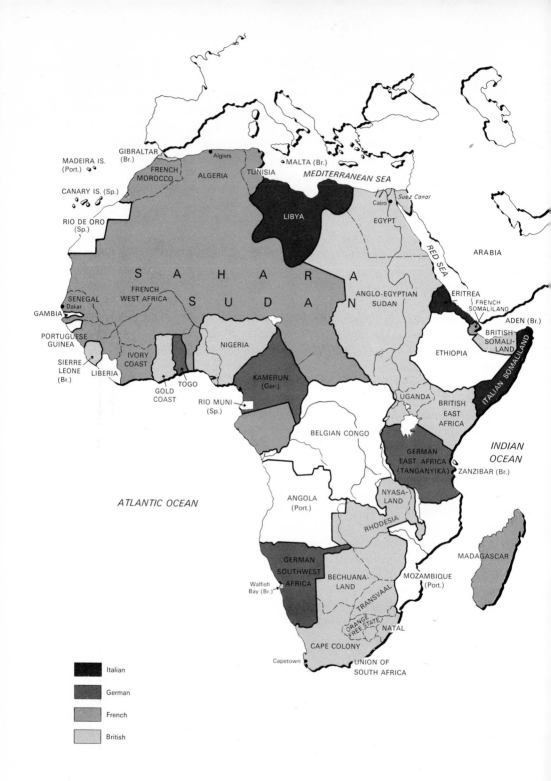

MADEIRA IS. (Port.)

GIBRALTAR (Br.)

CANARY IS. (Sp.)

RIO DE ORO (Sp.)

FRENCH MOROCCO

ALGERIA

Algiers

TUNISIA

MALTA (Br.)

MEDITERRANEAN SEA

Suez Canal

Cairo

EGYPT

ARABIA

LIBYA

RED SEA

S   A   H   A   R   A

SUDAN

SENEGAL

FRENCH WEST AFRICA

Dakar

GAMBIA

PORTUGUESE GUINEA

SIERRE LEONE (Br.)

LIBERIA

IVORY COAST

GOLD COAST

TOGO

RIO MUNI (Sp.)

NIGERIA

KAMERUN (Ger.)

ANGLO-EGYPTIAN SUDAN

ERITREA

FRENCH SOMALILAND

ADEN (Br.)

BRITISH SOMALI-LAND

ETHIOPIA

ITALIAN SOMALILAND

UGANDA

BRITISH EAST AFRICA

BELGIAN CONGO

GERMAN EAST AFRICA (TANGANYIKA)

ZANZIBAR (Br.)

INDIAN OCEAN

ATLANTIC OCEAN

ANGOLA (Port.)

NYASA-LAND

RHODESIA

MOZAMBIQUE (Port.)

MADAGASCAR

GERMAN SOUTHWEST AFRICA

Walfish Bay (Br.)

BECHUANA-LAND

TRANSVAAL

ORANGE FREE STATE

NATAL

CAPE COLONY

Capetown

UNION OF SOUTH AFRICA

Italian

German

French

British

IMPERIALISM IN AFRICA, 1914

the lesser peoples rise to civilization—defined in European terms, of course; or, if they could not rise, and there was some doubt about this, at least they should be controlled by civilized powers. A number of strands of European culture went into this sentiment. There was a strong Christian sense of the need to convert heathens to Christianity and to other aspects of European life; this was the great age of missionary activity, both Protestant and Catholic. Liberalism, despite a general bias against empire, could be enlisted for programs of pacification, economic development, and education in colonial areas. Imperialist arguments coincided with Social Darwinism, in the stress on the rule of the fittest, and with the growing belief in a hierarchy of superior and inferior races. And certainly, there was ample support for imperialism in the rising nationalism of the period. The white man's burden could be seen as largely the Englishman's burden, because of his superiority to other Europeans; and national honor seemed to call for constant expansions of empire.

There was a general, though by no means universal, popular enthusiasm for imperialism, heightened by propaganda from imperialist organizations and by the attention of the new mass press. Many clerks and workers found their lives brightened by exciting tales of imperial adventure and felt a vicarious satisfaction at the evidence of the superiority of their nation and culture.

Furthermore, two other, related arguments were used to support imperialism, which had some influence on general public opinion and which particularly served special interest groups that could exert pressure on politicians. There was a widespread belief that great nations were great particularly because of large navies; and navies needed coaling stations throughout the world. All the major nations stepped up naval programs by the early 1890's. In Germany, the Navy League, combining business and military men, became one of the principal advocates of associated imperial and naval expansion.

A number of economic arguments were put forward for imperialism. In particular, groups of industrialists cited the need for more markets and for a secure supply of resources. There was also some feeling that expanding populations needed new outlets for settlement, without having to leave the jurisdiction of the mother country. It is possible to show that all of these arguments were wrong: the colonies acquired were almost uniformly unsuited for European settlement or were already overpopulated; market opportunities were limited in the backward areas, and trade continued to flow primarily to other industrial countries; resources, although available in a few cases, such as the Congo, could have been acquired at less expense in a free market. Though individual concerns could make a fortune from empire, the total cost of administration far exceeded the return. But many people believed the economic arguments, and they served as a final justification for imperial policies.

Europe's sense of confidence, then, permeated the imperial effort. The conviction that it was valid to impose one's own culture universally and the belief in national economic and military strength made up the imperialist mentality. But imperialism also reflected serious uneasiness in Europe. Christian missionaries were supremely confident in "backward" areas, but Christians in Europe grew increasingly concerned about the decline of religion. Aristocrats found jobs in imperial administrations that could only partially compensate for their loss of power at home. The nationalism and racism that supported imperialism were also being used to express vague new political and economic grievances. Finally, the economic arguments employed to support imperialism reflected not only a sense of economic vigor but also a new fear of declining economic opportunities, a fear reflected in other aspects of government policies as well. Imperialism did not, as Lenin argued at the time, represent the last stage of capitalism exactly, but it did reveal some serious economic weaknesses.

THE ECONOMY

Total production rose significantly during the period from 1870 to 1900, aided by new inventions and new products. Heavy industry continued its rapid advance. Coal production doubled in Britain and rose fifteen times in Germany, while chemical and electrical industries grew to gigantic proportions. New consumer products, such as bicycles, artificial fibers, and automobiles were introduced. National and international trade rose rapidly, with the extension of railroad networks and steamshipping, and new sales outlets, such as department stores, arose to handle the increased volume of goods. Germany was now clearly in the industrial big leagues. France suffered from the loss of Alsace-Lorraine, but in the 1890's began an unprecedentedly rapid growth. Austria in the 1880's and Italy in the 1890's initiated substantial industrialization. Even Russia was launched in factory industry by the 1890's.

With increasing production came increasing wealth. Real wages rose significantly in most urban areas, by 30 per cent or more in most cases. Profits advanced even more rapidly. Better diets, clothing, housing, and recreation all reflected the new wealth, and the lower classes could now afford luxuries such as newspapers or union dues.

New Economic Trends. The structure of the economy was changing. Big business, suggested in the previous period, took firm hold. New equipment, such as electric turbines, was extremely expensive, and only large firms based on corporate organization and relying on industrial investment banks could usually afford it. Beyond this, manufacturers increasingly realized that size had its own advantages, allowing firms to control markets and resources to a substantial degree. Particularly in Germany, a movement of cartellization developed, in which giant individual companies cooperated on such matters as pricing and market allocation. In the major industries, the days of economic individualism and the competition of small units were clearly over. Two firms, in Germany, controlled 90 per cent of the total production of electrical machinery. Huge steamship companies and the department stores spread the principles of big business into commerce. The growth of firms and the new restraints on competition accounted for the great rise in profits. They had political implications too, for big companies and industrial combinations increasingly influenced government economic and social policies. And the power of big business helped call into being a powerful labor movement, itself organized along lines of great size and centralized control.

The economic trends of the period were disturbing to many groups. Most professional people and small businessmen suffered at least in their relative economic standing, compared to industrialists and bankers, and many were directly threatened by the new business forms. Traditionalists were shocked by the decline of economic individualism and by the orgies of speculation that accompanied the exchange of corporate shares. Many workers resented the huge, anonymous managements that employed them, resented the rising wealth of the barons of industry. The economic dynamism of the period, while a source of rapid material advance, had many unsettling effects.

Economic Crises. Furthermore, there were weaknesses in the economic structure itself. An agricultural crisis began in the mid-1870's that lasted to some degree until World War I. This was not due to crop failures, as in the early nineteenth century, but to an overabundance of production. Grain from the New World and eastern Europe poured into European markets, and European farmers could not compete with its low price. Some switched to other forms of production, but there was a real decline in agricultural earnings and in land values. Even British landlords, long at the forefront of commercial agriculture, felt the pinch. Many producers converted to livestock or dairy farming; cooperatives were formed to promote agricultural modernization; new techniques were introduced in all branches of production—the rural population was not without resources. But the agricultural sector remained relatively depressed, and this limited one of the most obvious markets for industrial goods. In the cities, the wages of the lower classes, though rising, failed to keep pace with the increase in production; this, too, restricted the market. The simple fact was that industrial countries had created the capacity for mass production, but even in banishing poverty for most people they had not created a mass market, in which most people had money to spend well beyond their subsistence needs.

The most tangible result of this imbalance between output and market was a series of economic crises, particularly in the mid-1870's and the early 1890's; Britain, whose economy faced increasing competition, suffered also in the 1880's. Recessions began now with a financial collapse, due to overspeculation, which dried up investment funds on which heavy industry depended for its sales. The results were unemployment and falling production. Recessions did not cause the misery that occurred in their counterparts earlier in the century, mainly because there was no famine, but hundreds of thousands of workers might suffer and many

ANNUAL OUTPUT OF COAL, IRON, AND STEEL: 1867—1913.

In millions of metric tons

COAL

BRITAIN
- 292 (1913)
- 184.5 (1900)
- 11.8 (1871)

GERMANY
- 279 (1913)
- 89.3 (1900)
- 37.9 (1871)

FRANCE
- 40.8 (1913)
- 26.1 (1900)
- 13.3 (1871)

RUSSIA
- 36.3 (1913)
- 16.5 (1902)
- .4 (1867)

IRON

BRITAIN
- 10.2 (1913)
- 8 (1900)
- 6.5 (1871)

GERMANY
- 19.3 (1913)
- 4.7 (1900)
- 1.5 (1871)

FRANCE
- 4 (1910)
- 2 (1900)
- 1.4 (1871)

RUSSIA
- 4.6 (1913)
- 2.6 (1902)
- .3 (1867)

STEEL

BRITAIN
- 8 (1913)
- 6.5 (1900)
- 1.3 (1880)

GERMANY
- 18.9 (1913)
- 13.1 (1900)
- 8 (1880)

FRANCE
- 4.7 (1913)
- 3.4 (1900)
- .4 (1880)

RUSSIA
- 4.3 (1913)
- 2.3 (1900)

small businessmen went under. And the increasingly international character of the industrial market guaranteed that a crisis in one area would spread widely.

Industrialists, realizing the new tightness of the market, took a number of remedial steps. Cartels and other market arrangements were one response. Oppressed by a sense of declining opportunities at home, many businessmen invested abroad; France poured over a third of its total capital into foreign ventures during the period. Investors might well earn handsome interest rates from their loans, but they contributed to the lack of full development of the home market by withdrawing their funds. Businessmen sought and received assistance from their governments to modify economic pressures. A new wave of protectionism spread in Europe. France, Germany, and Italy reversed previous policies of free trade, and Austria and Russia raised their tariffs, to protect both agriculture and industry. Business groups, as we have seen, pressed also for imperial conquests and often played a major role in increasing military expenditures, for government spending on armaments provided an obvious market for heavy industrial goods that might be difficult to dispose of otherwise.

Political Implications. Clearly, the economy of the period created major problems beyond the economic sphere. There is no need to suggest a capitalist conspiracy to drive Europe to war; but efforts by capitalists to counter the pressure they felt had definite political and diplomatic implications. New tariffs contributed to the growing sense of national hostilities; foreign loans had diplomatic implications and contributed to national rivalries; certainly, imperialism and rising armaments did the same thing. Internally, the new interaction of business and government strengthened the forces of conservatism, for businessmen, often cooperating now with landed aristocrats to win tariffs and other gains, saw that a strong government was definitely in their interest. Finally, groups that suffered from big business and its politics were driven to a mounting sense of protest. By 1890 the social question dominated the political scene, overshadowing any remaining disputes between conservatives and liberals. The social question was, very simply, what to do with and for the lower classes in industrial society.

SOCIAL TENSION: THE LEFT

There was irony in the growing agitation of workers in the period. In a real sense, they had never had it so good. Wages were up. City and national governments were making increasing efforts to regulate the conditions of work and of life, to provide protection in illness and old age, and to offer new public facilities, such as schools and public parks. Obviously, the new prosperity was a precondition of worker protest. Higher wages helped provide dues for worker organizations; nearly universal literacy opened the door to the spread of new ideologies; shorter hours of work meant more time for protest activities; universal suffrage both forced and permitted the growth of political consciousness. All these gains heightened the appetite for more, by creating a belief in the possibility of further progress.

Grievances abounded for the working class. Workers failed to maintain their share of national incomes, due to the huge rise in profits. Bitter poverty remained; in the 1880's, it was estimated that almost a third of London's population was in real distress. Industrial work grew increasingly dull and disciplined. The work day was still long, from ten to twelve hours in most countries.

Workers, then, had both reason and ability to protest; and the persistent propaganda of socialist agitators gave increasing coherence to their discontent. The rise of socialist parties and a union movement took time, for both emerged fully only in the 1890's. Often, the first steps were taken by a minority of the middle class, which saw in socialism a means of protesting big business and political conservatism or unidealistic liberalism; this was clearly the case in France and Italy. Gradually a labor movement did take shape, and even in the 1880's it changed the framework of political debate.

Marxist Politics. The leading socialist parties were Marxist, which implied a methodological as well as doctrinal orientation. The parties were well organized, controlled by a central leadership through a clear chain of command. Though often pressed for funds, they organized vigorous campaigns of propaganda and set up a variety of publications. They also, during this period, worked to establish a unified, orthodox Marxist ideology. In the First International, Marx himself gradually drove out competing movements, such as anarchism; the result was an ideologically pure organization, but one so weakened that it collapsed in 1876. National Marxist parties had greater success. In Germany, compromises at first had to be made with Lassallean socialists, but in 1891 the Marxists captured the Social Democratic party completely. Native strands of French socialism, particularly the Proudhonist tradition of opposition to the state as well as to capitalism, were severely weakened by the repression following the Commune. The Marxist party founded in 1879 had, initially, no major socialist rivals. In Italy, Austria, and elsewhere, Marxist organizers introduced the first major socialist movement, and their parties, founded in the 1880's and 1890's, faced no real doctrinal opponents. Only in Britain, of the leading industrial countries, did Marxism fail to gain a significant foothold. There, a group of intellectuals, the Fabian Society, devised in the 1880's a more moderate approach that sought the complete socialization of all property used for production, but by gradual, democratic means. A clearly socialist political party developed only after 1900.

Except in Britain, then, socialism by 1890 meant Marxism, and Marxism meant a firm belief in class war and revolution to produce a totally new society. There could be no compromise with capitalism, and the capitalist system included existing political as well as economic structures. These structures were doomed by the inexorable forces of history; but probably a violent revolution, in which the workers seized the state and turned it against their oppressors, would be required to tumble the last pillars of the capitalist order. Then, ultimately, a new society would be built, without class war and therefore without formal government, in which each man produced what he could for society and received from it what he needed.

The political environment for early socialism confirmed the revolutionary approach to which the founders of the parties were ideologically committed. French socialists saw the brutal suppression of the Commune as clear evidence that even republicans were tools of the capitalist system. German socialists faced elaborate repression from 1878 to 1890, in which their papers and meetings were banned and many of their number arrested. Italian socialists encountered comparable persecution in the 1890's. And the revolutionary message won support, often in the face of government resistance. The German Social Democratic party led the way: between 1878 and 1890, its votes rose from 437,158 to 1,427,298, and its representation in parliament rose from nine to thirty-five. Italian socialists had over thirty deputies by 1900, French socialists over fifty. The parties were minority groups still, even within the working class itself, but their strength was mounting steadily. To hopeful socialists or to fearful conservatives the new movement could easily seem the wave of the future.

Rise of the Labor Movement. Nor was political socialism the only aspect of the labor protest in the period. A mass union movement developed, reaching industrial and unskilled workers for the first time. In Britain, unskilled dockers struck in 1889 and showed that even the most depressed segments of the working class were capable of organization. Major strikes by miners and railroad workers on the continent opened a new era of industrial relations; everywhere, the number and size of strikes mounted. Unions grew rapidly. By 1900 they had over a million members in Germany, over two million in Britain. Their organization improved, as national unions were formed in all the major industries and usually federated to provide some central direction for the whole movement.

The rise of the labor movement thrust social questions to the forefront of political debate. Conservative and liberal parties alike had to decide on some mixture of conciliation and repression to meet the new threat. The spate of new welfare legislation, initiated by Germany, was the main form of conciliation; regulation protected workers in many aspects of factory life and insurance plans helped relieve obvious hardships of accident and illness. Yet these measures failed to head off the labor movement, just as repression failed. Social tension, translated into politics, continued to mount as Europe entered the twentieth century.

CULTURAL TENSIONS: THE RIGHT

An attack on the existing order was also developing on the right, though it was more vague and less massive than the socialist movement. It, too, was led by intellectuals, and it found some popular response. The radical conservative critics damned some of the same features of the existing system that the socialists did, but they also condemned socialism. They looked to a new and rigorous imposition of political authority as the cure to social ills, and this meant major changes in the organization of the state as well.

The intellectual basis for the conservative attack was a further development of the war on rationalism. Three points must be stressed here. Many intellectuals, including most socialist theorists, continued to believe in the powers of reason and in an ultimately rational universe. But much of the work done by men in the rationalist tradition now called aspects of rationalism into doubt, without producing a clearly antirational system. Finally, by no means all the antirationalists were politically minded or committed to the radical conservative attack; the purely intellectual aspects of the revulsion against reason must be remembered.

Many discoveries in science and the social sciences continued the rationalist tradition. Study of the behavior of electrons, by Joseph Thomson and Hendrik Lorentz, seemed to confirm Newtonian laws of the regularity of motion. The work of Louis Pasteur and others on the germ theory and the discovery of the X ray showed that rational investigation could produce greater understanding of the physical environment and major improvements in the human condition. The burst of activity in the social sciences was based on the rational investigation of man and society. A new school of physiological psychology clearly sought to apply science to the study of the human mind. Sociologists tried to find generally applicable laws of social organization and usually believed that their discoveries would not only increase human understanding but also lead to rational social planning.

But science now opened pitfalls for any rational view of man. Most basically, Darwinian biology had shown man's animal origins. Some Darwinists translated the theory of evolution into a view of steady biological and social progress, but increasing numbers of social scientists turned their attention to irrational aspects of individual and social behavior, to the persistence of animal characteristics in human nature. Social psychologists claimed that crowds were controlled by frenzied impulse; Freud began his work on the unconscious irrationality of much of human nature.

Rationalism and the Arts. In art and literature, the leading works tried to appeal to man's senses or his subjective consciousness, without carrying any rational, intellectual message. The Impressionist painters were followed, in the 1890's, by Postimpressionists such as Vincent van Gogh, who moved further away from representational art and who sought visual impact above all. Canons of literary and poetic style, the whole idea that any clear standards could be applied to literature, were increasingly attacked by symbolist writers, who sought a personal style to convey their emotional consciousness.

Finally, there were direct attacks on the assumptions of rationalism. Friedrich Nietzsche condemned the materialism and petty politics of his age, which he related to a false belief in human reason. He saw society

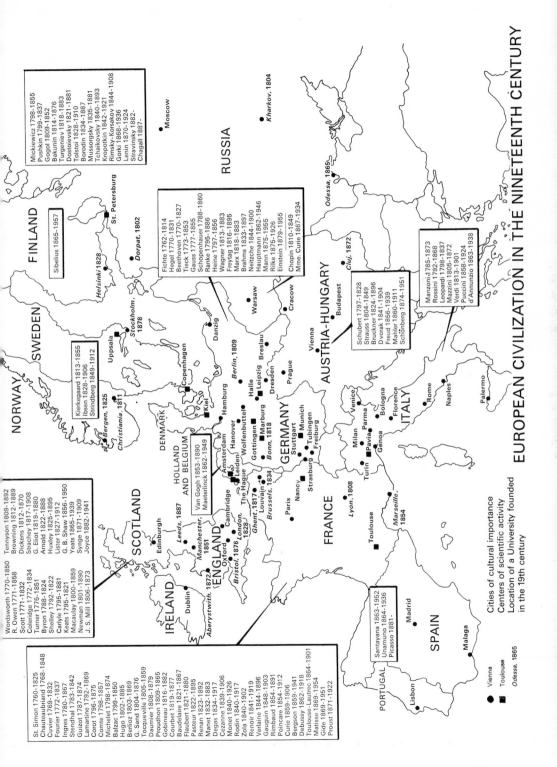

EUROPEAN CIVILIZATION IN THE NINETEENTH CENTURY

RUSSIA

Mickiewicz 1798-1855
Pushkin 1799-1837
Gogol 1809-1852
Bakunin 1814-1876
Turgeniev 1818-1883
Dostoievsky 1821-1881
Tolstoi 1828-1910
Borodin 1834-1887
Mussorgsky 1835-1881
Tchaikovsky 1840-1893
Kropotkin 1842-1921
Rimsky-Korsakov 1844-1908
Gorki 1868-1936
Lenin 1870-1924
Stravinsky 1882-
Chagall 1887-

Moscow
Kharkov, 1804
Odessa, 1865
St. Petersburg
Dorpat, 1802

FINLAND
Sibelius 1865-1957
Helsinki 1828

SWEDEN
Stockholm, 1878
Uppsala

NORWAY
Bergen, 1825
Christiania 1811

Kierkegaard 1813-1855
Ibsen 1828-1906
Strindberg 1849-1912

Fichte 1762-1814
Hegel 1770-1831
Beethoven 1770-1827
Tieck 1773-1853
Gauss 1777-1855
Schopenhauer 1788-1860
Ranke 1795-1886
Heine 1797-1856
Wagner 1813-1883
Freytag 1816-1895
Marx 1818-1883
Brahms 1833-1897
Neitzche 1844-1900
Hauptmann 1862-1946
Mann 1875-1955
Rilke 1875-1926
Einstein 1879-1955

Warsaw
Cracow
Danzig
Breslau
Berlin, 1809
Leipzig
Halle
Dresden
Hamburg
Kiel
Hanover
Wolfenbüttel
Göttingen
Marburg
Bonn, 1818
Tübingen
Stuttgart
Munich
Freiburg
Strasbourg

DENMARK
Copenhagen

HOLLAND
AND BELGIUM
Van Gogh 1853-1890
Maeterlinck 1862-1949
Amsterdam
Leiden
The Hague
Ghent, 1828
Louvain
Brussels, 1834

GERMANY

AUSTRIA-HUNGARY
Vienna
Budapest
Cluj, 1872
Prague

Schubert 1797-1828
Strauss 1804-1849
Bruckner 1824-1896
Dvorak 1841-1904
Freud 1856-1939
Mahler 1860-1911
Schönberg 1874-1951

Manzoni 1785-1873
Rossini 1792-1868
Leopardi 1798-1837
Mazzini 1805-1872
Verdi 1813-1901
Puccini 1858-1924
d'Annunzio 1863-1938

ITALY
Rome
Naples
Palermo
Venice
Bologna
Florence
Milan
Parma
Pavia
Turin
Genoa

FRANCE
Paris
Nancy
Lyon, 1808
Toulouse
Marseille, 1854

SCOTLAND
Edinburgh

ENGLAND
Leeds, 1887
Manchester, 1851
Oxford
Cambridge
Bristol, 1876
London, 1828
Aberystwyth, 1872

IRELAND
Dublin

Wordsworth 1770-1850
R. Owen 1771-1858
Scott 1771-1832
Coleridge 1772-1834
Cuvier 1769-1832
Fourier 1772-1837
Ingres 1780-1867
Stendhal 1783-1842
Guizot 1787-1874
Lamartine 1792-1869
Corot 1796-1875
Comte 1798-1857
Michelet 1798-1874
Hugo 1802-1885
Berlioz 1803-1869
Tocqueville 1805-1859
Daumier 1808-1879
Proudhon 1809-1865
Gobineau 1816-1882
Courbet 1819-1877
Baudelaire 1821-1867
Flaubert 1821-1880
Pasteur 1822-1895
Renan 1823-1892
Manet 1832-1883
Degas 1834-1917
Cezanne 1839-1906
Monet 1840-1926
Rodin 1840-1917
Zola 1840-1902
Renoir 1841-1919
Verlaine 1844-1896
Gauguin 1848-1903
Rimbaud 1854-1891
Poincaré 1854-1912
Curie 1859-1906
Bergson 1859-1941
Debussy 1862-1918
Toulouse-Lautrec 1864-1901
Matisse 1869-1954
Gide 1869-1951
Proust 1871-1922

Tennyson 1809-1892
Browning 1812-1889
Dickens 1812-1870
Strachey 1817-1908
Arnold 1822-1888
Huxley 1825-1895
Lister 1827-1912
G. B. Shaw 1856-1950
Yeats 1865-1939
Synge 1871-1909
Joyce 1882-1941

St. Simon 1760-1825
Chateaubriand 1768-1848
Keats 1795-1821
Macaulay 1800-1859
Newman 1801-1890
J. S. Mill 1806-1873
Turner 1775-1851
Byron 1788-1824
Shelley 1792-1822
Carlyle 1795-1881
G. Eliot 1772-1834
Balzac 1799-1850
G. Sand 1804-1876

SPAIN
Santayana 1863-1952
Unamuno 1864-1936
Picasso 1881-
Madrid
Malaga

PORTUGAL
Lisbon

Cities of cultural importance
Centers of scientific activity
Location of a University founded
in the 19th century

● Vienna
■ Toulouse
Odessa, 1865

183

declining to a common mediocrity, based on an assumption of rationality in all men. To replace this, he preached a new philosophy of the will, in which strong men could trample all conventions in their quest for power and emotional fulfillment. Their standards would be personal, violent, and irrational, for it had to be recognized that man was basically evil and rationalist notions of human perfectibility were nonsense.

Few thinkers stressed a purely individual defiance of reason and convention; increasingly, they looked to racial superiority and unity as the antidote to rationalism. For them, the key problem of modern society was the assumption that man could stand alone, relying on his reason. Because men were not rational, they needed a collective loyalty to give focus to their lives, and this loyalty should be to the race. The race would offer collective traditions to guide men's lives and, in its efforts at self-assertion, would provide an atmosphere of conflict and violence necessary to satisfy real human nature.

All of this had obvious political implications. The racists attacked parliamentary politics because they promoted individual selfishness and divided the race, making it ineffective. They attacked the materialism of the age, which detracted from man's true loyalties, and the exploitations of the capitalist system, which split men into hostile, selfish classes. They attacked liberalism, which had sponsored both parliamentary politics and capitalist economics. They wanted a strong state under a strong leader, capable of resolving the political and social disputes and leading the race to unity and glory. Writers like Julius Langbehn in Germany and Maurice Barrès in France translated the attacks on rationalistic liberalism into fervent appeals for a return to the traditions of the national past and a strong, hierarchical regime that could keep the passions of ordinary men in proper check.

Antiliberal politics won some popular support in the period. The very fact that most conservative parties had compromised with liberalism drove some traditionalists into a sweeping attack on the existing order; the participation of many legitimists in the Boulanger movement was one symptom of the new politics of the traditionalists. The bickering and corruption of some parliamentary politicians repelled many people. Economic grievances drove some professional people and shopkeepers to protest. The universities were turning out more doctors, lawyers, and journalists than the economy could then support, and many professional men and students now turned against a system which provided neither the income nor the status which they expected. Shopkeepers and other small businessmen were threatened by the new, big units of production and distribution, and financial crises hurt many small pensioners. On yet another front, many Christians bemoaned the growing secularization of society. Most of these groups were also frightened by the rise of socialism and the unions, which represented yet another form of big organization and which threatened the property and position on which their lives were based. They were open, therefore, to movements that criticized the present order from the right.

Nationalism and Anti-Semitism. The clearest signs of restiveness on the right were a heightened, belligerent nationalism and a growing wave of anti-Semitism. Pan-national movements arose in Germany and Russia that sought to embrace the whole of the Aryan or Slavic races and demanded on authoritarian government to push these expansions forward. In France, a League of Patriots was formed, with over 100,000 members by the 1890's, which urged that revenge against Germany was the chief duty of the French state and sought a dictatorship to replace a divided and corrupt parliament. Even in Britain, as an appendage of the Conservative party, Randolph Churchill founded Primrose leagues to arouse popular enthusiasm for imperialism and for defense of the established order.

Anti-Semitic movements grew in the 1870's and 1880's in France, Germany, and Austria; they obviously appealed to racist sentiments, but they also used Jews as scapegoats for all the grievances against parliaments, big business, and socialism. Many artisans and shopkeepers, students, and Christians were attracted at least to the slogans of the movement. In Germany, a Protestant pastor, Adolph Stöcker, formed a political party based on anti-Semitism, antiparliamentarism, and anticapitalism; Stöcker sought a strong state, firmly in control of the economy in the interest of the nation as a whole, and a cessation of individual selfishness and social bickering. By 1898, his party could claim almost 300,000 votes.

The Radical Right. The new or radical right of the late nineteenth century is difficult to assess. Its intellectual bases had been set in the vigorous attacks on rationalism and liberalism. A few formal movements had been launched, though they were fairly small. There were some signs of a broader appeal, particularly in the growth of anti-Semitism and fervent nationalism. These sentiments could remain apolitical, of course, and they were held by some on the political left as well as on the right.

But there were signs that a new kind of conservatism was developing at the end of the century, a conservatism that differed both from the traditionalism of the earlier nineteenth century and from the new, semiparliamentary conservatism of this same period. This radical conservatism stressed authority and was at best suspicious of the parliamentary form; it preserved some links with religion but was not tightly bound to it; it was vigorously antisocialist, yet urged social reforms to end the evils of capitalism; and of course it was enthusiastically nationalist and, usually, anti-Semitic. Furthermore, the radical conservatism sought to enlist mass support by a variety of popular organizations and ballyhoo. In Britain, this new strand of conservatism remained within the Conservative party and did not go so far as to attack the parliamentary structure; but the heightened nationalism of some Conservative politicians and the new youth groups and women's groups, with their uniforms and parades, showed that one wing of the Conservative party was looking toward a new approach. At the other extreme, in republican France, radical conservatives refused to participate in politics at all, but they played a role in the major crises, in the Boulanger and Dreyfus affairs, where the stress on nationalism and authority was obvious. In Germany, conservatives of the radical stripe helped form Stöcker's group and others like it, but there were some also in the Conservative party who were anxious to do away with parliament altogether. In Austria, finally, the Christian Socialist party, formed in the 1880's, gained massive support from shopkeepers, clerks, and peasants with a program of German nationalism, anti-Semitism, antisocialism, and practical welfare legislation.

The radical conservatism of this period foreshadowed fascism in many ways, but it was not fascist. When they gained power in the city of Vienna, for example, the Christian Socialists forebore from any attacks on the Jews and concentrated on an extensive urban welfare program. Yet, unquestionably, radical conservatism pointed in new directions. It appealed more to shopkeepers and peasants than to the upper classes; hence its real concern with social reform as well as its opposition to socialism. It talked of order and authority, as other conservative movements had done, but it searched for new ways to achieve these. Still small, still disorganized in most cases, still in its most formal aspects almost exclusively an intellectual movement, radical conservatism constituted nonetheless an important dissent from the established order.

UNREST IN EASTERN AND SOUTHERN EUROPE

Conditions in eastern and southern Europe reflected the pressures of early industrialization combined with some of the economic and social problems of contemporary western Europe. The economic changes were partly comparable to those of western Europe earlier, but they occurred amid far greater rural hardship; and political structures were far less flexible than they had been in the West. All this was complicated by the collapse of agricultural prices, which affected eastern and southern Europe from the late 1870's, and by extensive foreign investment and entrepreneurial activity that introduced sophisticated forms of capitalist enterprise while returning many of the profits to foreign hands. Modern doctrines of socialism and nationalism were imported from industrial countries too, which further promoted unrest.

The result was a social and political situation that simply cannot be compared to that of western and central Europe. Not only workers but also peasants and even middle-class elements were bitterly aggrieved and often willing to use violence. Liberalism remained to some extent a revolutionary doctrine in these regions, for though it was a weak force, because of the small size of the middle classes, it had as yet little reason to compromise with or work through the existing order. Similarly, there were few modifications in traditional, repressive conservatism. Russia returned to a fully repressive system after the reform period of the 1860's and 1870's; parliamentary regimes were largely façades in Spain, Hungary, and several of the

Balkan states; even southern Italy was gripped by oppression from the North. The terms of political conflict, then, differed greatly from western patterns. Here there were massive social tensions, rural as well as urban, and dispute about the nature of state structure as well. Add to this, in many cases, divisive nationalist agitation, and the growing instability of the peripheries of Europe becomes clear.

Peasants were trapped by increasing hardship. The populations of eastern and southern European areas were growing rapidly after 1870; in Russia, for example, peasant population rose a full third, without any significant increase in available land. Emigration and movement to the cities reflected population pressure, but still there was not enough land. In addition, outside Russia, large estates dominated what land there was. Peasants in southern Italy and Spain were squeezed by sharecropping arrangements, while the majority of Rumanian peasants had to work at least part-time as miserably paid labor on the estates. Estates loomed less large in Russia, though they were a source of complaint, but the continuing obligations of redemption payments for former manorial dues added a distinctive and bitter grievance. In most countries, governments increased taxes on the peasantry, in order to gain revenues necessary to support industrialization and the modernization of military establishments; yet peasants still found it difficult to produce for the market, because they lacked capital and technical training, and market prices were down anyway. Finally, the difficulties of the peasantry were not only economic. The landlords had political powers too, and they enveloped peasants in many areas in supervision by the priests, policemen, and magistrates whom they appointed; in Russia, village and *zemstvo* bodies were increasingly subjected to aristocratic control.

Growth of the Middle Class. A sort of middle class was growing up in eastern Europe at the same time, dominated by professional people. State bureaucracies required growing numbers of lawyers and even doctors, and university enrollments rose fairly steadily, drawing increasingly on nonaristocratic elements. The professional group, always self-consciously intellectual and open to ideas, was now numerous; in Russia, it included over half a million people by 1900. A business group arose as well. By the 1890's, Russia was engaged in a process of rapid industrialization. Encouraged by government support for railroad development and manufacturing and by massive foreign loans, production of coal, metals, oil, and textiles advanced quickly. In the Balkans, there was little factory industry but, again spurred by foreign investment, a basic railroad system was established and trade increased rapidly, through export of agricultural goods and import of manufactured products; a local merchant group was not slow to develop. Around Barcelona in Spain, industry and trade advanced notably.

The new and diverse middle class, though often prospering from commerce and government work, had grievances of its own. It resented continued aristocratic power; it wanted more modern and efficient government; it wanted a parliamentary system; often, it sought new national identity as well. The new middle class was small. Its business elements, particularly, were often timid because of their dependence on government support. But it, too, contributed to protest movements in the period, and from its ranks came not only liberal and nationalist leaders but also socialist agitators.

Finally, population pressure and the advance of trade and industry created a large urban proletariat. Cities such as Moscow, Budapest, Lodz, and Barcelona grew rapidly. The new workers suffered the usual early industrial ills of crowded housing, low wages, and long hours; they faced also government prohibitions on unions and strikes, and they had no real political representation. Small wonder that some workers were won by protest doctrines even more extreme than Marxism.

Anarchism. In Spain, there were two large pockets of anarchism, among workers in Barcelona and among over a million peasants in the south. Workers struck with increasing frequency and anarchist peasants rose almost once a decade after 1870, attacking churches and government officials, seizing land, and setting up egalitarian village communes. At the same time, many businessmen in Barcelona were attracted to a Catalonian nationalism that preached its own hatred of the government in Madrid. The diverse strands of protest did not unite, but their combined attack severely challenged the state.

There was more limited anarchism in Italy, which expressed its defiance of government by a number of assassination attempts. Socialism was more important here, winning votes from disgruntled segments of the middle class. In 1893, urban socialists in Sicily led the peasants in an outright revolt, the Fasci rising, against landlords and government agents. Five years of social unrest followed, capped by the May rebellion of 1898, in which Milanese workers set up barricades and held out for five days against the government.

The Spanish government responded to unrest by growing repression. The church controlled education and censorship. There was a parliament, with universal suffrage after 1885, but this was made meaningless by police and landlord intimidation of voters and by outright rigging of elections. Regularly, for example, election results showed that whole cemeteries full of departed citizens had revived long enough to vote for the right people. A corrupt bureaucracy, in which position was obtained by bribes and used for personal profit, a privileged landlord element, a privileged church—all this kept Spain in an essentially unrevised old regime. Repression was also the Italian answer to protest in the 1890's; the government imposed censorship, arrested many socialists, and virtually suspended parliament between 1898 and 1900, in favor of military rule. But here the reaction was short-lived, and if little was done about basic social problems at least the liberal political regime was restored. It remained true that the governmental system seemed almost irrelevant to the disenfranchised lower classes; Italy was to reap the harvest of this disaffection in the first decades of the next century.

Nationalist Protests. Parliamentary regimes existed in the Balkan countries, and where the assemblies had real power, as in Rumania, liberal, middle-class protest was muted. Authoritarian rule created great tension in Bulgaria and Serbia; the Bulgarian prime minister and the Serbian king were both assassinated near the turn of the century. None of the governments, including that of the Ottoman Empire, tried to cope with peasant problems, with the result that brigandage and riots were endemic and there were major risings like the one in Bosnia in 1875. Much of the social tension of the region was expressed through nationalism. Intellectuals and businessmen led in demands for an independent Bulgaria, in the 1870's; in established states, such as Greece and Serbia, they pressed for an aggressive foreign policy. Secret societies, such as the Ethnike Hetaireia in Greece, insisted on national expansion and could put real pressure on the governments. Nationalist sentiment even spread to sections of the peasantry, particularly where there were Moslem landlords as in Bosnia. The social instability of the Balkans and endemic nationalism made the area a diplomatic trouble spot as early as the 1870's, and promised to do so again.

Nationalist protest increased in other parts of eastern Europe. A new Young Czech nationalism arose in the 1890's, which refused the sorts of compromises that the Taaffe government had offered and demanded Czech autonomy at the very least. Austrian politics were virtually paralyzed after 1890 by the obstructionism of Czech nationalists and mounting German sentiment against any concessions; new demands by other Slav nationalities only added to the ferment. And again, nationalism now had spread well beyond landlords, merchants, and intellectuals; workers and particularly peasants joined nationalist groups as well. A socialist movement arose in Austria and Bohemia too, with the advance of industry, but its demands were overshadowed by the nationalist disputes. Even in Hungary, where the Magyars used their autonomy to oppress minority groups, a new Magyar nationalism developed in the 1890's that demanded virtual independence.

In Russia, almost all the forms of protest arose, and with increasing intensity. Nationalist movements spread among Ukrainians, the Baltic peoples, and the Finns. Peasant rioting mounted, particularly in the 1870's and again in the 1890's. Strike movements among industrial workers, though illegal, were frequent after 1880. Finally, students and other educated groups, the intelligentsia, participated in a variety of radical movements. In the 1870's, a populist movement attracted greatest attention. The populists held that capitalism could be avoided if the existing system were overturned in favor of rural communism, and they went out to the villages to educate the peasantry in the principles of true community. When it became obvious that the peasants were not interested in such an abstract message, the populist movement became more radical. After 1878 several groups were formed, which preached action by an elite in the interests of the masses and established secret terrorist cells for purposes of political assassination; in 1881 one such group managed to kill the czar. In the 1880's also, a number of intellectuals in exile were attracted to Marxism.

The response of the Russian government to lower-class discontent and the organization of the intelligentsia was almost completely repressive. After 1881, under the ministry of Pobiedonostsev, all notions of reform or concession were abandoned. Only in its encouragement of industrial development did the government show any interest in change, and even this policy was resisted by many conservatives and pursued largely at the expense of the heavily taxed peasantry. Pobiedonostsev believed in absolute monarchy, associated with the Orthodox Church. He actively persecuted racial and religious minorities. He increased the secret police and set up military courts to deal with political crimes. The powers of the *zemstvos* were severely limited, and of course there was no national parliament at all. This was full reaction, untempered by even the façade of liberal government.

Most clearly in Russia but to an extent throughout eastern and southern Europe, mounting unrest was met by a purely repressive conservatism, backed by traditionalist churches and by a social hierarchy still dominated by a landholding aristocracy. Liberal, western political institutions, where they existed at all, were largely sham. Yet forces of westernization were irresistibly felt. Western capital and entrepreneurs were welcomed by governments eager to enhance their military and economic power. But almost certainly, the combination of economic advance and political traditionalism could not be maintained. Already, revolutionary and nationalist crises were brewing. When they came, they would embroil the whole of Europe, not just the peripheries. For if Europe was profoundly divided in political and social structures, it was united in its diplomatic system; and the diplomatic system proved only as stable as its weakest members.

SUGGESTED READING

Economic and social studies of this period include: G. W. Edwards, *The Evolution of Finance Capitalism* (1938); H. Feis, *Europe, the World's Banker, 1870-1914: An Account of European Foreign Investment and the Connection of World Finance with Diplomacy Before the War** (1930); C. Kindleberger, *The Economic Growth in France and Britain, 1851-1950* (1964); W. R. Bruck, *Social and Economic History of Germany, 1888-1938* (1938); G. M. Young, *Victorian England: Portrait of an Age** (1954). E. Hobsbawm, *Primitive Rebels** (1965), presents a compelling picture of social unrest in southern Europe.

Two recent studies in cultural history most clearly suggest the intellectual turmoil of the period: F. Stern, *Politics of Cultural Despair* (1965) and H. S. Hughes, *Consciousness and Society* (1958). See also: H. E. Barnes, ed., *An Introduction to the History of Sociology** (1948); H. Alpert, *Émile Durkheim and his Sociology* (1939); J. P. Mayer, *Max Weber and German Politics: A Study in Political Sociology* (1944); H. A. Reyburn, *Neitzsche: The Story of a Human Philosopher* (1948); G. P. Gooch, *History and Historians in the 19th Century** (1949); E. Wilson,

*Available in a paperback edition.

Axel's Castle: A Study of the Imaginative Literature of 1870-1930* (1931); E. Zimmer, *The Revolution in Physics* (1936).

Nationalism as a political current in the period has been rarely treated, but there are now some good studies. H. Rogger and E. Weber, eds., *The European Right** (1966) is extremely useful. Also, E. Weber, *Nationalist Revival in France* (1959); R. Byrnes, *Antisemitism in Modern France* (1950); P. Pulzer, *The Rise of Political Anti-Semitism in Germany and Austria: 1867-1918** (1965).

On socialism, see Carl Landauer, *European Socialism* (Vol. I, 1959) for a comprehensive, sensible treatment. Also, A. Noland, *The Founding of the French Socialist Party, 1893-1905* (1956); C. Schorske, *German Social Democracy, 1905-1917** (1955); P. Gay, *The Dilemma of Democratic Socialism; Eduard Bernstein's Challenge to Marx** (1952); J. Schumpeter, *Capitalism, Socialism, and Democracy** (1950). On labor unions, see W. A. McConagha, *The Development of the Labor Movement in Great Britain, France, and Germany* (1942), for a summary; also, G. D. H. Cole, *A Short History of the British Working Class Movement* (1947), and L. L. Lorwin, *Syndicalism in France* (1914).

For two views of Bismarck's diplomacy, consult W. L. Langer, *European Alliances and Alignments, 1871-1890** (1950), and J. V. Fuller, *Bismarck's Diplomacy at its Zenith* (1922), the latter highly critical of the German statesman. An excellent summary of the whole period is R. J. Sontag, *European Diplomatic History, 1871-1932* (1933). C. Sforza, *Fifty Years of War and Diplomacy in the Balkans* (1941), is useful.

*Available in a paperback edition.

Rhodes: The Granger Collection   Peters: European

PETERS AND RHODES

Carl Peters (1856-1918) and Cecil John Rhodes (1853-1902) were leaders in Europe's imperial expansion in Africa at the end of the nineteenth century. Peters, in fact, was responsible for Germany's first major entry into the imperial field. He was intended for an academic career, but a long stay in England aroused his interest in empire. In 1884 he founded the Society for German Colonization, which replaced a tamer imperialist organization and was designed to reverse the government's policy of disinterest in overseas territories. Peters long led the combination of business, military, and nationalist figures that served as a powerful pressure group in matters of empire. But political pressure was not Peters' main contribution. He went out, by himself, to East Africa, to explore the districts of Useguha, Ukami, Nguru, and Usagara—a territory of 60,000 square miles. By various bargains and treaties he won the allegiance of many tribal leaders to German rule. Bismarck's government did not immediately recognize Peters' efforts, and for a few years the colonies Peters had claimed for Germany really belonged to him alone. But Peters' continuing expeditions in East Africa and along the Nile roused British opposition; on this basis, Peters was able to request and receive direct German protection and explicit recognition of the African colonies, of which he was made imperial commissioner.

192

As a colonial administrator, after the establishment of the German holdings, Peters was authoritarian; to the natives he was indeed brutal. German opponents of empire, notably the socialists, seized on reports of his awful cruelty. In the political battle that ensued, Peters was dismissed, in 1894, and retired to England. Though the government restored his reputation and imperial office in 1906, Peters' role in German policy was ended.

Cecil Rhodes went to South Africa as a young man, for reasons of health. He quickly obtained an interest in the Kimberley diamond mines and led the consolidation of the fields into the De Beers mining company. He was also active in politics in the Cape Colony; and he constantly pressed for British expansion into neighboring areas. He helped the British take over Bechuanaland and in 1899 organized the British South Africa Company, to obtain the territory later named Rhodesia. The Company reflected Rhodes' two sources of power: it was supported by De Beers funds and had an official charter from the British government as well. Rhodes' immediate concern was the possibility of German expansion in the area —the reflection of Peters' activities—and of resulting pressure on existing British holdings. In the longer run, he envisaged a chain of British territory from the Cape to Cairo. He helped launch, in fact, railroad and telegraph lines along this south-north route.

Rhodes was also an opponent of the Boers. The Boers might block the interests of Britain, and of Rhodes, in northern expansion. They might ally with the Germans. Rhodes was a racist and feared the racial kinship of Boers and Germans, for there were sporadic efforts by Boers and Germans alike to combine their opposition to the British in Africa. Moreover, Rhodes was developing a massive economic interest within the Boer republic, having formed the Consolidated Gold Fields Company to develop deep mines in the Rand.

·Like Peters, Rhodes had no compunction about committing his government to any policy he deemed proper, whether he had authorization or not. He encouraged revolts against the Boers and sponsored a raid into Boer territory that he hoped would lead to war. And he actively supported the war against the Boers when it did come in 1899. The war actually curbed Rhodes' power, for the British government now took a more active hand in South African administration. The era of the freewheeling imperial promoter was over.

Peters and Rhodes, though representing opposing national interests, were men of a similar type. They had few friends; they were hard to know; they were reckless, strong-willed. Rhodes at least had a somewhat mystic temperament, a belief in a personal destiny which he could easily equate with that of England. Both men used African natives with complete callousness. Peters' brutality was matched by Rhodes' bloody repression of native rebellion in Rhodesia and by his exploitation of native labor in the mines. Both men were adventurers, both enamoured of power. Peters was the more clearly nationalist of the two; he worked for Germany's interest even when, in his view, Germany did not recognize it. Rhodes worked for Britain, to be sure, but even more for his own great wealth and political power.

These were the sorts of men without whom the imperial expansion of the period would have been impossible. It was they, not their governments and certainly not popular pressure, who initiated major imperial gains. It was they who had the ruthlessness to expand and to make expansion profitable, at least to themselves. Their role in imperialism is clear enough, but broader questions remain: what produced such extraordinary personal dynamism at this time? What diverted it from normal domestic and diplomatic outlets, into the quest for empire? ∎

Chapter 6

Prelude to Disaster
1900–1914

In 1900, many European publicists took the occasion to look back on the previous century. What they saw was good, and it gave promise of further advances in the future. The rationalists' belief in progress, enhanced by the optimistic interpretation of the evolutionary process, seemed amply confirmed. There had been clear advances in knowledge, particularly in biology and physics, and many of the discoveries had been applied to produce technical and medical improvements. New products and new wealth had spread to many elements of society. Famine and catastrophic epidemic disease were things of the past. Education had been vastly extended and, along with new learning, had pushed back the boundaries of superstition. A variety of liberties had been extended, most clearly in the area of freedom of religion and of expression, but also in the abolition of the slave trade and in new civil rights for women; and liberties were generally protected by a division of governmental powers between parliament and the executive. There had been no general European wars since 1815, and it seemed possible that peace might be permanent; the establishment of the World Court, following an international peace conference in 1899, seemed a promising step toward a system of law among nations. Many of the benefits of European civilization, from new technology to humane justice, were being extended to the rest of the world. The rational European man had gained control of society and nature; there were no clear limits to his future development.

Eighteen years later, this facile optimism seemed nonsensical, for the World War shattered many hopes. Even in 1900, only a minority fully believed in it. Militant nationalists might believe in progress, but not of the humanitarian, pacific sort; and they were restlessly dissatisfied with the present. Socialists believed in progress, but they had scant confidence in the achievements of the nineteenth century. For most people in southern and eastern Europe, deterioration, not progress, was the overwhelming trend in economics and, often, in politics as well. In diplomacy, there was little change in basic motives or methods, nothing to justify exaggerated hopes for peace; the conference that established the World Court also failed to limit national armaments, which had been its purpose. Yet, for the most articulate segments of society in western and central Europe, for the middle classes particularly, there were few clouds on the horizon in 1900. The economic and political structure was stable and good.

In less than two decades after 1900, much of this structure broke down. The failure of orderly diplomacy, which led to world war, caused this breakdown most directly. Related to diplomatic failure was the political collapse of eastern Europe, which had never achieved the compromise in the system of government or the industrial success of the West. But there were symptoms of disorder in western Europe itself, which carried forward earlier, subordinate themes of disarray; and these, too, contributed to the diplomatic breakdown.

WESTERN AND CENTRAL EUROPE

Most of the states of industrial Europe were politically stable after 1900, more so in many cases than they had been in the 1890's. In France, the Radical party continued to rule after the settlement of the church-state question. It was able to cooperate to a degree with the socialists and with more conservative republicans. There seemed some hope that a balance might be struck among these three political forces, all of which accepted the republic. The regime was able to carry through a number of important army reforms, including a three-year general conscription law in 1913, and several limited welfare measures.

In Italy, the chaos of the 1890's gave way to the stable leadership of Giovanni Giolitti. Giolitti was a liberal who was eager to develop a new consensus in Italian politics and was willing to undertake democratic and some social reform in order to achieve this. He wooed the socialists, with partial success, by legalizing trade unions and passing a number of factory laws. He won increasing cooperation from the Catholics, for the church, frightened by socialist gains, now relaxed its restrictions on Catholic political participation. Admittedly, there was still no strong party structure in Italy, and much of Giolitti's consensus depended upon rigging elections and bribing delegates; Giolitti was the last but not the least successful practitioner of transformism. But a tone of stability and gradual progress could not be denied, at least until 1911.

German politics, from the fall of Bismarck, suffered from a lack of able leadership. The chancellors were weak, unable to restrain either the military or the unpredictable emperor, William II. But parliament was, on the whole, content, and of course its power was limited anyway. Conservatives, liberals, and the Catholic Center party united to support the government on most occasions, proud of Germany's new diplomatic power and anxious for governmental favors such as the high protective tariff of 1902. The socialists remained in opposition and their strength grew steadily, but they could not seize power and they showed increasing willingness to compromise on some issues.

In Britain, the Conservative party was firmly ensconced between 1895 and 1905. It stood for a strong imperial policy, some limited reforms such as increased state aid to education and an old age pension law, and general preservation of the status quo. The Liberals seemed to lack an issue, particularly because their traditions opposed major social reform. On their left, a new Labour party took shape in 1900, through the collaboration of trade unionists and Fabian socialists, and it began to make slow but steady gains. This situation prompted a last flowering of British liberalism, on a program of substantial welfare legislation, in partial cooperation with the Labour party. The power of the House of Lords was cut down, to weaken opposition to reform, and a number of factory acts and social insurance measures were introduced. The National Insurance Act of 1911, backed by new taxes on high incomes, insured workers against accident, sickness, and unemployment. British politics seemed capable of continued adaptation.

Socialist Revisionism. Crucial to the political stability of the period was the new attitude of socialism. Socialist parties continued to gain support; by 1914 they represented sizable minorities in all the parliaments, and in Germany the Social Democrats were the largest single party. Without question, these gains indicated substantial protest against the existing order. But the socialists themselves became increasingly mild. Few socialist parties had ever actively worked for revolution, and now they even stopped advocating it seriously.

A revisionist movement grew up, most explicitly in Germany but in effect throughout industrial Europe. The revisionists held that Marx was wrong in many respects. The workers were not getting poorer; the capitalist system was not collapsing. At the same time, a democratic, parliamentary structure allowed socialists, in cooperation with friendly middle-class parties, to win major gains for the workers, as existing welfare legislation already proved. There was no need for revolution, no possibility of revolution, and every reason to work vigorously for improvements within the existing system. A vision of a perfected, socialist society was not abandoned, but it was to be attained gradually and, for now, was not nearly so important as limited, practical reform. The growing power and influence of the socialist parties and the clear desire of most socialist voters for benefits here and now supported the revisionist position.

Except in Britain, where Marxism was unimportant, the leading socialist parties formally voted revisionism down. The German party insisted on a theoretical commitment to class warfare. Italian socialists refused Giolitti's invitations to enter the government. French socialists did support the government during the Dreyfus affair, when the republic seemed threatened, and a few socialists even became ministers. But the

Marxist wing of the movement disapproved of this compromise and the party was reunited, in 1905, only on the promise that it would no longer participate in bourgeois regimes. Without doubt, a minority of all the parties really wanted a revolutionary stance. But the parties as a whole, even aside from the formal revisionists, looked to revolution only in theory. In practice, they cooperated with leftwing liberals and supported parliamentary, democratic regimes. Some socialists even voted for war credits and colonial expansion; and when World War I came, almost all the parties supported their governments despite their commitment in principle to international class solidarity. The conversion of socialism to a reformist approach was a major political development. True, socialists still frightened many conservatives by their talk of revolution, and a radical wing of socialism remained unreconciled. But tentatively, at least, socialism had accepted the existing political system.

Economic and Cultural Grievances. In most industrial countries, the problems of the period were not fully expressed within the political system, and that in itself was dangerous. Economic difficulties and continued cultural dissent promoted various expressions of grievance, for which existing politics did not seem entirely relevant. There were no prolonged economic crises in the period, but there was a slowing of industrial growth, particularly in Germany and Britain, though French and Italian industry was booming still. Coal and textile industries, particularly, found it difficult to expand their sales. More generally, there was a decline or stagnation of real wages. Giant companies succeeded in driving up their prices while holding money wages down. Profits were not hurt as a result, but this simply meant that inequalities in income became still more pronounced. Social insurance measures were inadequate in this situation. They covered too small a portion of the working class, in most cases, and their benefits were too low; further, they were almost entirely financed by the workers themselves. Conceived in a conservative spirit, as palliatives, they could not correct the growing disequilibrium in the capitalist system.

There was no abatement, either, of the intellectual attack on rationalism and liberalism. In science, the rediscovery of Mendelian genetics added to the notion that man could not control his destiny; Einstein's studies of relativity would sweep away much of the Newtonian physics on which the view of an orderly universe had depended. In art, Cubism represented a further step away from realistic portrayal. And one new artistic movement, Italian Futurism, drew directly political consequences from antirational art. The Futurists held that, just as style should defy convention and express the individuality of the artist, so should politics and morality be shaped by individual will. There were no standards in politics or art, only force and motion. Society should be based on action instead of thought, and the highest expression of society was war.

A New Wave of Agitation. The growing stress on violence was the most important note of the antirationalist political philosophy, though it was not entirely new. Georges Sorel, in France, preached violence for its own sake, as a basic human need. Enrico Corradini, in Italy, urged a new

Caesar to lead his people to war. In 1911 German General Friedrich A. J. von Bernhardi predicted and welcomed imminent world war, for he felt that war purified the soul of man and particularly the preëminently war-like German. Again, it is possible to note some popular interest in these new doctrines of action. The growing popularity of professional sports, of scouting and hiking clubs can be seen as a heightened interest in action for its own sake. Certainly the widespread initial enthusiasm for the World War itself showed that the preachers of violence had not lacked an audience.

Increasing agitation on the left was a natural outgrowth of economic difficulties and the concern for action. The growing socialist vote was one symptom of working-class dissent. But many workers felt that socialism was not enough, particularly in its newly tame revisionist form. There was a huge rise in the strike rate all over industrial Europe. Workers in France and Germany conducted well over a thousand strikes a year on the average. Industry-wide strikes, often violent, occurred in mining, railroads, and on the docks; nation-wide strikes took place in Belgium, Holland, and Sweden. Most strikes were not directly political, and their demands were often limited; but there was a new impatience abroad. Beyond this, a syndicalist movement developed that preached the strike as a weapon against the state as well as against capitalism. Violent general strikes would tumble the whole system, which could then be replaced by an egalitarian society with no formal government. Syndicalism captured major segments of the union movement in France, Italy, and Spain, and its influence was felt elsewhere. Finally, a new leftwing socialism arose in several countries that rejected the compromises of even modified revisionism and insisted on a pure, revolutionary approach. A segment of the German socialist party, under Rosa Luxemburg, turned to this approach; and, after universal suffrage was extended in Italy, the Italian party was largely captured by revolutionaries, led by Benito Mussolini, who rejected the whole parliamentary system.

In Britain, massive strike movements were supplemented by the rise of violent feminist agitation, in which women seeking the vote attacked property and persons in huge demonstrations. Earlier feminism had relied primarily on petitions, but now there was a growing abandonment of legal political action in favor of violence. Finally, Irish agitation for home rule had been growing more intense since the 1880's; it included rent strikes, thefts, and outright murder. To some observers, British society in 1914 seemed on the verge of revolution, from which only the War saved it. This view is perhaps exaggerated, but there is no doubt of the rising and violent challenge to the existing order.

On the continent, attacks from the right were added to those of the left. Stöcker's movement collapsed in Germany, but the Conservative party itself took on an increasingly anti-Semitic, authoritarian tone. As in the case of Austrian Christian Socialists, now the largest party in Austria, this meant that the grievances associated with anti-Semitism were toned down to some extent and brought into the political arena; but they were perhaps all the more dangerous in that they now penetrated one of the major political groupings. In Italy, small and violent rightist groups gathered around the Futurists and the poet Gabriele d'Annunzio, who preached national war under an authoritarian government. In France, finally, the *Action française* was founded during the Dreyfus affair to attack the parliamentary regime. Its doctrine urged authoritarian rule under a revived monarchy and church, which would do away with democracy and individualism and would abolish capitalist exploitation. Its methods stressed lively propaganda and violence, spearheaded by a strong-arm group called the *Camelots du roi,* to attack socialists and republicans and make the peaceful working of the regime impossible. The *Action française,* like all the extreme rightist organizations, was small and limited in impact. It revealed, nevertheless, a radical discontent that could spread and that already, in certain circumstances, could influence political and diplomatic decisions.

For all their political stability, then, the regimes of western and central Europe were increasingly pressed. There were attacks, outside the system and on the system, from left and right. The political structure was out of tune with the falterings of the economy and with the vanguard of intellectual activity. These countries were not on the verge of collapse; conscious dissent was still too limited and too vague. But there was an uneasiness, an uncertainty, even among the ruling groups themselves.

EASTERN EUROPE

In Spain, Russia, and the Hapsburg monarchy, collapse did seem imminent; and nationalist agitation increased in the Balkans. There was a major worker revolt in Barcelona in 1908; peasant agitation continued; and a strong Marxist movement developed among workers in Madrid and Bilbao. Several peasant risings occurred in the Balkans; it took 140,000 troops to quell the Rumanian revolt of 1907, and over 2000 people were killed. Socialist and union movements began to develop in the cities. Nationalist societies gained strength everywhere. In Serbia, a new dynasty, the Karageogevitch, came to power in 1903, committed to a violently anti-Austrian policy. With its support, secret societies such as the Black Hand grew and extended their agitation to South Slavic areas in Austria. Bulgarian, Serbian, and Greek societies tried to stir up the Macedonian population against Ottoman rule, and a specifically Macedonian society arose as well. All of these groups received some government backing, but they were not simply agencies of official policy. They expressed bitter social grievances: the Serbian ex-peasant, Prinzip, who assassinated Archduke Francis Ferdinand in 1914, explained his action very simply: "I am a peasant's son and know what is happening in the villages." The governments could not escape the pressure of the nationalist agitation precisely because they knew no other outlet for the discontent it expressed.

Nationalist ferment mounted steadily in the Hapsburg monarchy. Demonstrations periodically disrupted the Austrian parliament, and deputies themselves often broke chairs and engaged in fist-fights. Efforts to conciliate the Czechs, by granting them a greater role in the bureaucracy, only aroused the Germans to indulge in their own agitation and parliamentary disruption. There were rising demands by other minorities in the Empire, and added to this was a new social tension in politics. A partial extension of the suffrage in the 1880's had already produced the Christian Socialist party, which was hostile to liberalism but not conventionally conservative either. In 1907 universal suffrage was granted in Austria, which led to the rapid rise of the Socialist party and drove the Christian Socialists toward the conservative nationalists. The Magyars raised continued difficulties also. Their oppression of their own minority nationalities, notably the Croats, a South Slavic people, raised internal pressures with diplomatic implications, since it fed South Slavic nationalism outside the Empire. The Magyars themselves continued to have visions of still greater power in the empire. In 1905, the Hungarian parliament refused to vote credits for the imperial army, unless the Magyar language was used by all officers commanding Hungarian troops.

The impression of weakness in the Empire should not be overdrawn. The Hungarian crisis was resolved by forcibly dissolving the parliament and threatening to extend universal suffrage to Hungary, which would have swamped the Magyars. The two largest parties in Austria, the Socialists and the Christian Socialists, both supported the empire. A number of smaller nationalities' disputes were resolved in Austria, and if the Czech problem still refused solution — because of the competition between Czechs and Germans — it grew no worse, and growing numbers of Czechs were in fact obtaining government positions. Finally, if parliament was still periodically disrupted in Austria, necessitating rule by decree, Austria enjoyed a wide variety of civil liberties and an advanced code of welfare legislation. Was the empire doomed? Could multinational states no longer survive? The undeniable weakness of the empire, the fact that it did collapse after four years of war, should not lead to a too hasty affirmative. But many Austrian statesmen, notably Baron Aehrenthal, the foreign minister after 1908, were conditioned by decades of instability to feel that collapse was imminent. They felt that only a daring foreign policy could save the situation. This attitude, in turn, did in the end make the dissolution of the empire inevitable.

Unrest in Russia. Russia was now the most obviously unstable of the major powers. The conditions of the workers remained miserable and their grievances intense; strikes and illegal labor unions both indicated their discontent and exposed them to leaders and doctrines that spurred further protest. Significantly, strikes increasingly included demands for governmental reform and parliamentary democracy. Professional people, many of them employed by the *zemstvos,* began to urge liberal reforms at the national level. The peasants, finally, though still largely apolitical, rioted with rising frequency against government restrictions and impositions.

Two revolutionary ideological currents played upon this varied unrest. The Social Revolutionaries, organized formally after 1905, continued the agrarian communist tradition. They hoped to rouse the peasantry against the existing regime and replace it by egalitarian rural communes; and in the meantime they espoused and, often, practiced political terrorism and assassinations. The Marxist Social Democrats were a smaller group, whose leaders were largely in exile. In 1903, they split over issues raised by Nikolai Lenin, an intellectual turned devoted revolutionary. Lenin and his group, the Bolsheviks, stressed the importance of revolutionary purity without any taint of cooperation with bourgeois parties. They urged a small, tightly knit party filled with an elite group of professional revolutionaries who would lead the workers without being contaminated by their interest in immediate reforms; the duties of the party required rigid central organization and discipline. Lenin's ideas of method and organization were his most important contribution to Marxist theory and, put into practice, they allowed the Bolsheviks to play a role in the Russian revolutionary movement out of proportion to their numbers.

The defeat of Russia by Japan, in 1904 and 1905, followed four years of industrial slump. The demonstration of government ineptitude combined with economic grievances to bring revolutionary ferment to a boil. Professional men organized a variety of associations to press for political reform. A strike in St. Petersburg in January 1905 was brutally attacked by the government, leading to a general strike in most major cities and to the formation of worker councils called Soviets. Rural revolts followed for the next several months, as peasants seized land and attacked government officials. The Revolution of 1905 was a massive protest comparable in scope if not in result to the wave of revolutions in western Europe a century before.

In October 1905, Czar Nicholas II seemed to yield to the protests, for he guaranteed protection of liberties and called a national legislative assembly, the Duma. A number of moderates were satisfied by these concessions. But a Kadet party was formed by liberals who wanted greater parliamentary power, and the Social Democrats and Social Revolutionaries remained hostile to the existing order. The divisions within the opposition and the rallying of aristocrats and churchmen enabled the government to put down the revolution and withdraw many of its concessions. The Duma was forbidden to legislate on military matters, and even its powers over the budget were restricted; in 1906, many of the most vigorous defenders of parliamentary rights were removed from the Duma, and by 1907 it had become a purely consultative body, with no real influence over the government.

During the next decade, the government devoted itself primarily to a vigorous attack on revolutionary organizations. The bureaucracy deteriorated as appointments were made by favoritism and the czar's family underwent the influence of the reactionary monk Gregory Rasputin; even the glaring weakness of the military went largely unremedied. One minister, P. S. Stolypin, did attempt to correct some of the grievances of the peasantry. Redemption payments had been abolished during the revolution. Stolypin further eliminated most restrictions on the movement of peasants and tried to encourage individual farming by promoting consolidation of land holdings. His measures were clearly successful; by 1914 a tenth of the land in European Russia had been consolidated, and peasant production had risen. Stolypin's measures were popular, at least among a decisive minority of the richer peasants. Rural disorders, as a result, decreased sharply.

As with the Hapsburg monarchy, it is easy to see Russia in 1914 in the light of the events of the following four years. Many historians have argued that revolution was inevitable. Certainly, the weakness and corruption of the government were open invitations to attack. The revolutionary organizations were not snuffed out, and many workers were drawn by socialist appeals. Lenin had been convinced by the Revolution of 1905 that Russia could go directly from a feudal to a communist society; and he realized that the peasantry as well as the workers could be a potent revolutionary force. These decisions were crucial to the success of the Bolsheviks in 1917. Yet a Duma existed, even if its powers were hollow; a reform of its position could easily have contented the liberals. Some of the leading demands of the peasants were being satisfied. Russia's industry was booming once again. Would the system have collapsed without the pressure of war? This is a fascinating question, but an idle one; the continuing instability of Russian society helped drive the government to a fatally aggressive foreign policy which contributed to a war Russia could not endure.

REALIGNMENT OF DIPLOMACY

Between 1900 and 1914, a number of major diplomatic changes occurred in Europe. Britain entered the alliance system; Russia turned its attention to the Balkans; the Balkans themselves entered a new phase of turmoil; Austria undertook a more dynamic foreign policy; Germany began to dabble directly in the Near East. Behind most of these changes was a basic alteration in Europe's diplomatic framework—the closing off of imperial expansion. Already there were signs of heightened local resistance to the advance of empire. During the 1890's the British were hard pressed in the Sudan, the French in Madagascar; and Italy was actually defeated by the Ethiopians, at Adowa in 1896. An antiwestern rebellion of nationalist Chinese, the Boxers, in 1900 was put down only after considerable violence. In South Africa, the Boer War between Britain and the Dutch settlers lasted for three years, until 1902, and tied up a large British army. Except in the Ethiopian case, local resistance could be put down, but its suppression demanded resources that inhibited further expansion.

More serious still were the direct clashes between imperial powers.

Africa was so fully divided that almost no further gains were possible without confrontation with other European states, as had already been threatened when Britain and France met at Fashoda. Tension between Britain and Germany in southern Africa, particularly over Germany's espousal of Boer interests, fed the general growth of hostility between these two powers. Spain was deprived of most of its empire not by native uprisings but as a result of war with the United States. Most notably, the rise of Japan cut Russia off from further expansion in the Far East. Japan, long resenting Russia's advance in Manchuria, went to war in 1904, and won easily over the inefficient Russian army and inadequate Far Eastern navy. Here was a symbol of the end of imperialism: the defeat of a white nation by a yellow one. Here was a fact: Russia was forced to turn its expansionist interests back toward Europe, toward its traditional goals in the Dardanelles and the Balkans.

The end of easy imperial gains, indeed, brought every power's diplomatic attention back to Europe. But imperialism had changed purely European diplomacy. It was tempting to apply a sense of national mission to Europe itself. Russian pan-Slavs talked of Russia's duties to aid its Balkan brothers; pan-Germans preached the inclusion of racial Germans in Holland and Scandinavia into a greater German state. These notions colored official policies to some degree and clearly frightened other powers. More specifically, rivalries created in the imperial sphere were now extended to European alignments. German-British conflicts of interest in Africa and the Pacific were greatly heightened by a new naval competition. Most states expanded their navies in the 1890's, because of the need to protect the new empires and the general belief that navies were basic to national greatness. Germany, however, had never built a substantial navy before; its leaders, including the Emperor, proclaimed an interest in challenging British supremacy on the seas by a fleet smaller than the British but capable of inflicting unacceptable damage in case of war. By 1900, Britain and Germany were engaged in active economic, imperial, and naval competition, due to Germany's lust for greatness and Britain's unwillingness to recognize a diminution of its own world status.

The Boer War forced Britain to reconsider its position. Britain was completely isolated, for European opinion cheered the underdog Boers, and its army was so weak that it had trouble suppressing a few thousand Boer troops. Britain could no longer stand alone. A 1902 alliance with Japan showed British interest in cooperation against Russia in Asia. More important, the 1904 Entente Cordiale with France brought Britain into the European alliance system. Both France and Britain were anxious to end their mutual imperial rivalries. Britain wanted a firmer defense against possible German ambitions in Europe and on the seas. France wanted to supplement its alliance with Russia, whose weakness was increasingly clear. The Entente settled Franco-British imperial disputes, particularly by setting recognized spheres of influence for each state in North Africa.

The Moroccan Crisis. Germany, frightened by this clearly unfavorable change in the balance of power, tried to disrupt Franco-British friendship, but succeeded only in solidifying their understanding. France had long been interested in controlling Morocco, particularly to prevent incursions into Algeria. France now had British agreement for this, and had won Spanish and Italian consent as well. But in 1905, Germany firmly opposed the French plans, and insisted on a conference at which the Kaiser hoped to humiliate France and show the hollowness of British support. At the Conference of Algeciras, however, France was backed by all the powers except Austria and Germany; and the British were so antagonized by German bluster that they entered negotiations for defensive military arrangements with France.

This First Moroccan Crisis revealed the new tensions in Europe, even over imperial matters, and the growing isolation of the Central Powers. In 1907, British-Russian hostilities were buried through an extension of the Entente. Both powers wanted to end conflicts in the Far East, where Russia was blocked by Japan anyway, and both were urged by France, their mutual ally, to come to terms. Britain was increasingly preoccupied by the problem of Germany, while Russia, reattracted to the Balkans, faced Austria as the natural enemy and now feared German economic influence in that region as well. The prewar system was complete.

On paper, the system seemed nicely balanced, three against three. But Italy was weak and untrustworthy, from the German standpoint, and only Germany was threatened on two sides, by Russia and by France. Certainly, Germany's big talk, its sense of unfulfilled mission, had largely created this unfavorable balance. Its naval policy and extensions of economic and military assistance in the Near East inevitably created new antagonisms, even if more traditional great powers were pursuing similar policies. Germany was unwilling to abandon its initiatives; repeated British efforts to end the naval race failed, for Germany insisted on a strong fleet and Britain insisted on a fleet twice as large as the German. But from 1907 onward, German policy was dominated by a defensive, not an aggressive mentality. Because Germany was surrounded, it could afford no further changes in the European diplomatic structure. Yet Germany's great power and the fears its government had aroused, abetted by the wild talk of the pan-German militarists, created a similar defensive mentality in France and Britain. No one could afford change; yet change was inevitable, particularly because of the instability in the Balkans. The weak powers of the alliance – Austria, Russia, and Italy – actively sought change to counter internal dissent and maintain or assert their great-power status. The tragedy was that the leading powers, by the rigidity of their defensive stance, left the initiative to their less stable allies.

As the result of the Second Moroccan Crisis in 1911, France, backed by its allies, finally acquired Morocco despite vigorous German opposition. French nationalism was so inflamed that the government was forced out for negotiating with Germany at all, even successfully, while Germany was left with a feeling of diminished power. Every crisis now created new tension and reduced the flexibility possible in the next crisis. The French protectorate over Morocco prompted Italy to declare war on the Ottoman

Empire to acquire Tripoli, which Italy had long coveted and which France and Britain had agreed it could take. The Italian government was pushed also by riotous agitation of the authoritarian nationalists led by d'Annunzio. With Turkey distracted by Italy, the Balkan states saw their chance to win other Turkish territories for themselves; and their war against Turkey led to World War I. Every diplomatic change now had fateful repercussions, and an aura of inevitability dominates any account of diplomacy after about 1907. The Balkans were bound to be inflamed once again, and the great powers were bound to come to blows over a Balkan crisis.

Conflict in the Balkans. Great-power interference in the Balkans was nothing new. Britain and France had some interest in the area; Britain was particularly anxious to protect its route to India. These powers and Germany had long competed for influence among the Balkan states by offering loans for railroad building and extending guidance for economic and military projects. This heightened the rivalries within the Balkans and created an often false sense of great-power support for local ambitions. Italy had more direct Balkan interests, particularly along the Adriatic, though its influence was slight. The leading great powers in the area were the territorially contiguous ones, Austria and Russia. Both had reason to fear any hostile power in the Balkans. Both had traditional interests in expanding in the area, with Russia especially eager to gain access to the Mediterranean by controlling the Straits of the Dardanelles. Both now had new opportunities in the area because of Balkan nationalism. Russia honestly felt its kinship to the Balkan Slavs, and Russian agents constantly incited the Serbs and others. Austria, equally honestly, feared Slavic nationalism because of its impact on national disputes within the Hapsburg monarchy.

In 1908, Austria annexed Bosnia-Herzegovina, which it had previously only administered. The Austrian foreign minister, Lexa von Aehrenthal, felt that Austria required diplomatic glory to soften internal dissent. He also wanted fuller control over the Serbs, both by gaining greater authority over the Serbs in Bosnia and by humiliating the nationalists in Serbia, who naturally were affronted at the Austrian move. Russia had agreed to the annexation on Aehrenthal's promise that Austria would accept a Russian sphere of influence at the Straits; here was Russia's chance for new power in the region and a glorious diplomatic gain to erase the memory of the defeat by Japan. But Aehrenthal tricked his Russian counterpart, declaring the annexation before Russia was ready to act. Russia was aggrieved, and Serbia, outraged, mobilized its army; Russia and Austria both feared general war enough to avoid further conflict, but the situation was highly unstable.

In 1912, prompted by the Italian attack on the Ottoman Empire and urged on by Russian diplomats, a Balkan League was formed by Serbia, Bulgaria, and Greece to attack Turkey. All three countries coveted Macedonia, still held by the Turks, and all three had sponsored agents to promote their nationalisms in Macedonia for the past twenty years. Bulgaria was promised a substantial share of Macedonia by the new alliance;

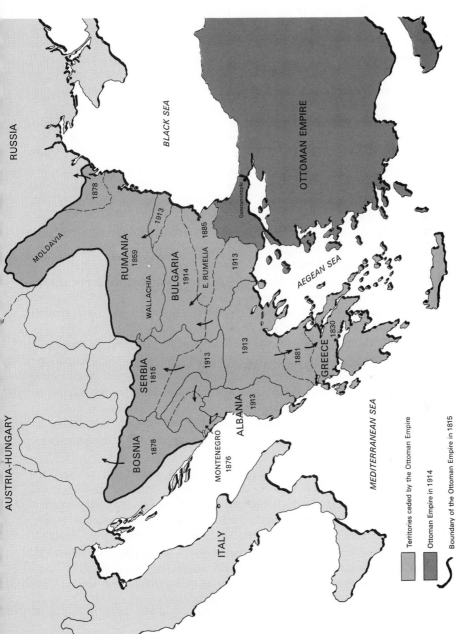

RUSSIA

BLACK SEA

MOLDAVIA

1878

RUMANIA
1859

1913

WALLACHIA

BULGARIA
1914

1885

E. RUMELIA

1913

Constantinople

OTTOMAN EMPIRE

AEGEAN SEA

SERBIA
1815

1913

1913

1881

1830

GREECE

BOSNIA
1878

AUSTRIA-HUNGARY

1913

ALBANIA
1913

MONTENEGRO
1876

MEDITERRANEAN SEA

ITALY

Territories ceded by the Ottoman Empire

Ottoman Empire in 1914

Boundary of the Ottoman Empire in 1815

THE BALKANS

Serbia, besides looking to a part of Macedonia, hoped for a general war between Austria and Russia in which it could gain Austria's South Slavic holdings. Greece was to obtain part of Macedonia, and Montenegro, a rival of Serbia for South Slavic leadership, entered the alliance as well and actually started the war against Turkey. Here, then, was the classic Balkan formula: intense nationalisms goaded by nationalist organizations and supported by opportunist monarchs; intense mutual rivalries, which combined at this point only because the opportunities seemed so great and because no power trusted another to act alone; intense hatred of the Turk and, on Serbia's part, of the Austrian; and Russian prompting, which gave everyone a sense of great-power sponsorship.

Austria tried to prevent the Balkan war, for it feared any gains for its Slavic neighbors, and even Russia tried to prevent actual conflict; but their actions came too late. The League attacked Turkey in October 1912, and won easily. Russia and Austria now acted more forcefully. Austria contemplated preventive war against Serbia, but Germany refused support in case of trouble with Russia. Russia was itself concerned about Bulgaria's advance near the Dardanelles. Austria successfully insisted that, in exchange for its acquiescence in the conquest of Macedonia, its friend Rumania be given some Macedonian territory too and a free Albania be created, to block Serbia from the Adriatic. Serbia was bitterly disappointed, having failed to cause a more general war and having occupied much of Albania in vain. As a result, Serbia and Greece refused to turn most of Macedonia over to Bulgaria, for, precisely because Bulgaria had done most of the fighting against the Turks, Serbia and Greece had been able to seize most of the territory. The result was the Second Balkan War, of 1913, in which Bulgaria attacked Serbia and Greece; the Turks and Rumania joined against Bulgaria also, and the new allies won easily. In the Treaty of Bucharest (August 10, 1913), Serbia and Greece obtained most of Macedonia, Rumania gained territory at Bulgaria's expense, Turkey recovered a bit of Thrace, and Bulgaria was left, after two wars, with tiny fragments of Thrace and Macedonia.

Bulgaria now bitterly hated Serbia and Russia, the latter as Serbia's sponsor; it drifted rapidly toward the central powers. Russia and France increased their support to Serbia, their logical ally in the region and a natural enemy to Austria. Serbia was more aggrieved than ever, for it had not gained access to the Adriatic or Bosnia-Herzegovina. Serbia's nationalists were exalted by two successful wars, its leaders confident of great-power support and convinced that aggression was a successful policy. In 1913 Serbian troops reëntered Albania, a direct provocation to Austria. Austria had been the main loser in the Balkan Wars, particularly because of the expansion and new nationalist fervor of the Serbs. It could not endure a further setback. Russia, having backed down so often in past Balkan crises, could not endure one either. The lines of Balkan diplomacy were now interwoven with those of great-power policies.

On June 28, 1914, the Austrian Archduke Francis Ferdinand was assassinated by a Serbian nationalist. The assassination convinced Austria that Serbia had to be attacked, at all costs. On Russian urging, Serbia made a substantial apology, but this was not enough for Austria. Austria's strong stand was supported by the German government, particularly the military. Many German leaders felt that world war was inevitable and that this was the best time for it, for both France and Russia were augmenting their military strength; and all realized that Austria, the only major ally, was unstable and had to be supported by strong German friendship. Austria, then, actively sought a local war and was willing to risk a general one. The German government felt that preservation of the alliance was more important than peace, and a large group pushed for a preventive European war.

Russia saw that to abandon Serbia to Austria would erase Russian influence in the Balkans. When Austria declared war on Serbia on July 28, Russia followed two days later by declaring mobilization. Russia's mobilization procedures were slow, so it sought a head start without, as yet, declaring any war. This mobilization frightened Germany in turn, for German strategy called for a quick defeat of France, before Russia's build-up was complete. So Germany declared war on France and Russia on August 1. France had supported Russia throughout the crisis; like Germany, France felt that its main ally was weak and required all-out support. Naturally, France responded to the German declaration by mobilization of its own. Britain hesitated, tried various negotiations for peace, and may have misled the Germans into thinking that it would not intervene. But Britain was definitively tied to France; even their fleets were coordinated, with the French defending the Mediterranean and the British the North Sea. Germany's invasion of neutral Belgium, a longstanding part of the German military plan against France, made it easy for Britain to declare war on August 4.

After the war, there was much discussion of who was to blame for the whole catastrophe. The argument must, at this point, seem rather sterile. The only clearly aggressive power was Serbia, and even its leaders softened their approach on Russia's advice. Austria felt it was defending its interests against Serbia, Russia its against Austria, and so on. Even the German advocates of preventive war were reacting defensively against encirclement. All the states had territorial ambitions: the French wanted Alsace-Lorraine, the British wanted Germany's empire, and pan-Slavs and pan-Germans had even greater hopes. But none of the powers was, during the crisis, motivated directly by its ambitions. The statesmen erred in many ways. The British were too vague, the Germans too dominated by the presumed requirements of a prearranged military plan. But their defensive arguments were genuinely felt. At least in this immediate crisis, they were trapped by the inflexibility of the alliance system, by the sense that no further adjustment was possible.

No catastrophe so massive as World War I, no such blow to the morale and values of a whole continent, can be simply explained. The details of diplomacy and of military build-ups in the preceding decade can be easily outlined, but this is not enough. The War resulted from a change in the European power balance that began at least forty years before. For the Germans and the opponents of the Germans, it was a war stemming from confusion over the place which so great a new nation could and should assume in the world. Never had Europe seen a new state rise to continental dominance so quickly. Naturally, this rise created diverse resistance by older states; naturally also, it created grandiose hopes on the part of many Germans. The War resulted also from confusion over the decline of traditional powers. A persistent overestimation of Russian strength played a major role. More subtly, war came in part from Britain's decline and the steps it took to avert this.

Diplomatic background alone cannot explain the war. World War I caused or furthered major changes in society, politics, even philosophy; it resulted from changes in these areas also. Internal instability played an obvious part in the diplomatic policies of eastern Europe and Italy. The Italian, Serbian, and Bulgarian desires for diplomatic glory, all directly involved in the events of 1911 to 1914, were responses to internal social tension. The Austrian foreign minister publicly stated that his country was doomed unless it attacked the Serbs and that a world war was not only worth the risk but actually represented a far better way to fall than through an otherwise inevitable internal collapse. Russian foreign policy had been dominated for decades by internal pressure, and certainly the sense in 1914 that diplomatic concessions were impossible was rooted in the fear that a new revolution would be their reward.

Internal tension played a more subtle role in motivating the western powers. It is impossible to say what influence labor agitation had in France or Germany. Diplomatic policy was not directly used to counter pressure in parliament or in the streets. But the statesmen's sense of alternatives may have been narrowed by the attacks on the existing order. In the longer run, certainly, the diplomatic setting had been created partly to guard against internal disorder. Imperialism and nationalism owed much to the desire of conservatives to distract the masses. The atmosphere of violence created by labor unrest, as well as by many intellectuals on the radical right, may well have eased the resistance of statesmen to violence in diplomacy. Discontent on the right played a direct role in diplomacy. Pan-German leagues were filled largely by bureaucrats and professional men who saw in nationalism an enhancement of their own status; rightist organizations pushed for imperial gains from the 1880's through the French and Italian expansion in North Africa in 1911. The new sense of constriction in the industrial economy contributed to diplomatic tensions by promoting active business support for imperial ventures and increasing armaments.

Europe faced a crisis by 1914 far greater than diplomatic tension alone. Without the war, the structural weaknesses of the economy might have been remedied, alleviating much of the unease on both the left and right of the political spectrum. Without the war, the intellectual challenge to the liberal and rationalist traditions of the nineteenth century might have been met. But without the social and cultural ferment in all parts of Europe, the impulse to war—or at least to the total conflict which the war became—might have been checked. The end of nineteenth-century civilization was not accidental. Its principles had never spread uniformly in Europe, and those regions and classes that had been excluded from its benefits now called them into question, by social protest and diplomatic adventures. But even in western Europe, even in the middle classes who had led in shaping nineteenth-century society, there was new uncertainty. Not all the values of the middle-class revolutions in politics and the economy were lost, of course; the World War itself was not a total disruption. But confidence in orderly parliamentary politics, in the advance of general enlightenment, in steady economic progress was harder to maintain in 1914 than it had been in 1900. Hopes for peace were clearly illusory, and some pessimists were even beginning to question whether Europe could maintain its position in the world. The nineteenth century, which had continued in spirit for fourteen years beyond its allotted span, was now over.

SUGGESTED READING

General political studies include: D. W. Brogan, *The Development of Modern France, 1870-1939* (1940); the more readable D. Thomson, *Democracy in France* (1952); G. Chapman, *The Dreyfus Affair* (1955); B. Croce, *A History of Italy, 1871-1915* (1929); A. W. Salomone, *Italian Democracy in the Making: The Political Scene in the Giolittian Era, 1900-1914* (1945); A. Gerschenkron, *Bread and Democracy in Germany* (1943), on Junker politics; R. C. K. Ensor, *England, 1870-1914* (1949); G. Dangerfield, *The Strange Death of Liberal England* (1935), an excellent study on tensions between 1910 and 1914; H. Seton-Watson, *The Decline of Imperial Russia, 1855-1914* (1952); and M. T. Florinsky, *The End of the Russian Empire* (1931).

There is an ample and controversial literature on imperialism. Two works basic to the debate are J. A. Hobson, *Imperialism: A Study* (1948) and V. I. Lenin, *Imperialism, the Highest Stage of Capitalism* (1949). A balanced, general discussion is W. L. Langer, *The Diplomacy of Imperialism, 1890-1902* (2 vol., 1935). See also: L. C. Robbins, *The Economic Causes of War* (1939); E. Staley, *War and the Private Investor: A Study in the Relations of International*

*Available in a paperback edition.

Politics and International Investment (1935); E. M. Winslow, *The Pattern of Imperialism: A Study in the Theories of Power* (1948); P. T. Moon, *Imperialism and World Politics* (1926); R. Maunier, *The Sociology of Colonies: An Introduction to the Study of Race Contact* (2 vols., 1949); J. A. Schumpeter, *Imperialism and Social Classes** (1955); and Stewart C. Easton, *The Rise and Fall of Western Colonialism* (1964).

The controversies on who was at fault in causing World War I seem rather sterile now. A summary of them is conveyed in D. Lee, *Origins of World War I* (1958). For comprehensive treatments and varying points of view see: S. B. Fay, *The Origins of the World War** (1930); P. Renouvin, *The Immediate Origins of the War* (1928); L. Albertini, *The Origins of the War of 1914* (2 vols., 1952-1953); B. E. Schmitt, *The Coming of the War, 1914* (2 vols., 1930); and N. Mansergh, *The Coming of the First World War: A Study in the European Balance, 1878-1914* (1949).

*Available in a paperback edition.

William II: The Granger Collection
Marinetti: Wide World Photos

WILLIAM II AND MARINETTI

William II (1859-1941) was Emperor of Germany and king of Prussia from 1888 to 1918. He was educated in the Prussian military tradition, having entered the army in 1880, but also received university training in law and political science. He believed firmly in the power of monarchy, which he felt was justified by divine right. Filippo Tommaso Marinetti was neither king nor soldier. Far from esteeming tradition in politics or anything else, he led a vigorous, often violent campaign against established principles in art, in government, and in diplomacy. Yet both William II and Marinetti helped shape the character of the two decades before World War I and helped bring on the war itself. They had no contact with each other and certainly cannot be compared in political importance. But their personalities had some common qualities of impatience and flamboyance. They shared interests in force and in war. Marinetti was one of the most articulate artists who attacked reason and urged violence in its stead. William II was the most powerful representative of the old order of monarchs and military men who resisted political change and, to some extent, expressed their resentment at modern politics in diplomatic and military adventures. It would be far too simple to say that war resulted from the confluence of the discontented intellectuals and the beleaguered traditionalists. But both groups accepted and even favored war, and both attracted large segments of society to the banners of militarism.

William II, from childhood, displayed a willful and aggressive personality. As Emperor he sought personal rule; his dismissal of Bismarck cleared the way for this, as did a succession of compliant ministers thereafter. Yet William's politics internally were defensive. He resisted liberalization and even altered the German school curriculum to stress conservative and religious principles. Initial hopes of conciliating the working classes gave way to bitter antagonism to the rise of socialism. William's great interest was in diplomacy. His actions in this field were far more modest than this words, but he consistently sought to advance Germany's interests throughout the world. He felt and reflected the growing industrial and military might of his Empire. He worked to expand German influence in the Near East, in Asia, and in Africa. He was a prime supporter of a great German navy. His speeches on German naval power, on the rivalry with Britain, on hostility to France in Morrocco, and even on a German-led crusade against the "yellow peril" of Asia, all played a major role in creating the impression of an unsatisfied, belligerant German nationalism. All of this was more than poor policy, though certainly William had little sense of tact. It expressed the frustrated thirst for glory of the Emperor himself, whose personality Theodore Roosevelt aptly described as "a curious combination of power, energy, egotism, and restless desire to do, and to seem to do, things."

Marinetti (1876-1944) was born into a rich business family in northern Italy and educated first in Jesuit schools, from which he was expelled, and then at the University of Paris. He began writing epics and plays in the early 1900's, and though his literary work was not outstanding, he showed an ability to capture and organize many of the themes of Europe's contemporary writers and artists. His doctrine, first expressed in the Futurist Manifesto of 1909, was defiance of all conventions. There were no permanent standards in art or morality or politics. Every rule had to be broken. The essence of life was movement, expressed in the modern machines whose energy captivated Marinetti and his fellow Futurists. Any artistic style was appropriate that conveyed power and violence. Religious and moral codes were absurd. In politics, the timidity and corruption of parliamentary systems and the materialism and internationalism of the socialists roused Marinetti's ire equally, though he sensed a violence in socialism that he respected. The state should be organized for war. Marinetti greeted Italy's invasion of Tripoli with vast enthusiasm: "We can admire nothing else today except the formidable symphony of the shrapnel and the wild bursts of our inspired artillery."

Marinetti was in no sense an original thinker or writer. His importance rests in his ability to sum up many of the intellectual interests of his day and to publicize the slogans of the preachers of violence even beyond the intellectual community. He directly spread many of the principles of Futurism to France, England, and Russia. In Italy, his efforts in journalism, his sensationalist novels, and his ability to organize violent demonstrations kept him in the public eye. He played no small role in creating the public mentality that urged and welcomed the war for Tripoli, Italian participation in World War I, and later fascism itself. He reflected the total impatience with the present, the desire for blind movement, that affected many socialists as well as radical conservatives, many common people as well as intellectuals, all over Europe.

From two quite different points of departure, then, from the powerful German emperor and the wild Italian writer, came a restless energy and a distaste for the political and diplomatic conventions of the day. From them, in quite different ways, came the sorts of pressures that led to war. ■

Conclusion

The key legacies of the nineteenth century to the twentieth were the expansion of government and the related extension of political awareness to almost every segment of society, both undergirded by industrialization.

The sources of government growth were twofold. From the French Revolution onward, almost every significant political movement had urged new government functions. Traditional conservatives of the Metternichian variety had not greatly expanded government, for they relied on aristocrats and churchmen to supply many political services, but they increased the police apparatus at least. Liberals resisted governments in many ways, but outside Great Britain government activities invariably increased under liberal regimes. Liberals wanted education and economic encouragement from the state, and they played a major role in creating efficient government bureaucracies that were capable of handling new functions. Socialism and nationalism obviously encouraged a strong state, and this helped account for the particularly rapid extension of government services and bureaucracies after 1870. Even in Britain, state expenses and personnel more than doubled in the two decades before World War I.

Ideologies and political movements provided the motive for state expansion. They provided opportunity as well, by removing many traditional units such as guilds and manors, which had performed political functions. Economic development created the means to seize the new opportunities. New transportation and communication systems increased the contacts between states and their citizens. New wealth provided vast new revenues for taxation. The power of industrial states would be massively revealed in the First World War.

The question for the twentieth century was whether the political consciousness of the various classes in society was sufficiently active to resist undue state power—or at least to guide it in useful directions. Liberalism, the political force most appropriate for the limitation of government activities, was in decline. Many liberals were too satisfied with their place in society to protest the erosion of liberal values. Many businessmen simply abandoned liberalism, for they saw that a strong state was essential to protect their economic interests. Other liberals, particularly in

Britain, maintained greater vitality, but only by bowing to the popular demand for new government services.

Socialism by 1914 commanded far greater support than liberalism did. For the most part, socialists worked not to limit the state but to channel its power to the benefit of society. However, within many socialist parties and other labor organizations, some people sought less to channel the state than simply to destroy the whole existing order. Some were opposed to the state altogether, while others wanted to build a totally new state to create a new society. Both of these impulses stemmed from grievances that were too great to be expressed within the existing order. For this very reason, they goaded some governments into new activities to choke off or divert their pressure. In sum, the political awareness that had spread to many workers and others usually worked through and supported democracy. For a minority all over Europe, it led to a rejection of parliamentary democracy as inadequate and frightened others into rejecting it as well.

Nationalism was usually joined to a desire for a responsible state. The earliest forms of nationalism, in the French Revolution, stressed the importance of a state that earned popular loyalty by serving the citizenry. By the later nineteenth century, many conservative as well as liberal nationalists urged governments to assist all segments of the population. They did not encourage a severely limited state, obviously, but they wanted state activities to be justified by a higher purpose.

However, two types of nationalism pointed to an authoritarian state. Robespierre had long ago suggested that state authority might in practice be its own justification, thus removing all real limits to its power. Far more intellectuals and politicians directly advocated state power for its own sake by 1914. Fascination with power grew as power did itself, and already it provided some statesmen and military leaders with boundless ambitions in diplomacy. Many other people were authoritarian nationalists because they saw a strong state as the only way to restore older values in society. People who hated big business, who detested the presumption of the lower classes, who disliked political pragmatism and perhaps the modern political process itself could see a strong state as the way out. Some who wanted to return to older Christian values and to traditional family structures, so disrupted in industrial society, now looked to the state. They were wrong to do so, for they did not know how powerful a state could now be and they did not realize that a strong state could not really attack industrial society, for to do so would be suicidal. This was a lesson still to be learned, however, and in 1914 there was already some tentative contact between people who opposed the modern world and those who joyfully accepted the power that the modern world had created.

In western Europe, political outlets had largely kept pace with political consciousness after 1789, though not without some major disruptions. First the middle class, then other groups had learned to accept a state that gave them some voice and was sufficiently responsive to their demands. Further, industrialization had flowed from the structure of society, rather than being imposed upon it. Peasants with small holdings adjusted to commercial agriculture gradually; artisans who did not depend on guilds could adapt to new forms of manufacturing; a large preindustrial middle class provided personnel and appropriate values for new business ventures. There was massive disruption and hardship even so, and there was protest. Political outlets developed fairly soon after new grievances were felt and were largely adequate to express them. Despite economic difficulties and social tensions in the later nineteenth century and afterwards, there was little doubt that the states of western Europe could maintain some balance between their new power and the varied interests of their citizens.

From Germany eastward, economic innovation in the nineteenth century was a great shock, even though it sometimes brought less physical suffering than it had in the West. Governments were the prime movers of economic change, precisely because neither agriculturalists nor manufacturers were ready to undertake it spontaneously. So the power of states grew unusually rapidly, and the confusion of many traditional producers was great. Political consciousness spread, but it was sometimes inadequate to express the grievances of new workers or landless peasants or displaced shopkeepers; and effective political outlets were slow to come.

Much of Europe, in 1914, was approaching a mature industrial society. Differences in social structure were far less great than they had been in 1789. Political ideas and artistic styles spread easily across national boundaries. This had been true among intellectuals even before the French Revolution, but now a more general public was open to European cultural currents. European states were engaging in many similar activities, from diplomacy to social welfare. Similar ideologies and economic experiences did not, however, produce similar results. The choice for Europe, the question of how to use the modern state, was a general one, but the answers would not be the same. The political values of statesmen and common people alike differed greatly. Europe, divided now by war, was divided even more by the expectations of its people.

INDEX

Social change, French Revolutionary decade, 35, 36; increasing pace of, 73
Social Darwinism, 8
Social Democratic Party, 157, 180, 181; establishment of, 122
Social tensions, leftist movement, 179-181
Socialism, 86, 87; consolidation years of 1870-1900, 158, 180, 181; conversion to, 7; Marxist theory of, 141; moderation of, 7; revision of attitudes, 197, 198; rise of, 6, 10; twentieth-century support of, 216; end of utopian period of, 113
Sorel, Georges, 198
Southern Europe, conditions between 1850-1870, 123, 124; political interests, 6; unrest during 1870-1900, 186-190; increase of violence in, 4
Spain, anarchism in, 188; opposition to Napoleon, 59; post-Revolution reaction in, 77; twentieth-century agitation, 200
Speranski, Mikhail, 57
Staël, Mme. de, 59
State power, growth of, 5
Stein, Baron Karl von u. zum, 56
Stolypin, P. A., 202, 203
Subversion, French Revolution, 25
Suffrage, property requirements for, 19; universal male, 158
Syllabus of Errors, 125
Széchenyi, Count István, 91

T

Taaffe, Count Eduard, 160, 166
Taxes, alterations in, 2
Tennis Court Oath, 17
Territorial grab, 30, 31
Terror of French Revolution, 24-30
Thiers, Adolphe, 94, 160
Third Coalition, 49, 50
Third estate, 16, 17
Thomson, Joseph, 182
Transition period, 1848-1870, 113 ff. (*see also* Revolutions of 1848); agricultural gains, 119, 120; new and old styles of conservatism, 124-134; Crimean War, 137-139; eastern European conditions, 123, 124; economy during, 119-124; industrial gains, 119-122; intellectual developments, 141; liberal dilemma during, 131-134; middle-class gains, 122, 123; nationalism and diplomacy, 136-140; new realism, 140-142; Piedmontese policies, 125; Prussia after 1848, 127-129; abolition of serfdom, 123, 124; society during, 119-124; southern European conditions, 123, 124
Treaty of Adrianople, 79
Treaty of Bucharest, 208

Treitschke, Heinrich von, 131
Turner, Joseph, 83
Twentieth century, 1900-1914, agitation arising anew in, 198-200; growth of anti-Semitism, 199; Balkan conflict, 206-209; central Europe developments, 196-200; cultural grievances, 198; eastern Europe developments, 200-203; economic grievances, 198; legacies of nineteenth century to, 215; Moroccan crisis, 204-206; new wave of agitation, 198-200; political stability, 195-197; prelude to disaster, 195 ff.; realignment of diplomacy, 203-209; socialist revisionism, 197, 198; western Europe developments, 196-200

U

Union movement, reforms of, 5
Universal military service, principle of, 28
Universal Workingman's Association, establishment of, 122
Urban population, changes in, 3
Utopian socialists, 87

V

Valmy, battle of, 26
Van Gogh, Vincent, 182
Vendée, rebellion of, 28
Versailles, siege of palace of, 17
Violence, decline of, 4; increase in, 4; rise among working class, 7
Voltaire, 20

W

Waterloo, Napoleon's defeat at, 61
Watt, James, 22
Welfare programs, 6
Western Europe, age of revolution, 9; boom between 1850-1870, 119, 120; conservatism in, 80-82; effect of French Revolution, 20; industrialization in, 90; liberalism during 1850-1870, 133, 134; Napoleon's introduction of revolutionary principles in, 53, 54; orderliness in, 4; political interests, 6; population growth in, 3; transformation of conservatism, 130, 131; twentieth-century developments, 196-200; universal male suffrage, 158

3 4 5 6 7 8 9 10 11 12 13 14 15 16 17 18 19 20 21 22 23 24 25   75 74 73 72 71